YORUBA BELIEFS
AND
SACRIFICIAL RITES

YORUBA BELIEFS AND SACRIFICIAL RITES

J. Ọmọṣade Awolalu, B.D., S.T.M., Ph.D.

Senior Lecturer in African Traditional Religion,
University of Ibadan

Longman

LONGMAN GROUP LIMITED
LONDON

Associated companies, branches and
representatives throughout the world

First published 1979

ISBN 0 582 64203 5 (cased)
ISBN 0 582 64244 2 (paper)

0069298

Phototypeset in V.I.P. Plantin by
Western Printing Services, Bristol.
Printed in Great Britain
by Lowe & Brydon

DEDICATION

To my late friend Dr Keith Kibblewhite of the University of London, for his encouragement in producing this book

LIST OF ILLUSTRATIONS

CONTENTS

FOREWORD

The Yorùbá people who live in Nigeria and some neighbouring countries are among the most numerous and coherent of the peoples in Africa. The importance of their contributions to art, social order and religion has been increasingly recognised in recent years. William Fagg, in his foreword to *Yoruba Religious Carving*, writes that the Yorùbá are 'the most prolific in art of all the tribes, and if statistics were available would be found to have produced more sculptures per thousand persons than any other'.

The Yorùbá are also well known in the Americas, where in some places they have maintained their ancient customs virtually intact, in what Roger Bastide calls 'preserved religions' to distinguish them from mixtures like Voodoo. This great authority says that 'of all the African religions that have been preserved in America, it is undoubtedly that of the Yorùbá which has remained most faithful to its ancestral traditions' (*African Civilisations in the New World*, p. 115). The importance of Yorùbá culture is international as well as local, and therefore not only the popular artifacts but the religious ideas which inspire them deserve to be better documented.

Yorùbá religion has never received a full-scale study with the attention that has been devoted to the religion of other West African peoples such as the Ashanti, Ga or Nupe. There have been books on Yorùbá history, new religions, oracles or the Supreme Being, but no exposition of Yorùbá religion as a whole and in its sacrificial practices. This is what Dr Awolalu has attempted and he is to be congratulated on presenting such a comprehensive, systematic and attractive picture of the traditional religion of his own people.

Dr Awolalu began his work with a study of sacrifice, and this was valuable in itself as original and first-hand research, but he came to add the opening chapters on religious beliefs and this gave the necessary background to the sacrifices and provided a clearer general picture of the religion. Dr Awolalu refers to the works of earlier writers who have described various aspects of Yorùbá religion and most, though not all, of these were Europeans or Americans who tried to understand the customs of the people they visited or lived among. Dr Awolalu has the great advantage of writing about his own people, whose language he therefore speaks and whose traditional prayers and songs he understood without the intermediary of an interpreter. Sometimes he differs even from other Yorùbá writers and plainly there are different religious practices in various places as well as divergent points of view. But his work is fair and scholarly, and he has both a systematic and a critical approach. Where the future, or the present, is not clear he recognises that precise answers to problems cannot always be given.

This book deserves a wide market among those who are interested in African culture, among students of religion as a whole, and among the general public. It will repay careful attention, and it sheds light not only on religions but also on social and political concerns. When my own studies of African religion were made, over a period of twenty years, I expressed the hope that pioneer work would be followed by studies that would show more of the religion from the inside. I am glad to commend Dr Awolalu's work on his own people and I wish it every success.

Geoffrey Parrinder,
Professor of the Comparative Study of Religions,
University of London.

PREFACE

The people whose beliefs and rites we are considering are concentrated in South-Western Nigeria (in the Oyo, Ondo, Ogun, Lagos and Kwara States) and in a section of the Bendel State of Nigeria. Some of them are also to be found in neighbouring Dahomey (now Republic of Benin) and Togo, the adjacent countries to the west of Nigeria. They constitute one of the largest ethnic groups in West Africa. The descendants of the Yorùbá are also found in Sierra Leone where they are known as '*Aku*', in Cuba where they are called '*Lucumi*' and in Brazil where they are known as '*Nago*'. Perhaps no African group has had greater influence on the culture of the New World than the Yorùbá. Today, their descendants still preserve Yorùbá culture and traditions in parts of the Caribbean and South America, particularly in Cuba and in Brazil as well as in North America. In many parts of the Caribbean and South America, for example, Yorùbá religion has been accommodated to Christianity; Yorùbá divinities have been identified with Catholic saints.[1]

This book sets out to describe, in brief compass, the beliefs and the most important religious rites – namely, sacrificial rites – of the Yorùbá of West Africa. The work is a revision and an expansion of a Ph.D. thesis submitted to the University of Ibadan in 1971. Entitled 'Sacrifice in the religion of the Yorùbá', it was the result of many years of field research carried out among my own people – the people whose language I speak and in whose culture I was brought up.

A number of scholars advised me, when I was revising the thesis for publication, to spell out the beliefs of the Yorùbá which lead them to give such a prominence to sacrifice. This would not only teach readers about the 'special' theme of sacrifice, but also give them a basic knowledge of the beliefs of the Yorùbá.

In the 1973–74 academic year, I spent my sabbatical leave at the

Center for the Study of World Religions, at Harvard University in the
U.S.A. About that time, a group of black Americans who 'colonised' a
place in South Carolina and called themselves the 'Yorùbá' group,
began to attract public attention in the U.S.A. They claim to be
'living' the Yorùbá way for, according to them, to live the Yorùbá way
is to re-discover the culture of the black Americans because most
black Americans have their origin in West Africa, particularly
Yorubaland.

The students and faculty of the Harvard Divinity School who got to
know that I was a Yorùbá from Western Nigeria seized every chance
to ask me questions concerning the Yorùbá and their beliefs and
whether or not certain statements made by the 'Yorùbá' of South
Carolina were true and acceptable. We used to have very interesting
discussions.

A greater opportunity of discussing the Yorùbá came when, in the
spring semester 1974, I was invited by the Harvard Divinity School to
give a course on the 'Beliefs and sacrificial rites of the Yorùbá of West
Africa'. That enabled me to consider seriously revising and expanding
my thesis along the lines of the course taught. The response of
students who took the course convinced me of the great enthusiasm of
American students (particularly Afro-Americans) to learn about the
religion of Africa in general and the religion of the Yorùbá in particular; the latter they consider very close to their traditional culture.
They expressed the desire for a textbook such as is here presented.

Since Professor E. G. Parrinder introduced the teaching of African
Traditional Religion into the University of Ibadan in 1949, there has
been increasing interest in the subject at university level in many
African universities, seminaries and theological colleges. In recent
years, with the introduction of 'West African Traditional Religion'
into the syllabus for the General Certificate of Education of the West
African Examinations Council, teachers and students of African
Religion have wanted to have basic textbooks on the different ethnic
groups in West Africa. This book will, therefore, be of use to students
taking the General Certificate of Education in West Africa,
theologians and seminarians, undergraduates and graduates in universities in Africa, Europe, America and other parts of the world, and
to general readers eager to learn about the rich culture of one of the
advanced ethnic groups in Africa.

Throughout this book, I have chosen my material *mainly* from
personal research conducted among my people and first-hand infor-

mation gathered from informants. In other words, the work is based on what the people *actually* believe, practise and say and not on what they are *supposed* to believe, practise or say. The fact that I am myself a Yorùbá facilitated my research, enabling me to travel freely among the people, to meet them and discuss freely with the elders, chiefs and priests and to watch and participate in some of the religious festivals and cultic practices. To obtain the facts and information relevant to the study, I was able to interview rulers of various communities, and their knowledgeable attendants, the priests of the various cults and other well-informed citizens. Besides seeking information from these groups of people, I was privileged to make direct observation and to draw conclusions.

I have sought to emphasise that religion is never to be thought of in the abstract; rather it should be seen as something practical and meaningful for those who practise it. The Yorùbá world-view is reflected in the sacrificial rites performed by the people. In other words, sacrificial rites constitute the outward and visible signs of the inner beliefs of the people. The beliefs and rites are closely related, hence they are treated together in this book. When I speak of belief in the first part of the book, I mean to emphasise the firm persuasion of the truth of a body of religious tenets held by the people; it is the faith that keeps them going; it is the full acceptance of what they hold to be true.

In the process of writing this book, I have received inestimable help from a number of directions. My main difficulty is to know whom to thank first and to whom I am most grateful.

For my field work, I owe many thanks to several paramount chiefs in Yorubaland for their readiness to answer my questions and for making it possible for me to meet priests and individuals who are knowledgeable in things traditional, and to watch many of the rituals.

I wish to express my deep sense of gratitude to Professor E. Bọlaji Idowu, for his encouraging interest in the study and particularly for his painstaking supervision of the thesis which, in a modified form, now results in this book.

I am greatly indebted to the late Dr Keith Kibblewhite, formerly of the University of London, for all the encouragement and help that he gave me. Not only did he read through the final typescript and offer valuable suggestions, but he also made very useful contacts on my behalf.

I am also grateful to Professor Bill Stevenson, Professor of English at Boston University (formerly of Ibadan) and Professor Noel King, Professor of History and Comparative Religion at Merril College, Santa Cruz, California, who read through the typescript at different stages and offered me very useful suggestions.

I wish to express my profound gratitude to the University of Ibadan for granting me the study leave that took me to Harvard University for one year when I had the chance of working on this book. My thanks also go to the Harvard Divinity School, the Center for the Study of World Religions and the Peabody Museum Library for placing all their resources at my disposal.

I must express my deep gratitude and warm appreciation to Professor E. G. Parrinder for readily agreeing to write a foreword to this book.

I thank the many scholars who have, in the past, written on the Yorùbá beliefs and whose works have encouraged me to make a research into the beliefs of my people and to correct some erroneous ideas where they have occurred.

My deep gratitude also goes to the Rev. Dr S. A. Adewale who spent time preparing the index; Mr I. K. Dawodu, who organised the typing of the final draft; Mr Leonard Obeifoh and Mr Samuel Olatunji who actually did the bulk of the typing; Mr G. O. Àjàmú who scrutinised the Yorùbá orthography, and the members of staff of Longman Group who made the publication of this book possible.

Finally, my sincere gratitude is due and it is hereby given to my wife, Bósèdé, whose sympathy, love and understanding continue to sustain me during these arduous years of study and research.

I send out this book with the hope that it will contribute to the knowledge of African Traditional Religion in general and Yorùbá beliefs in particular.

J. Omosade Awolalu
Department of Religious Studies,
University of Ibadan,
Ibadan, Nigeria.

1. W. R. Bascom, 'The Yoruba in Cuba', *Nigeria*, xxxvii, 1951, pp. 14–20; P. Verger, 'Yoruba Influences in Brazil', *Odu*, i, 1955, pp. 3–11.

Part One
Beliefs

Chapter One

BELIEF IN THE SUPREME BEING

Among the indigenous Yorùbá people, the existence of the Supreme Being is taken as a matter of course. It is rare, if not impossible, to come across a Yorùbá who will doubt the existence of the Supreme Being or claim to be an atheist. If there is anyone like that, further investigation will reveal that he has been exposed to non-African cultural influences. In other words, we are suggesting that an indigenous Yorùbá has a belief in the existence of a self-existent being who is believed to be responsible for the creation and maintenance of heaven and earth, of men and women, and who also has brought into being divinities and spirits who are believed to be his functionaries in the theocratic world as well as intermediaries between mankind and the self-existent Being.

Review of scholars' views:

Before giving further details about the people's belief in the Supreme Being, it is useful to make a critical review of what previous scholars have said about the Yorùbá concept of God. It is not possible to refer to them all; but we shall attempt to examine as many of them as possible – if only to show the amount of interest that has been shown in the discussion of this all-important subject, and how difficult it is to assess people of other faiths and cultures. Some of these writers, certainly, have made thorough research into this concept, and what they wrote was based upon well-established facts. But others who were handicapped by ignorance, total or partial, of the Yorùbá language and culture, and who approached their study with preconceived notions, constantly went wide of the mark.

P. Baudin, a French scholar writing in 1884, claimed that:

The Blacks have neither statues, nor symbols to represent God. They consider him as the Supreme Primordial Being, author and father of the gods and spirits. At the same time, they think that God, after beginning the organisation of the world, charged Ọbàtálá to finish it and to govern it, then withdrew and went into an eternal rest to look after his own happiness . . .[1]

Although no direct mention is made of the Yorùbá here, we know that this is implied because it is only among them, and those who are closely related to them, that we have the archdivinity, Ọbàtálá, referred to by Baudin. He is quite correct to say that 'the Blacks' have no statues of the Supreme Being. This is because He is too great and awesome to be pictured or formed into a concrete mould. But we have to be careful when we speak of symbols. 'A symbol', according to P. Gardner, 'is a visible or audible sign or emblem of some thought, emotion or experience, interpreting what can be really grasped only by the mind and imagination by something which enters into the field of observation.[2]

The Yorùbá believe that the Supreme Being is pure, and they associate the colour white with Him. According to E. Bọ́lájí Ìdòwú:

The worshipper (Yorùbá) makes a circle of ashes or white chalk; within the circle, which is a symbol of eternity, he pours a libation of cold water, and in the centre he places his kola-nut on cotton wool . . .[3]

Although this ritual practice is now rare to come by, one can rightly say that ashes, white chalk, cotton wool, and the like symbolise purity among the Yorùbá, as a circle symbolises eternity.

When we examine Baudin's statement further, we discover that he does not appreciate the fundamental idea of God as conceived by the Yorùbá, especially with regard to the creation and government of the world. This we shall take up at a more appropriate place in this book.

R. P. Bouche, another French scholar, writing in 1885, claimed that:

A Yorùbá man thinks that God is too great to deal with him and that he has delegated the care of the blacks to the Òrìṣà. Master of heaven, God, enjoys abundance and gentle rest, keeping his favour for the white man. That the white man attends God is natural. As for the blacks, they owe their sacrifices, their offerings and their prayers to Òrìṣà only . . .[4]

From Bouche's statement we see that he holds the view that God is partial, in favour of the white and against 'the blacks'. It seems that Bouche's personal opinion is inspired by racial pride and blindness. Here again we have to deal with the kind of stubborn ignorance which is incapable of seeing, or refuses to see, things as they are. A study of any depth would have shown Bouche that it is the Yorùbá belief that all human beings are created by God and are, in fact, members together of one human race.

In Bouche, we find another writer who does not understand the relationship between the Supreme Being and the divinities, and for this reason, he has been led astray in his comments on offerings and prayers. The divinities (Òrìṣà), as we shall show later, are in no way independent of the Supreme Being; in actual fact, they act as intermediaries between man and the Supreme Being.

A. B. Ellis, a British officer in the late nineteenth century, claims that:

> Ọlọ́run is the sky god of the Yorùbá; that is, he is deified firmament, or personal sky . . . He is merely a nature-god, the personally divine sky, and he only controls phenomena connected in the native mind with the roof of the world. . . . Since he is too lazy or too indifferent to exercise any control over earthly affairs, man on his side does not waste time in endeavouring to propitiate him, but reserves his worship and sacrifice for more active agents. . . . In fact, each god, Ọlọ́run included, has, as it were, his own duties; and while he is perfectly independent in his own domain, he cannot trespass upon the rights of others. . .[5]

We choose to quote Ellis at length because he raises a number of issues on which he displays ignorance. The most glaring error in Ellis' statement is his associating Ọlọ́run with 'a nature god'. In an attempt to substantiate this mistaken notion, Ellis shows his ignorance of the language by translating Ẹlẹ́dàá as 'He who controls rain', and Olódùmarè as 'Replenisher of brooks'. These are far from the true meanings of the two words which we shall deal with later on. Suffice it to say here that 'Ẹlẹ́dàá' means 'He who creates', that is, the Creator. This has nothing to do with 'causing rain to stop'. Olódùmarè is the origin and ground of all that is: the Almighty, the Supreme Being.

Furthermore, Ellis ranks Ọlọ́run with the other divinities when he said, 'Ọlọ́run cannot trespass upon the rights of others'. By others,

Ellis means other divinities. Ọlọrun, according to him, is in no way superior to the divinities; they are altogether independent of him. This notion is false. The Yorùbá clearly believe that Òrìṣà (the divinities) have no existence apart from the Supreme Being. As we hope to show, they are only ministering spirits and intermediaries between man and the Supreme Being. Ellis showed more ignorance of the basic principles of worship among the Yorùbá when he claimed that worship is rendered entirely to agents who are more active than Ọlọrun. It is also wrong to say that the Supreme Being is too lazy, distant and indifferent. We agree with Fádípẹ̀ when he wrote:

> No remark could have thrown into greater prominence the ignorance of Ellis of the everyday routine life of the Yorùbá. Far from Ọlọrun being a distant conception to the people, the average Yorùbá uses the name, often in proverbs, in prayers and wishes, in promises, in planning for the future, in attempts to clear himself of accusations, in reminding his opponent of his duty to speak the truth, and the like. Indeed, for all general purposes, it is more natural to invoke the name of Ọlọrun than that of òrìṣà.[6]

Talbot knows that the Supreme Being among the Yorùbá is 'Awlawrun' (Talbot's way of writing Ọlọrun), and that He is the creator of the universe. 'Beneath him is a hierarchy of Òrìṣà who are deputed to rule human beings, administer the various departments of nature and mediate between mankind and the supreme god . . . He also asserts that God is deemed to be too far away to take interest in mankind; hence prayers and sacrifices are offered to the Òrìṣà, 'and if necessary, through these mediators, to the *Awlawrun*'.[7]

One wonders why Talbot chooses to write 'supreme god' in small letters. If this is deliberate and arises from the notion that the Supreme Being as conceived by the Yorùbá is a sort of inferior deity, one who is other than the universal God, Talbot is wrong.

He does, however, realise and point out that Ọlọrun is the Supreme Being and that He is the creator of the universe. Furthermore, he is right in saying that in the administration of the world, Ọlọrun has the Òrìṣà (divinities) as His functionaries. He also states that prayers and offerings, more often that not, go to the divinities, although they are conveyed to Ọlọrun only 'if necessary'.

We must admit that Talbot, as a stranger on the scene, has done his best to interpret the basis of worship, but at the same time we must point out that he, too, has been somewhat confused about the relation between Ọlọrun and the divinities, as we shall see.

S. S. Farrow proves himself a very thorough investigator of the Yorùbá concept of God. 'We find among the Yorùbá', he declared, 'a belief in a Being called Ọlọrun whose position is unique in several respects'. . . . This idea is not due to Mohammedan or Christian influence.'[8] Farrow knows the various names by which the Supreme Being is called, and he is not unaware of some of the attributes of this Being.

One hesitates to criticise the work of such an honest researcher; nevertheless, it must be pointed out that the phrase 'A Being called Ọlọrun' seems to suggest that Farrow believes that God as conceived by the Yorùbá is different from the Supreme God, Who is the Creator of all the earth.

Lucas confesses that he is deeply impressed by Farrow and 'firmly believes that Dr Farrow is right' in what he writes about the Yorùbá concept of God. But the puzzling thing is that Lucas, himself a Yorùbá, believes that the idea of God as conceived by the Yorùbá (who are described by him as primitive) is too lofty and too sublime to be native to Yorubaland. He therefore suggests that this idea must have been borrowed from Egypt.[9] This is contrary to Farrow's claim that the idea is native to these people. Lucas is reasoning from the premise that whatever culture is noticeable in Yorubaland originated in Egypt, the cradle of civilisation. Westcott, after pointing out Lucas' weaknesses, concludes that Lucas has done this out of sheer patriotism mainly to associate Yorùbá with Egypt. Lucas 'appears to feel that any but the most ancient pedigree would be unworthy of his people'.[10] But Ògúnbà believes that Lucas' 'mistakes, monstrous and disconcerting, are more of ignorance that of patriotism'.[11] Lucas' idea of Ọlọrun is not clearly defined. In one breath he says, 'Love for the Deity certainly does not exist', and in another, he says 'The Yorubas attribute their preservation to the direct agency of Ọlọrun'.[12] One wonders why there should be no love for a Being who is responsible for the preservation of life and to whom people pray from time to time. There seems to be a contradiction in these two statements. The true position of things with regard to the worship of the Supreme Being will be taken up towards the end of this chapter.

While Lucas maintains that the concept of God as held by the Yorùbá is not native to the people, Parrinder, like Farrow before him, says that the belief in the Supreme Being is ancient among them.

'They call Him Ọlọ́run. No cult is offered to him, and there are no temples or priests of Ọlọ́run. He is not called Òrìshà, a god; he is above and beyond the other gods.' According to Parrinder, references are made to Ọlọ́run 'in proverbs, salutations, oaths and blessings.'[13] This is, to some extent, an apt description of the concept of God among the Yorùbá. But, in a particular statement made earlier in the same book, Parrinder disappoints us when he says that the Supreme God is 'sometimes above the gods, sometimes first among equals'.[14] We must emphasise the fact that the Yorùbá never rank Ọlọ́run who is Ẹlẹ́dàá (the Creator) with the divinities or the creatures. They know that He is over and above all divinities and men. That 'no cult is offered to him' is also an overstatement.

The best recent research into the concept of the Supreme Being among the Yorùbá, so far, is that of Ìdòwú. In his lucid and informative book, *Olódùmarè – God in Yorùbá Belief*, he claims that Olódùmarè is the traditional name of the Supreme Being and that Ọlọ́run, though 'commonly used in popular language appears to have gained its predominating currency in consequence of Christian and Moslem impact upon Yorùbá thought.'[15] Here we have to go warily. Elders among the Yorùbá who are non-Christians and non-Muslims claim that the name (Ọlọ́run) is as indigenous as Olódùmarè. And, as we shall show below, the two words are frequently used together or interchangeably.

Olódùmarè, according to Ìdòwú, 'is the origin and ground of all that is . . . ; the Yorùbá have never, strictly speaking, really thought further back than Olódùmarè, the Deity. . . . The existence of Olódùmarè eternally has, for all practical purposes, been taken for granted as a fact beyond question. It is upon this basic faith that the whole superstructure of Yorùbá belief rests.'[16]

Fẹlá Ṣówándé, in his attempt to prove that Olódùmarè is not the name of the Supreme Being, as put forward by Ìdòwú, confuses himself and his readers. He struggles to distinguish between Ọlọ́run, Ẹlẹ́dàá, Orí and Olódùmarè, failing to see that all these names refer to the same being. Ṣówándé develops his own hierarchy – the Supreme Being, according to him, is called Ọlọ́run, and next to Ọlọ́run is Ẹlẹ́dàá, and next to Ẹlẹ́dàá is Orí, and next to Orí is Olódùmarè. According to him there are 'at least two Olódùmarès'. Yet he sees in this hierarchy a trinity. Like the Gnostic Philosophers, Ṣówándé speaks of *emanation*. 'Ọlọ́run', he says, 'is not directly involved in human affairs, because the Spiritual Force emanating from Him is of such potency that it would shatter our human bodies. . . . Hence Ọlọ́run keeps His distance for our safety, but it is His life, His everything that we use.' Because of this potency, 'Ọlọ́run has decided to have as His Lieutenants Ẹlẹ́dàá, Orí and Olódùmarè.'[17] We consider this as quite unacceptable, suggesting little serious and systematic attention was given to this all-important matter.

However, from our own investigation, we know and uphold that Ọlọ́run is the same being as Olódùmarè as well as Ẹlẹ́dàá. Orí is a complex concept. It is the physical head as well as that force that is responsible for controlling one's being.[18] The physical head represents the inner head or inner person and has its correlation with Olódùmarè because it derives from Olódùmarè and is kept in being and wholeness by maintaining its correlation. But it cannot be made identical with Olódùmarè. At best, it is only a part which cannot be equal to the whole. It should also be emphasised that in the day-to-day life of the Yorùbá, the Supreme Being is never referred to as Orí in the same way as He is called Ọlọ́run or Olódùmarè. We are, however, convinced that when the Yorùbá speak of Orí they mean something more than the physical head. They are referring to the personality-soul which is believed to be capable of ruling, controlling and guiding the life and activities of man. The people believe that success or failure in life depends on Orí and its quality. Generally, a fortunate person is called olórí-ire (one who possesses good orí) while one who is unfortunate in life is described as olórí-burúkú (one who possesses a bad orí).

Furthermore, the word Orí which is used to describe the personality soul is also used to describe man's *double* (*alter ego*) *over-soul* or *guardian spirit*. When a Yorùbá says *Orí mi bá mi ṣe é* (my head has enabled me to do it) he is referring to the fact that it is the *alter ego* that has helped him. If a person miraculously escapes from harm, he will say *orí mí yọ mí* (my orí has saved me). If, on the other hand, a strong boy maltreats a weaker one and the former, in an attempt to run away, dashes his toe against something, the latter will say '*orí mi ló mú ẹ yẹn*' (it is my orí that has caught you). In other words, it is my 'head' that has passed judgment on you. If an enemy plans some mischief against a person, and the mischief is miscarried, people will say of the fortunate person, '*orí rẹ̀ kò gbàbọ̀dì*' (his orí does not compromise with the evil one; that is, his Orí wards off evil). When a father says to his son, '*Orí mi á gbè ọ́* (may my orí support you), he is praying that his guardian spirit may also guard and support his son. In all these usages,

Orí refers to a different personality that is capable of warding off evils, guiding and guarding a person and retaliating where need be.[19]

In reviewing the scholars' views of the Yorùbá concepts of God, we pointed out errors in the scholars' assertions. What, then, is the correct view of the peoples' concept of the Supreme Being? To answer this question, we should examine two areas which can facilitate our establishing the correct concepts of the peoples' views of God: the names and attributes of the Supreme Being. It is difficult to distinguish between the names of the Supreme Being and His attributes. And if there is an instance of a name appearing under the attributes of God and *vice versa*, we should appreciate the nature of the problem.

The names of the Supreme Being

Among the Yorùbá, names are very significant. Nearly every name is actually a complete sentence. This is very unlike the culture of Europeans who bear such names as Box, Cox, Drinkwater, Hunter, Johnson, Wood and the like to distinguish one person from another.

The Yorùbá attach great importance to names. Nearly every name given by the Yorùbá depicts a significant character as well as the circumstance of the birth of the bearer of the name. For example, the name *Olúṣìnà* (the Lord has opened the gate) shows that the parents of the child have long desired to be blessed with a child, and the birth of one into the family testifies to the fact that the barrier (that is, barrenness) has been removed by the Lord. If on the other hand a daughter is called *Yétúndé* (mother has come back), the Yorùbá know that such a child is born after the death of a grandmother in the family circle; and the newborn child is believed to be a reincarnation of the deceased. This is a pointer to the people's belief in the transmigration of the soul.[20] As a further example, if a child is called *Babárímisá* (father dodged me, or ran away at my approach), we know that the father of a child so called died when the child was still in the womb.

We take the trouble of examining these secular names in order to emphasise the fact that names are not just given, but that they are given with definite intentions. When we turn specifically to examine the names of the Supreme Being, we discover that each of the names depicts the people's concept of Him.

Olódùmarè

The origin of the word, *Olódùmarè*, cannot easily be determined. Attempts made in the past to break up the word into syllables for easy analysis have not been entirely satisfactory.[21] But tradition, as held by the elders among the people, confirms that the name connotes one who has the fullness or superlative greatness; the everlasting majesty upon whom man can depend.

Olọ́run

The name, *Olọ́run*, is self-explanatory. It means either the owner of *ọ̀run* (the heaven above) or the Lord whose abode is in the heaven above.

It is to be pointed out that in ejaculatory expressions, the Yorùbá use Olọ́run Olódùmarè together (but not in the form Olódùmarè Olọ́run). This double expression means the Supreme Being whose abode is in the heaven above and who is almighty and dependable. The two words can also be used interchangeably.

Besides these two words, a number of other names are used of the Supreme Being. Among these could be mentioned:

Ẹlẹ́dàá

The word, *Ẹlẹ́dàá*, means the *Creator*. This name suggests that the Supreme Being is responsible for all creation – that He is the self-existing Being and the Source of all things.[22]

Alààyè

The word *Alààyè* means the *Living One*. This suggests that the Supreme Being, as conceived by the Yorùbá, is ever-living or everlasting. In other words, the Supreme Being never dies. This is why the people say, '*A kì ígbọ́ ikú Olódùmarè*' ('We never hear of the death of Olódùmarè').

Ẹlẹ́mìí

Ẹlẹ́mìí means the Owner of life. The name, as applied to the Supreme Being suggests that all living beings owe their breath of life to Him. In other words, without the Supreme Being no creature can live. When the owner of life takes away the breath of a living soul, that soul dies. Hence, in planning for the future the Yorùbá usually add the conditional statement: '*Bí ẹlẹ́mìí kò bá gbà á, èmi yóò ṣe èyí tàbí èyìinì*' ('If the owner of life does not take it, I shall do this or that').

Ọlọ́jọ́ Òní

The name *Ọlọ́jọ́ Òní*, means the owner or controller of this day or of the daily happenings. To call Him the owner of the day or of the daily happenings is to emphasise total dependence of men and women together with their plans on the Supreme Being. He is supreme over all in an absolute sense.

From our study of these names, we can say that the Supreme Being as conceived by the Yorùbá is the Creator of heaven and earth, the One who has everlasting majesty and superlative greatness, who has tabernacles in the heavens above and who determines man's destiny. But it should be pointed out that though His abode is said to be in the heavens above, He is not removed from the people and He is not inaccessible. This will be elaborated when we examine the attributes below.

Attributes of the Supreme Being

He is the Creator

Among the Yorùbá the myth of creation (which lacks details) holds, among other things, that earth was a marshy waste, Olódùmarè and some divinities living in heaven above. But heaven and earth were so close that the denizens of heaven used to descend and ascend by means of a spider's web or a chain. They frequented earth for their pastimes, particularly for hunting.

When Olódùmarè decided to create the solid earth He summoned Òrìṣà-ńlá (the arch-divinity) to his presence and charged him to go and create it. For materials He gave him some loose earth in a snail shell (or tied in a napkin), and as tools, He gave him a hen and a pigeon. Òrìṣà-ńlá came to the marshy waste, threw the earth on the spot and let loose the hen and the pigeon who immediately spread the earth. Thus a great deal of the waste was covered and it became land. Òrìṣà-ńlá reported to Olódùmarè that the work has been accomplished. Olódùmarè then despatched Chameleon to go and inspect the work. He came and inspected and reported that the earth was wide enough but was not yet solid enough. On the second inspection, Chameleon reported that the work was ready for further action.

Olódùmarè then instructed Òrìṣà-ńlá (the arch-divinity) to go and equip the earth. When he was going, he took Ọrúnmìlá (the oracle divinity)[23] with him as his adviser and counsellor. For the purpose of equipping the earth, he was given the primeval palm tree to be planted. This was to provide food, drink, oil and leaves for shelter. He was also given three other trees that are full of juice to supply drinks for the inhabitants of the earth for as yet there was no rain. In addition, the original birds (the hen and the pigeon) were to increase on earth.[24]

After this, Òrìsà-ńlá was asked to lead to the earth sixteen persons already created by Olódùmarè. The head of these first human beings was Òrèlúeré. To have more human beings on earth, Olódùmarè instructed Òrìsà-ńlá how to mould human forms. Òrìsà-ńlá moulded human forms and kept the lifeless things in one place. Occasionally, Olódùmarè would come and put life into them. Thus, Òrìsà-ńlá could create human forms but that was all he could do; the principle of life was given only by the Supreme Being.[25]

There is another version of the creation myth which is very popular in Ilé-Ifè, the traditional home of the Yorùbá. This emphasises the fact that when Òrìsà-ńlá was sent to create the earth, he became intoxicated with palm wine and fell asleep. Odùduwà, another divinity, was sent to go and find out what had happened. When he came and found that Òrìsà-ńlá was in a drunken sleep, he stealthily collected the equipment that had been given to Òrìsà-ńlá and he created the earth instead.

Two or three layers of tradition appear to be blended together here. We hope to look at this problem more critically when the two divinities (Òrìsà-ńlá or Obàtálá and Odùdúwà) are discussed in the next chapter. For the time being, however, let us examine the missing details in this myth. We are left with the impression that either the world was made out of pre-existent materials which the Supreme Being did not make, or that He had made already before He ordered the work of the solid earth. For example, anybody reading this story critically will ask how the earth, the birds, the napkin in which the earth was tied or the snail shell in which it was carried came into being. Furthermore, the divinities were already using the marshy waste upon which the solid earth was spread as a sporting ground; from where did the animals and fishes that they were hunting come? The myth also says that sixteen people were sent with Òrèlúeré to be the first set of people to occupy the earth; when were these people created? All this points to the fact that there are noticeable gaps in the creation myth.

But barring all these gaps in the account, we discover that the myth aims to explain some essential tradition – mainly to emphasise the important fact that Olódùmarè is the Creator of heaven and earth and of all beings and things. We find that whenever and wherever a lesser agent of creation comes into the picture, he has no absolute authority to act. Olódùmarè is the One responsible for the vital principle or the essence of vitality in man. He is the supreme Author of creation. Apart from Him, there is no other. This is why He is called Ẹlẹ́dàá (the Creator) and Ẹlẹ́mìí (the Owner of life). In their admiration of His work the Yorùbá say, 'Iṣẹ́ Ọlọ́run tóbi' ('God's work is great or mighty').

He is unique
This means that He is the only One and there is no other like Him. It is in consequence of His uniqueness that the people have no graven images or pictorial paintings of Him. There are symbols or emblems[26] of Him but no images, for nothing can be compared to Him. This may be one of the reasons why foreign investigators of the people's religion have made the mistake of thinking that He is a withdrawn God about whom men are uncertain (Deus remotus et incertus).

He is immortal
The Supreme Being is called Ọlọ́run Aláàyè (The Living God) because He is ever-living. It is unimaginable for Ẹlẹ́mìí (the Owner of life) to die. It is a thing which never happens. In their belief they sing: 'A kì ígbọ́ ikú Olódùmarè' ('We never hear of the death of Olódùmarè'). Hence He is described as 'Òyígíyígì ọta àìkú' (the great immovable rock that never dies).

He is omnipotent
He is One with whom nothing is impossible. He is described as 'Ọba a ṣè kan má kù' (the King whose works are done to perfection). The idea is that when the Supreme Being sanctions something, it is easily done; but when a thing does not receive His blessing, it becomes difficult, if not impossible. There is, therefore, the common saying 'A dùn íṣe bí ohun tí Olódùmarè lọ́wọ́ sí, a ṣòro íṣe bí ohun tí Olódùmarè kò lọ́wọ́ sí' ('easy to do as that which receives Olódùmarè's approval; difficult to do as that which Olódùmarè does not sanction'). This is to suggest that a thing is quite easily done, a position is quite easily attained, a prayer is easily answered, or a success is easily achieved when this is approved by Olódùmarè who is 'almighty'. This is why He is called

Ọlọrun Alágbára (the powerful God). He is also called *'Ọba tí dandan rẹ̀ kì ísélẹ̀'* (the King whose biddings are never unfulfilled). He is *'Alèwí-lèṣe'* that is, He who can both propose and dispose as He wishes. In their realisation of the omnipotence of Olódùmarè the Yorùbá say, *'Àìsàn ló dùn íwò, a kò rí tỌlọjọ ṣe'* ('Illness can be cured, but pre-determined death cannot be averted'). The implication of this statement is that the Yorùbá believe that Ọlọjọ (the Controller of daily events), another name for the Supreme Being, has pre-determined what will happen to everybody in every moment of his life here on earth, including when he will die. If a person is ill, he can easily be cured if the appointed time of death has not yet come; but a time of death sanctioned by Ọlọjọ cannot be averted. This is to emphasise His omnipotence.

He is omniscient

The Supreme Being has knowledge of everything; He is all-wise, all-knowing, all-seeing and all-hearing. He is *'Elétí igbọ́ àròyé'* – He who is ever listening to (His creatures') complaints. He is also described as *'A-rínú-róde Olùmọ̀ ọkàn'* ('the One who sees both the inside and the outside (of a person), the Discerner of the heart'). He is also believed to be capable of seeing hidden things; hence in situations difficult to discern people say, *'Ohun tí ó pamọ́, ojú Ọlọrun tó'* ('that which is hidden to people is seen by the eyes of Ọlọrun'). The people praise His wisdom when they say, *'Ọlọrun ló gbọ́n, ẹdá gò púpọ̀'* ('It is God that is wise, creatures are very ignorant').

He is King and Judge

In their anthropomorphic conception of God, the Yorùbá see Him as holding the position of a very important King who is also an impartial Judge. They call Him *Ọba ọ̀run* (the King of heaven) and believe Him to be all-seeing. This is evidenced in the saying *'Bí Ọba ayé kò rí ọ, ti òkè ńwò ọ́'* ('if the earthly king does not see you, the One above sees you'). This shows His supremacy over the earthly rulers. He is also referred to as *Ọba a dákẹ́ dájọ́* (the King who sits in silence and dispenses justice). Olódùmarè as the Creator of all things and beings will also be the Judge of all. Actions of men and divinities do not escape His notice and judgment. Every one is to do His bidding, and failure to do so is punished as good deeds are rewarded. It is the people's belief that good will follow right conduct and evil will follow wrong conduct. People may not reap their rewards for good acts or suffer punishments for their evil deeds for a long time, but the consequences will come. This judgment is at two levels, here on earth and in the hereafter; the final judgment in the hereafter is given by the Supreme Being.

He is transcendent

The people believe that the Supreme Being is high and far above the heads of all. He is not one among many but wholly other. He is not of the rank and file of the divinities, neither can He be described as a nature god. It is the consciousness of the position of the Supreme Being which apparently enhances the significance of the divinities in the religion of the Yorùbá and which leads casual observers to conclude rashly that the Supreme Being is remote and uninterested in human affairs and has been displaced by the divinities. We need to emphasise that although the Supreme Being is transcendent, He is not removed from men. On the contrary, He is conceived as a social being interested in the life and events of the people. He is not unapproachable but quite accessible: no priest is necessary, on many occasions no intermediary, no building need be set apart for Him. He can be called upon any time and anywhere because He is omnipresent. In other words, His transcendence does not rule out His immanence.

In this position, He is conceived and described by the Yorùbá as atéreʠekáyé (He who spreads all over the world or He who covers the whole world or makes the whole world feel His presence). He is also described as Ògbìgbà tí ńgbà aláìlárá (the saving One Who comes to the aid of the helpless). He Who is believed to cover the whole world and to be capable of coming to the aid of the helpless at any time cannot be said to be removed from or uninterested in the people.

From our examination of what the casual observers of the Yorùbá religion have written we see that they wrongly emphasised the following:

(a) that the Supreme Being is remote, lazy and uninterested in what is happening on earth;

(b) that He is not worshipped;

(c) that the divinities who are more active agents receive better attention from the people than the Supreme Being.

We disagree with these writers and say that to the Yorùbá, God (the Supreme Being) is not remote. He hears people whenever they call on Him. For example, they pray to Him to watch over the travellers or those going to sleep. To the travellers they say *'Mo fi Ọlọrun sìn ọ́'* ('I pray God may go with you') and to those going to sleep: *'K'Ọlọrun ṣọ́ wa mójú o'* ('May Ọlọrun watch over us till daybreak'). He who can watch over somebody sleeping cannot Himself be said to be sleepy, idle or remote. He who can deliver somebody from an unexpected danger cannot be uninterested and lukewarm. Instead of the incorrect assessments made by casual observers, what ought to be emphasised is the sacredness of the Supreme Being and the reverence that goes with that sacredness.

It is not correct to say that the people do not offer any cult to the Supreme Being. If cult is seen solely as putting up a temple or erecting a sanctuary for the worship of the Supreme Being, it is true that this is not given any prominence among the Yorùbá. But if, in worship, prayer, adoration and invocation are given prominence, we will maintain that the Yorùbá worship Him. His name is on the people's lips at all times in prayers, spontaneous acts of thanksgiving for blessings received, in oaths and in proverbs.

It is regrettable that some people who write on Yorùbá religion cannot appreciate the interaction between culture in general and the religious beliefs of the people. They may not know, for example, that the Yorùbá society is hierarchical and that great importance is attached to old age and to those people in positions of authority. In Yorùbá etiquette, it was (and to a great extent still is) not correct for a young person to approach an elderly person directly when he wants a special favour. In the home, in practice, mothers are more accessible to children than fathers. Children tell their needs to their mother who later discusses them with their father. This does not mean that the father is remote from or disinterested in the child's affairs. In the same way, a boy who wrongs an elder appeals to another elder for whom the wronged person has great regard to speak on his behalf to the wronged friend.

We may draw further illustrations from the secular realm. In the Yorùbá political set-up, the Ọba is the traditional head of his people, the *pontifex maximus*, and the representative of the ancestors. In things secular and religious, he has the final say. Many festivals begin and end in or in front of the palace or the *ojà ọba* (ọba's market) and in the principal ones, the *ọba* has certain vital rituals to perform. Even when he is not physically present, there are those whom tradition has appointed to act on his behalf. Furthermore, in consequence of the sacred or *'numinous'* status of the *ọba*, the subjects do not as a rule, go directly to them but through minor chiefs (*ọba kékeré*), who act as intermediaries.

These analogies cannot be pressed too far. An earthly father for example, cannot be equated with the Supreme Being, neither can it be rigidly maintained that every appeal to a father or to the Supreme Being has to be channelled through an intermediary. The Supreme Being is not to be conceived as an unapproachable great Chief. What we mean to emphasise is the hierarchical set-up, as conceived by the Yorùbá, in the earthly sphere as well as in the spiritual realm. It is in the light of this that we can understand the status of the Supreme Being and the position of the divinities in the religious concept of the Yorùbá. They know that there is the Supreme Being who is the Creator, the Ruler of the universe and the Determiner of destiny. The kingdom of this world is a theocratic one in which the Supreme Being is Himself the Head, while the divinities that have no existence apart from Him are His intermediaries and functionaries. The role of these divinities will be taken up in the next chapter.

NOTES

1. P. Baudin, *Fétichisme et Féticheurs*, Lyon, 1884, p. 6 (translated by M. McMahon, *Fetishism and Fetish Worshippers*, 1885, pp. 9–10).
2. P. Gardner, 'Symbolism' (Greek and Roman), *Encyclopedia of Religions and Ethics*, (*E.R.E*), vol. 12, p. 138.
3. E. B. Ìdòwú, *Olódùmarè, God in Yoruba Belief*, Longman, 1962, p. 142.
4. P. Bouche, *La Côte des Esclaves et Le Dahomey*, Paris, 1885, p. 106.
5. A. B. Ellis, *The Yoruba-Speaking Peoples of the Slave Coast of Africa*, London, 1894, pp. 36–38.
6. N. A. Fádípẹ̀, *The Sociology of the Yoruba*, Ibadan University Press, 1970, p. 282.
7. P. A. Talbot, *The Peoples of Southern Nigeria*, Oxford University Press (O.U.P.), 1926, vol. 2, p. 29.
8. S. S. Farrow, *Faith, Fancies and Fetich*, London, 1926, pp. 23ff.
9. J. O. Lucas, *The Religion of the Yorubas*, Lagos, 1948, p. 34.
10. W. R. Westcott, 'Did the Yoruba come from Egypt?', *Odu*, 4, p. 15.
11. O. Ògúnbà, *Ritual Drama of the Ijebu People*, Ph.D thesis, University of Ibadan, 1967, p. 29.
12. Lucas, *Religion of the Yorubas*, pp. 45 and 46.
13. E. G. Parrinder, *West African Religion*, Epworth Press, London, 1949, p. 26 and p. 19 of 1969 edition.

14. *Ibid.*, p. 16 (1949) and p. 12 (1969).
15. Ìdòwú, *Olódùmarè*, p. 37.
16. *Ibid.*, p. 18.
17. Fẹlá Ṣówánde, *Ifa*, author's copyright, 1964, pp. 27–32.
18. This concept is elaborated by Ìdòwú in *Olódùmarè*, pp. 170–173. See also E. A. Adegbola in K. A. Dickson and P. Ellingworth, eds., *Biblical Revelation and African Beliefs*, 1969, pp. 122–124.
19. J. O. Awolalu, 'The African Traditional View of Man', *Orita*, vi, 2, December, 1972, pp. 108–109.
20. We shall examine this in greater detail under the Ancestral Cult in ch. 3.
21. See Lucas, *Religions of the Yorubas*, p. 41; Ìdòwú, *Olódùmarè*, pp. 33f; Fàdípẹ̀ *The Sociology of the Yoruba*, p. 281; T. A. Bamgbose, 'The Meaning of Olódùmarè', *African Notes*, vii, 1, 1972, pp. 25–32.
22. We shall examine the Creation Myth below.
23. For details about Yoruba divinities, see ch. 2.
24. Tradition among the people holds that the first place in the whole universe where habitable land appeared and first man landed was Ilé-Ifè, the traditional home of the Yoruba.
25. For more details of the Creation Myth see Ìdòwú, *Olódùmarè*, pp. 19ff.
26. See *circle* and *white* as emblems on p. 2.

Chapter Two

BELIEF IN DIVINITIES AND SPIRITS

The Yorùbá hold the belief that as the Supreme Being created heaven and earth and all the inhabitants, so also did He bring into being the divinities and spirits (generally called *Òrìṣà* or *Imọlè* and *Ẹbọra* respectively) to serve His theocratic world. The divinities and the spirits are best considered together because the Yorùbá do not make too clear a distinction between them. They are both divine and are both in the spirit-world. These divine beings are of complex nature. Some of them are believed to have been with the Supreme Being long before the creation of the earth and human beings, and can aptly be called 'Primordial Divinities'. Others are historical figures – kings, culture heroes and heroines, war champions, founders of cities, etc. who have been deified; and yet others represent personification of natural forces and phenomena – earth, wind, trees, river, lagoon, sea, rock, hills and mountains.

The actual number of the divinities is not easily determinable; it has variously been estimated to be 200, 201, 400, 401, 460, 600, 601, 1,700 or even more. Yorubaland is very rich in these divine beings. Some are widely worshipped while others are only of local importance. We cannot treat them all, but we shall select examples from the three categories enumerated above, stressing, however, that this is a flexible classification. It is not impossible that one divinity or spirit may belong to or fit into more than one category, depending on what tradition is emphasised. Ògún or Odùduwà, for example, may be seen either as a primordial divinity or as a deified ancestor. Let us now examine some of these divine beings.

Primordial divinities:

Ọbàtálá (Òrìṣà-ńlá)
Among the earliest divinities to be brought into being by the Supreme
Being was Ọbàtálá or Òrìṣà-ńlá. We have seen him, in the last chapter,
in connection with the creation story and the moulding of human
forms. He is the arch-divinity of the Yorùbá. His cult is widely
acknowledged all over the Yorubaland, and different localities call
him by different names. For example, he is called Òrìṣà-ńlá in Ilé-Ifẹ̀,
Ìbàdàn and some other places; and he is known as Òrìṣà Pópó in
Ògbómọ̀ṣọ́, Òrìṣà Ògìyán in Èjìgbò, Òrìṣà Ìjàyè at Ìjàyè and Òrìṣà
Onílẹ̀ in Ugbò, the ancient Ìlàjẹ town near Òkìtìpupa. Even though he
is called by different names, the worship accorded him is the same in
these different places. It is believed by the worshippers that he has the
power 'to make his worshippers great, to prosper them by making
them increase and multiply, and by conferring material blessings
upon them. . . . It is therefore said of him '*ó gbé ọmọ rẹ̀, ó sọ ọ́ dajé; ó nì
kì wọ́n rẹ̀rìnín, wọ́n rẹ̀rìnín*' ('He stands by his children and makes them
materially prosperous; he gives them cause for laughter, and they
laugh').[1]
     The divinity is popular for giving children to barren women and for
moulding the shape of the child in its mother's womb. Hence it is a
common thing to hear people wish a pregnant woman, '*Kórìṣà yanà ire
ko nio*' ('May the Òrìṣà (that is Òrìṣà-ńlá) fashion for us a good work of
art'). This is why Òrìṣà-ńlá is called the '*sculptor divinity*'. As a way of
explaining how certain people come to be ugly or deformed, the
Yorùbá claim that the albinos (*àfín*), the dwarfs (*iràrá*), the hunch-
backs (asuké), the cripples (*arọ*) and the dumb (*odi*) are created like
that by Òrìṣà to make them sacred to him. Such people are called *Ẹni
Òrìṣà* (those set apart for òrìṣà). The belief is that Òrìṣà, as the sculptor
divinity, sometimes produces beings with abnormal traits; and when
one sees such beings, one has cause to thank the sculptor divinity for
shaping one properly.
     Furthermore, Òrìṣà-ńlá is notable for his purity; he lives in a
whitewashed place and is robed in white. Hence people say of him:

Bàntà-banta n'nu àlà!	Immense in white robes!
Ó sùn ń'nú àlà,	He sleeps in white clothes,
Ó jí ń'nú àlà,	He wakes in white clothes,
Ó tinú àlà dìde	He rises in white clothes.

Ba ńlá! Ọkọ Yemòwó![2]   Venerable Father! Yemowo's consort!
Orìṣá wù mí ní bùdó   Orisa delights me as he is in state;
Ibi re lòrìṣá kalẹ̀   It is a delectable place where Orisa is
                         enthroned.[3]

Worshippers of Ọbàtálá are expected to be clean and upright; they may wear clothes of any colour but white is the most acceptable. Women worshippers wear strings of small opaque white beads (ṣéṣéefun) and white lead anklets and bracelets.

There is always a pot containing water in his sanctuary. The water is kept clean and pure, according to the people's understanding. Such water is fetched very early in the morning from a spring by either a virgin or a woman who has passed the child-bearing age. She does not greet anybody on the way and she carries a bell which she rings all the way to let people know that she is on a sacred errand. This sacred water is ceremonially given to the devotees, and among other benefits, it is believed to make barren women fertile. Most of the offerings at his shrine are bloodless, consisting of snails, bitter kola (orógbó), corn starch (ẹkọ tútù), well-boiled maize (ègbo) and coconuts. Food offered is usually cooked in shea butter – never in palm-oil – and may not be seasoned with pepper. His chief taboo is wine from the oil palm (ẹmu). One tradition holds that Òrìṣà-ńlá forbids offering palm wine at his shrine and forbids his devotees from taking it because of his (Òrìṣà-ńlá's) having got drunk on it when he was sent by Olódùmarè to go and create the solid earth, as mentioned in the previous chapter.

Before we leave our discussion of Òrìṣà-ńlá it should be pointed out that one oral tradition credits the arch-divinity with living on earth and being married to Yemòwó (not Yemúhú as put by Talbot[4]) and another suggests that his wife is Odùduwà; yet a third tradition sees Ọbàtálá (Òrìṣà-ńlá) and Odùdúwà as androgynous divinities. The two of them, according to this last tradition, are represented by a closed white-washed calabash – the lid (upper half) being Ọbàtálá and the bottom (the lower half), Odùduwà; they are symbolic of heaven and earth. We shall seek a solution to this enigma when we have examined Odùduwà below.

Ọrúnmìlà

Ọrúnmìlà is another of the primordial divinities. One oral tradition among the Yorùbá holds that when Olódùmarè was sending Ọbàtálá into the world to equip the earth, Ọrúnmìlà was also committed to accompany him and to give him necessary guidance. The tradition adds that after the world had been created, Ọrúnmìlà decided to move freely between heaven and earth to give advice like a counsellor. Hence he was given the appellation *'Gbáyé-gbọ́run'* (one who lives both on earth and in heaven).[5] As one who lives in and sees both heaven and earth, he is believed to be in a position to plead with Olódùmarè on behalf of man so that unpleasant circumstances may be averted or rectified. He is popularly acknowledged to be the oracle divinity among the Yorùbá. Among other sobriquets, he is called *'Ibíkéjì Èdùmàrè'* (next in rank to Olódùmarè). The method by which the oracle is ascertained is called *Ifá*. It is, therefore, misleading to call Ifa the oracle divinity as some past scholars have done.[6]

Ọrúnmìlà is believed to be specially gifted with knowledge and wisdom. He knew the secret of man's lot and could direct him how to rectify it because, as we have indicated above, he was present when man was created and his destiny sealed; hence he is called *'Ẹlẹ́rìí ìpín'* – one who bears witness to fate. The Yorùbá believe that men's fate is sealed by Olódùmarè before they come into the world. The people concerned do not remember what their allotted fate is on earth, but Ọrúnmìlà who was present when the fate was allotted, knows what the circumstances are and can therefore advise how to rectify it, wherever possible. This is why he is called *Ẹlẹ́rìí ìpín*.

Furthermore, Ọrúnmìlà is believed to know the tastes and taboos of the divinities and he is capable of giving guidance to them and mankind. He can speak for the divinities and communicate with human beings through divination. In addition, Ọrúnmìlà, through Ifá, is the one who interprets the wishes of Olódùmarè to mankind and who decides what sacrifice to offer on any given occasions. This is why he is consulted on all important occasions and his directives cannot be ignored.[7]

Some traditions claim that Ọrúnmìlà, rather than being a primordial divinity, was born a human being. His parentage was uncertain and hence the father's name is variously given as Jàkúta, Òrókò or Àgbọnnìrègún; and the mother's name as Alájèrù. The traditional home of the parents, according to this myth, is Ifẹ̀ from where he wandered all over 'the world' teaching men wisdom.

One of the myths described him as a poor lazy youth; another said that he was born a paralysed child who had to be carried from place to place to beg for his living; and yet another myth claimed that in the early days, the divinities were as limited in their power as men and depended upon men's offerings. When no offerings came, they starved. During this low period, Ọrúnmìlà met Èṣù (another divinity to be discussed later), who promised to teach Ọrúnmìlà the technique of divination on the condition that he (Èṣù) would be given a portion of every sacrifice prescribed and offered. Ọrúnmìlà agreed to the bargain. Èṣù then asked him to procure sixteen palm nuts from Ọrúngan's palm-trees. With the co-operation of Ọrúngan and his wife, Ọrúnmìlà got the nuts and brought them to Èṣù who used them in teaching the art of divination, popularly known as Ifá today. Ọrúnmìlà, in turn, taught Ọrúngan how to divine; hence Ọrúngan was Ọrúnmìlà's first disciple.

All we can say is that his origin was uncertain and various myths were invented to rationalise the origin of this primordial divinity who is gifted with supernatural knowledge and wisdom. All the traditions ended by indicating that Ọrúnmìlà became very popular as a true prophet and as a medical practitioner, and that many people in Yorubaland flocked to him to seek his guidance. It has been suggested by some Yorùbá elders that among the many people who came to him to learn of him he selected sixteen, who became his intimate disciples and after whom the sixteen *Odù* signs are named.

Ọrúnmìlà is widely worshipped in Yorubaland, and his shrine is to be found in almost every traditional home. Emblems consist of at least sixteen sacred palmnuts (called *Ikin*), which are put into a bowl with a lid, actual or graven pieces of elephant tusk, some cowry-shells, the divining tray (*ọpọ́n Ifá*) and conical bells or tappers (*Ìrofá*). These emblems are placed on a mound in the corner of a room and are curtained off from public view. The curtain is drawn or raised whenever there is to be worship which takes place regularly – daily, 'weekly' or on festival occasions. The Yorùbá have a traditional four-day week. The first day, according to popular tradition, is '*Ọjọ́ Awo*' – the day on which the oracle divinity is worshipped; the second is *Ọjọ́ Ògún* – the day the *òrìṣà* controlling iron and metal, of war and the chase is worshipped; the third is *Ọjọọ Jàkúta* – which is the day set apart for the worship of the *òrìṣà* controlling thunder and lightning; and the fourth is *Ọjọ́ Ọbàtálá* or *Òrìṣà-ńlá* – the day on which the arch-divinity is worshipped. It should be pointed out that even though these four days are set apart for the worship of the four divinities after whom they are named, other divinities are worshipped on one or the other of these sacred days, and others have their sacred days on every seventh, ninth or seventeenth day.

Besides the house shrine, there are sacred groves, called '*Igbódù*' where worship and divination take place on special occasions, particularly during an initiation rite.

The priest of Ọ̀rúnmìlà is called *Babaláwo* (Father of mysteries). He usually shaves his head, wears an amulet of palm fibre, carries a fly-whisk and commands the respect of the people. He is ranked as the highest of all Yorùbá priests, and he is approached on every important event, private as well as public. The traditional Yorùbá will not embark upon any important project until he has consulted the oracle and ascertained the wishes of the *òrìṣà*. The system of divination and the relevance of this to sacrifice we shall examine at the appropriate place in this book.

Odùduwà

According to some myths, Odùduwà is seen both as a primordial divinity and as a deified ancestor. He is, indeed, a controversial figure in Yorùbá belief, and different writers, and informants have different traditions to give, depending upon where they are making their investigations.

Some Yorùbá, especially those in Ilé-Ifẹ́, emphasise the tradition which claims that Odùduwà was the creator of the earth and its inhabitants as a result of Ọbàtálá's failure through drunkenness to carry out Olódùmarè's injunction.[8] Yet another tradition, which Ifẹ̀ people dislike, claims that long after Ifẹ̀ had been created and peopled, a group of wanderers led by a warrior, who came later to be known as Odùduwà, reached Ifẹ̀, conquered the original inhabitants and settled there. He begat many children who later became the progenitors of the various clans which today constitute the Yorùbá people.

This controversial figure, Odùduwà, becomes more controversial when we are presented with another tradition that sees Odùduwà as the wife of Ọbàtálá and the chief female *Òrìṣà* (divinity) as Ọbàtálá is the chief male *Òrìṣà*.[9] We are, therefore, confronted with two tricky questions: Who created the solid earth – Òrìṣà-ńlá or Odùduwà?, and was Odùduwà a male or a female divinity? In his own solution Lucas suggested that:

> The myths depicting the deity as a female *òrìṣà* are more original in character, and are more widely accepted. There is hardly any doubt that Odùduwà was originally, a female deity . . . with her

adoption as the progenitor of the Yorùbá race, there seems to have arisen a tendency to regard her as a leader and a 'hero' in consequence of which late stories transforming her to a male deity were invented.[10]

While there may be a grain of truth in Lucas' solution it overlooks another problem: that the progenitor of the Yorùbá race is never regarded as a female but a male – not a heroine but a hero.

Ìdòwú has a double solution to this problem:[11]

(a) that the name Odùduwà itself connotes 'the self-existent Chief who created being', and this connotation might have led people to conclude that it was Odùduwà who created the earth;

(b) that the name of the hero, who led his men into Ilé-Ifẹ̀ and conquered the original inhabitants, might have been forgotten, and that the name Odùduwà 'belonged originally to a divinity and not to the personage to whom the name was later given.'

Today at Ugbò, a very ancient Ìlàjẹ town in Òkìtìpupa Division, there is a strong oral tradition which stresses the fact that the Ugbò people were the original inhabitants of Ilé-Ifẹ̀. Here, as earlier indicated, Ọbàtálá is called Òrìṣà-Onilẹ̀, the divinity that owns the land. Ugbò people claimed that they had lived in Ilé-Ifẹ̀ long before Odùduwà and his party landed and drove them away. Elders among the Ifẹ̀ people are not unfamiliar with this struggle which took place long ago between them and the Ugbò people (called Igbò by Ifẹ̀ people). This struggle between the adherents of Ọbàtálá and Odùduwà was a fierce one and it is re-enacted annually at the Edì Festival in Ilé-Ifẹ̀ when the Ọbawinrin, draped in grass, and representing the Ugbò people, engages the Ọòni (the king of Ifẹ̀, representing the Odùduwà group) in a mock wrestling match. The former has to fall as a token of submission to the latter.[12] But it is to be noted that the first child born by the champion of the Ugbò people after the terrible struggle was called Ọrún-m'akẹn'jà (ọ̀rún mọ akin ìjà) – that is, heaven knows who the champion is in the duel. This tradition from Ugbò is very illuminating with particular reference to the complex question of Odùduwà vis-à-vis Ọbàtálá. There are places in Ilé-Ifẹ̀ today which cannot be seen by traditional Ugbò people; and it is also believed that if any Ifẹ̀ people should set eyes on Ugbò town they will die. Whenever Ifẹ̀ people need to pass by Ugbò, they cover their heads.

From the different strands of tradition at our disposal, we conclude:

(a) that the original inhabitants of Ifẹ̀ knew and acknowledged Ọbàtálá as the deity that created the earth and to whom worship was due and given;

(b) that at a stage in the early history of Ifẹ̀, some intruders who were migrating from somewhere, came into Ifẹ̀, and conquered the original inhabitants who were devotees of Òrìṣà-ńlá;

(c) that the newcomers suppressed the worship of Ọbàtálá and embraced that of Odùduwà who was possibly a female divinity;

(d) that at the death of the conquering leader, his followers and admirers deified him and called him 'Odùduwà' after the primordial divinity whose worship he had encouraged. Thus, Odùduwà is portrayed as a primordial divinity and as a deified ancestor.

Some elders among the Yorùbá who want to resolve this problem emphasise the idea of a division of labour between the two divinities. They maintain that Ọbàtálá is senior to Odùduwà and that he was the one commissioned by the Supreme Being to create the earth, but that it was Odùduwà who actually did the work of creation. When Òrìṣà-ńlá came to himself after his drunkenness and discovered that Odùduwà had done what he himself had failed to do, he picked a terrible fight with him. Olódùmarè, the Supreme Being, stepped in and confirmed that Ọbàtálá was still the older of the two, but that the credit of creating the earth had gone to Odùduwà. Olódùmarè, then, gave another assignment to Ọbàtálá – the moulding of human forms from clay. Thus, he made human forms into which Olódùmarè breathed the breath of life. Hence Òrìṣà-ńlá is known as the 'sculptor divinity', and people sing his praise:

Ẹní ṣojú ṣemú,	He who makes eyes and nose,
Òrìṣà ni ma sìn	It is the Orìṣa I will serve;
A-dá-ni bóti rí;	He who creates as he chooses.
Òrìṣà ni ma sìn	It is the Orìṣa I will serve;
Ẹní rán mi wá,	He who sends me here,
Òrìṣà ni ma sìn	It is the Orìṣa I will serve.

In a sense, both Ọbàtálá and Odùduwà are associated with the creation of the earth and its inhabitants. The importance of Ọbàtálá, however, lies in the fact that he is universally acknowledged and worshipped in Yorubaland under different names, as pointed out earlier, and this shows that wherever the original people from Ifẹ̀ went, they took the cult of the divinity along with them. In comparison, the worship of Odùduwà is limited. It receives prominence mainly in Ilé-Ifẹ̀ where Ọbadió, the chief priest of Odùduwà, is ever ready to tell the enquirer that Odùduwà indisputably descended from heaven on the very spot where he (the chief priest) is occupying today and from where Odùduwà created the whole earth.

Èṣù

Èṣù is one of the principal divinities, and he is very prominent in Yorùbá mythology. We have seen him in connection with Ọ̀rúnmìlà to whom he taught the Ifá oracle which is a means of ascertaining the wishes of the divinities and Deity as well as seeking spiritual guidance. If, according to this popular tradition, he was Ọ̀rúnmìlà's instructor, one would say that he was his contemporary and, therefore, one of the primordial divinities. It would be wrong to suggest, as Bascom did, that 'Èṣù is the youngest . . . of the deities. . . .'[13]

It is very difficult for a casual observer of Yorùbá religion to understand Èṣù and his place in Yorùbá beliefs. Èṣù is neither the 'devil' of the Christian concept nor the 'shaitan' of the Muslim faith. The 'devil' or 'shaitan' in these two religions is outright evil, but this is not so with Èṣù in Yorùbá beliefs. Furthermore, we must stress that there is no dualism in Yorùbá religion in the way Dennett described Èṣù as the 'Being of darkness while Ifá is the Being of Light and Revelation'.[14] Lucas is also wrong to call Èṣù the 'evil deity who stands in direct opposition to Ọlọ́run. . . .'[15] Èṣù is neither like *Ekwensu* that is an altogether evil force, according to the belief of the Ìgbò of Nigeria, nor like *Ahriman* of Zoroastrianism that is constantly opposing *Ahura Mazda* (the Lord of wisdom). In other words, the Yorùbá world does not know of totally opposing forces – one representing evil and the other good. Èṣù is not the personal embodiment of evil standing in opposition to goodness.[16] As one of the functionaries of Olódùmarè in His theocratic world, he is to be seen as 'that part of the divine which tests and tries out people. He tempts people, but that does not mean that he is against the human race or will do only harm. He is one who loves to try out what is in people's hearts and what their real character is'.[17]

Èṣù is to be seen as the 'special' relations official between heaven and earth. The Yorùbá tradition holds that he maintains relationships with the super-sensible world and with human beings on earth. With regard to the super-sensible world, he maintains close relationship with Ọ̀rúnmìlà who is notable for his wisdom and who knows the wishes of Deity and divinities and who conveys these to men through Ifá (which Èṣù had earlier taught to him). Whenever the oracle speaks, sacrifice is prescribed, it must be offered by men and women who want the favour of the gods. A portion of each sacrifice goes to Èṣù (according to the contract with Ọ̀rúnmìlà), and he makes sure that he carries the 'message' to the spiritual world. But if a person refuses to do the biddings of the Deity and the divinities, Èṣù will make life uncomfortable for him or her. Èṣù's chief function is to run errands for both men and divinities and to report their deeds to the Supreme Being. As the 'inspector-general', Èṣù is ubiquitous, found in the market-place, at road junctions and at the thresholds of houses. In his actions, he is ambivalent as he is ambidextrous. What is intriguing about Èṣù is that he does not discriminate in carrying out errands – good as well as evil – he can be used as an instrument of retaliation; he can create enmity between father and children or between husband and wife as he can do between two good friends. At the same time, he can provide children for the barren or good bargaining power for the market-women. He can cause a person to misbehave or to act abnormally as he can force a debtor to pay up a debt owed to a creditor (if the latter seeks his help). This is why the Yorùbá say of him, '*Kò ṣe ídúró dè, kò sì ṣe ísá fún*' ('One neither flees from nor waits for him'). He is seen as the divine enforcer, punishing those who do not offer prescribed sacrifices and making sure that those who do are amply rewarded.

It should be pointed out here that the Yorùbá believe that Èṣù can and does instigate men to offend the gods – thereby providing sacrifices for the angry gods. This is why some people say that without him (Èṣù), the gods will go hungry.

Early investigators of the Yorùbá religion who claimed that Èṣù's place is always at the road junctions and far from human habitations are wrong. We have discovered that the true position is that almost every traditional household, clan or village, every devotee (irrespective of the cult to which he or she belongs) has the symbol and worship of Èṣù. His cult transcends the limits of any group or lineage. No devotee of any divinity will omit to propitiate Èṣù first before offerings are made to the divinity being worshipped. No family head will fail to give the first morsel of a meal or the first drop of a libation to Èṣù before the ancestral spirits are 'fed'. He must be propitiated first so that, in turn, he can co-operate in the favourable development of the ceremony to be performed. No one wants him to 'spoil' things for him. He must be reckoned with seriously because, eventually, he will be the one to carry the offerings to their recipients – thus maintaining the relationship between the human beings making the offerings and the supernatural entities. In other words, without Èṣù the dynamic of ritual would not exist. If he did not receive the necessary elements needed to fulfil his constructive function, he would retaliate by blocking the way of goodness and opening up the ways that are inimical and destructive to human beings. Hence he is both feared and revered.

Individuals keep Èṣù to help them ward off evil things and bring them prosperity and peace. Parrinder likens Èṣù in this kind of relationship to a savage dog 'that will rarely bite the hand that feeds it but, it is hoped, may be relied upon to attack any evil that approaches. . . .'[18]

Èṣù has no regular priesthood because he is associated with all the other divinities. But, whenever these other divinities are worshipped, due homage is paid to him. *His* devotees wear black or maroon beads round their necks.

He is represented by different kinds of images. He may be seen in the form of a simple mound crudely shaped into human form with horns on his head, and a knife or club in his hand; or he may be represented by a piece of laterite or rock stuck into the ground; or an earthenware pot turned upside down with a hole in the middle.

Offerings made to Èṣù are of very simple type: they include a few grains of maize or beans, black chickens or fowls, he-goats and dogs. Dogs are particularly said to be 'sacred' to him because they physically eat the sacrifices placed at the shrines of Èṣù. Hence the common saying among the Yorùbá: *'Ohun tì ajá máa jẹ, Èṣù á ṣe é'* ('What the dogs will eat will be provided by Èṣù'). Over and above it all Èṣù loves palm oil (*epo*) but abhors oil extracted from palm-kernels (*àdín*); to offer the former is to curry his favour and the latter to incur his displeasure. The belief is that if Èṣù is 'dry', trouble will break out – there might be a fight or pestilience or outbreak of fire; hence daily palm-oil is poured over the 'pillar' representing him.

We see in Èṣù a personification of good and evil; and the way the Yorùbá pay attention to him is indicative of their acknowledge-ment of the presence and co-existence of good and evil forces in the world.

Ògún

Ògún is sometimes depicted as a primordial divinity and sometimes as a deified ancestor. Both traditions have support among the Yorùbá; but it seems that the tradition that depicts him as a primordial being is stronger than the other.

According to one myth, when the divinities were first coming to inhabit the earth, they came to a thicket and could not cut their way through. Each of the divinities tried but failed until Ògún volunteered his service and cut the path through with his sharp matchet. In consequence of this, all the divinities hailed him as great. The Yorùbá have a saying: *'Òrìsà tí ó wípé tÒgún kò tó ǹkan, á fọwọ́ jẹ iṣu rẹ̀ nígbà àìmoye'* ('Whichever divinity regards Ògún as of no consequence, will eat his yams with his hands (i.e. unprepared) for times without number'). This is to suggest that the other divinities pay due regard to Ògún as they do pay to Èṣù. In actual fact, he is called *'Oṣìnmalẹ̀'* – chief among the divinities.

Because Ògún is associated with clearing the way or removing barriers, the Yorùbá hold the belief that when one's path is not clear or when one encounters difficulties, appeal must be made to Ògún to help in making the path smooth in the same way as he did for the divinities in the beginning of days. He is also believed to be capable of providing prosperity for his devotees. And among other sobriquets, he is called *'Onílé owó, Ọlọ́nà ọlà, Onílé kángunkàngun òde òrun'* ('The owner of the house of money, the owner of the house of riches; the owner of the innumerable houses of heaven').

Another tradition claims an earthly origin for Ògún. He is said to be the son of Odùduwà (Odùduwà in Yorùbá tradition has a large number of these sons!) and that he was a powerful warrior who helped his father in fighting against many of his enemies (including Ọbàtálá). The tradition adds that in appreciation of Ògún's victories, Odùduwà gave him authority to go and reign over Ìrè, a town in Èkìtì. Thus he became the first king of Ìrè; and he is today called Ògún-Onírè. We should point out, however, that other places in Yorubaland, for example, Iléṣà and Oǹdó, where the worship of Ògún is given prominence, dispute this right with Ìrè and say disparagingly that Ìrè is not the home of Ògún, he only called there to drink palm-wine on one of his war campaigns.

The present king of Ìrè (Olírè of Ìrè) claims descent from Ògún and thus from Odùduwà. He has personally confirmed that Ògún was the first king of Ìrè and that once when Ògún was returning from one of his fiercest battles, he came upon a group of Ìrè people in *Àjọ Òrìkí* (a gathering where greeting was forbidden), and was surprised to see that none of the people greeted him. With his matchet, he touched the kegs of palm-wine standing at the centre of the gathering, but felt disappointed when he discovered that they were empty – normally, when kegs of palm-wine have been emptied of their content, they are turned upside down. The infuriated Ògún started beheading the people – his own subjects and children, destroying quite a large number before he came to himself. Realising his bloody deed, he decided to put a stop to his carnage in a dramatic way. He thrust his sword into the ground, sat on it and began to sink slowly into the bosom of the earth. But before he disappeared finally, he assured the people that whenever they needed him they should call on him. And the Ìrè people claim that they have called on him at the approach of enemies and he has not let them down.

Today at Ìrè, the chief priest of Ògún lives permanently at the very spot where it is believed Ògún went into the bosom of the earth. According to tradition, he and the Olírè of Ìrè must not meet face to face. But the king makes sure that he sends regular offerings to the chief priest for the worship of Ògún.

Thus Ògún was with the very early divinities and was useful to them but, at the same time, there is the oral tradition which claimed that he actually reigned over a territory in Yorubaland. But what is the significance of Ògún in Yorùbá belief? He is believed to be the divinity of iron and of war and pre-eminently the tutelary divinity of hunters, the blacksmiths, the goldsmiths, the barbers, the butchers and (in modern time) the mechanics, the lorry and taxi-drivers – indeed, all workers in iron and steel. No Yorùbá hunter goes on a hunting expedition without paying due regard to Ògún; no soldier goes to war without offering appropriate sacrifice to the divinity; no lorry driver considers himself safe until offering is made to Ògún and no smith feels comfortable until he has paid homage to Ògún. All these workers in iron and steel look up to Ògún for protection against accident and for help in their work. It is believed that Ògún has the matchet to clear the path and open the gate for wealth, health and prosperity. And, if he is neglected, he can cause ghastly accidents and bloody battles. To avoid such catastrophes, offerings to propitiate Ògún are offered by the Yorùbá. In this way, Ògún is seen as a symbol of the superior, conquering one. This is a concept that is universal;

but, behind the concept, there may be a human being. For example, the Romans have *Mars* as their god of war as the Greeks have *Apollo* as their god of the chase.

It is also believed that Ògún stands for absolute justice and so he is called upon to witness to a covenant or pact between two persons or groups of people. At present, when a Yorùbá who is an adherent of the traditional religion is brought to the law-court, he is asked to swear on Ògún (represented by a piece of iron) instead of on the Bible or the Quran. This he does by kissing a piece of iron as he declares that he will 'speak the truth, the whole truth and nothing but the truth'. The Yorùbá believe very strongly that anybody who swears falsely or breaks a covenant to which Ògún is a witness, cannot escape severe judgment which normally results in ghastly accidents.

The shrines of Ògún are usually located outside – in the open air at the foot of some sacred trees (e.g. *Pèrègún*, *Akòko*, *Àtòrì*, and *Ìyéyè*), by the side of a wall and in a smithy. The symbols include pieces of iron, matchets or guns, and the popular dress of Ògún, *Màrìwò* (the palm-frond).

Offerings made to Ògún include palm-wine, palm-oil, dogs, snails, rams, roasted yams and tortoises. Human beings were offered before the abolition of human sacrifice.

Deified ancestors

Usually, among the ancient Yorùbá, heroic men and women who have made useful contributions to life and culture of the people were deified. Instead of saying that such heroes or heroines died, the Yorùbá would say that they have metamorphosed themselves into stone or iron – *wón dọta* or *wón diírin*; sometimes they were described as going into the bosom of the earth or ascending by means of a chain into the heaven above. We have a number of such deified ancestors and all that we can do here is to examine two or three of them.

Ṣàngó
Popular legend among the Yorùbá claims that Ṣàngó was a human being and that he reigned as the fourth Aláàafin of Ọ̀yọ́. There are many legends associated with him, and each of them tries to explain how Ṣàngó came to be apotheosised and associated with the solar deity.

One version says that Ṣàngó discovered a charm by means of which he could call down lightning from heaven. One day, he went to a hill outside the city to try his new discovery. The charm worked wonderfully: lightning descended on Ṣàngó's own palace and destroyed it together with his wives and children. Ṣàngó was so horrified by this calamity that he went out and hanged himself.

Another version says that Ṣàngó's wives (Oya, Òṣun and Òbà) were very quarrelsome and gave him no end of trouble. Worse still, there were complaints from his subjects about his tyranny. Weary of the unrest in domestic and state affairs, Ṣàngó mounted his horse in anger and rode into the forest. His people sought for him in vain. As they called him, urging him to come back, they heard him saying from the distance, 'I will not come back to you; I will now rule you unseen'. The legend adds that Ṣàngó went up to the sky above by a chain, and has been manifesting his kingly rule by lightning and thunder ever since.

But the most popular of the legends (and which the Ṣàngó devotees detest) is that Ṣàngó was a tyrannical and powerful ruler versed in various magical arts. When he addressed his subjects, for example, fire and smoke used to issue from his mouth and his nostrils; and this instilled fear into his subjects.

The legend adds that he had two courtiers, Tìmì and Gbọ̀nkáà Èbìrì, who were becoming too powerful to control, and so he craftily planned to get rid of them by setting them to fight against each other hoping that they might both die in the encounter. While Tìmì died, Gbọ̀nkáà continued to live and to be an irritant to the king. He therefore ordered that Gbọ̀nkáà be cast into the fire; but to the king's discomfiture, Gbọ̀nkáà came out of the fire unscathed. As a result, Ṣàngó abdicated and fled his kingdom. On the way to the place of his voluntary exile, he discovered that even the most intimate members of his family were deserting him. He therefore decided to 'play the man' and committed suicide by hanging himself on a tree. The news quickly went round.

The king's opponents, delighted to hear the news, began to ridicule and taunt the king's supporters. To save face, the supporters went to the Nupe clan (Ṣàngó's maternal home) and procured some preparation by which lightning could be attracted. This means they then employed to bring the disaster of lightning upon many people in Òyó and its environs. Houses and compounds were often found in conflagration. The people consulted the oracle and discovered that the calamity was brought about by Ṣàngó who was angry because it was alleged that he had hanged himself. The only way to avoid the lightning, therefore, was to declare openly that the king had not hanged himself, and to bring a propitiatory sacrifice of fowls, sheep, rams, palm oil and bitter kola nuts (orógbó). People came to the spot where Ṣàngó was alleged to have been hanged, and declared, 'Ọba kò so' ('the king did not hang'). This has since become a very popular sanctuary of Ṣàngó in the outskirts of the present Ọ̀yọ́ and there the kings of Ọ̀yọ́, who claim Ṣàngó as their ancestor, are traditionally crowned. Thus, Ṣàngó, who was a human being, became deified and worshipped.

The most interesting thing is that the devotees do not remember Ṣàngó for his tyranny or magical displays; rather they remember and revere him as standing for justice and fair play. They strongly believe that he hates and forbids stealing, lying, witch-craft and sorcery. But we know that Ṣàngó had not such high moral standards in his life-time. The truth of the matter is that there was a solar deity among the Yorùbá called Jàkúta (one who hurls or fights with stones) who was a guardian of social morality and who hated immorality in any shape or form; indeed he was 'too good to behold iniquities'. Whenever people did wrong or did things contrary to the will of Olódùmarè, Jàkúta would hurl stones of fire. What we are suggesting is that there had been thunder and lightning before Ṣàngó was born and that there was a divinity associated with this phenomenon: Jàkúta. But what happened was that Ṣàngó's supporters, who became his first devotees, came to see in him attributes similar to those of the traditional solar divinity, Jàkúta. Thus, a kind of Euhemerism[19] took place. Ṣàngó, the man, came to assume the attributes of Jàkúta the original deity who was a manifestation of 'the wrath' of Olódùmarè. Today, among the Yorùbá, the devotees of Ṣàngó worship him on the sacred day of Jàkúta. And if one asks these devotees why they worship Ṣàngó on the day of Jàkúta, one will discover that they cannot give any satisfactory answer; rather, they will dismiss the question by saying that Ṣàngó is the same divinity as Jàkúta.

Thunder and lightning are usually hailed 'Kábíyèsí!' ('Hail your majesty!') as the paramount chiefs are hailed among the Yorùbá. This is because the people believe that whenever it thunders, the former Aláàdàfin of Ọ̀yọ́, who is now deified, has come for a visitation.

The belief of the Yorùbá (as we indicated in the last chapter) is that this world and all the inhabitants belong to the Supreme Being

(Olódùmarè) Who expects good behaviour and high moral standard of His creatures. If men do the wrong thing, there is a means whereby Olódùmarè will punish the evil doers. This is 'Karma', the law of cause and effect. And one of the ways by which the 'wrath' of Olódùmarè is manifested is Jàkúta who hurls stones on evil doers. This instils fear into men and women who are wicked and immoral. That is why the people say, 'Onímú ńṣímú, èké ńsá' ('the owner of the nose turns up the nose, and the liar flees'). Sometimes when there is a peal of thunder or a flash of lightning, people standing closely together will request in a jocular way (but backed up with some belief) 'Ẹ jẹ́kí á dúró lọ́tọ̀ọ̀tọ̀' ('Let us stand far apart'). The idea is that when people are standing together and the 'wrath' descends, it may not only land on the evil but the innocent who are close by may also be adversely affected.

However, it is strongly believed that only the wicked are struck by lightning. And, in consequence of this, whenever lightning strikes a person dead or descends upon a house, it is generally believed that such a person has committed some atrocious deeds and that the members of the house so struck are evil. Nobody, therefore, sympathises with the deceased's relatives or gives the deceased a proper burial. Only the Magbà, the priests of Ṣàngó, arrange the conveyance of such bodies to the 'bad bush' where they are ritually disposed of. The belongings of the deceased, if they have not been destroyed by lightning, revert to the priests (if authorised by Ṣàngó) or are conveyed into the bush with the deceased. A house struck by lightning cannot be used until the necessary propitiatory sacrifice has been offered. This is because Ṣàngó has taken possession of it and it would be dangerous to dispute it with him. Hence the Yorùbá say, 'Bí ó bá wọ̀ sílé, onílé a lọ wọ̀ lágbẹ̀dẹ̀' ('If he descends upon a house, the land lord has to leave for a smithy'). We can recall here the belief of the Nuer of the Sudan who hold a contrary view: among them, a victim of lightning is not considered to have died the death of a sinner, but he is believed to have been called away by God who needs his soul.[20]

Shrines of Ṣàngó abound in Yorùbá towns and villages. At such shrines can be found images of a man (representing Ṣàngó) surrounded by three smaller images (perhaps representing Ọya, Ọ̀ṣun and Ọ̀bà, his three wives); or the image of a man with a ram's head and horns, holding the handle of a double-headed axe (Oṣée Ṣàngó). There are also gourd rattles, (Ṣẹ́ẹ́rẹ́ẹ̀ Ṣàngó), inverted mortar, a big pot of water containing some celts, and, in some cases a tray or bowl holding celts and polished stones believed to have been hurled by Ṣàngó. Such symbols as may be at the shrine are screened off by means of a purple or maroon curtain which is the special colour of Ṣàngó.

Bitter kola (orógbó) is offered daily to Ṣàngó, but more elaborate offerings are made on the sacred day called 'Ọjọọ́ Jàkúta'. There is also offered to him plenty of palm-oil (epo) to calm his anger. And, on festival occasions, a ram, which is his favourite animal, and chickens are offered to him. Lucas is probably wrong when he claims that 'a ram must never be offered or eaten by his (Ṣàngó's) worshippers'.[21] It is a common belief among the Yorùbá that Ṣàngó eats àgbò (ram) as Ògún eats ajá (dog).

Orógbó (bitter kola) is also used as the principal means of divination by the priests of Ṣàngó. Such a bitter kola is cut into two halves longitudinally and cast on the ground after the appropriate invocation has been pronounced. The priest then reads the omen and interprets the oracle. The other means of divination used is the erìndín-lógún (divining by means of 16 cowries).[22] These are the two permissible means of divination as far as Ṣàngó is concerned.

Worthy of note in connection with the worship of Ṣàngó is the 'Ẹlégùn' (Ṣàngó's mount) – this is the person 'invaded' by the spirit of Ṣàngó. It is the belief of the Yorùbá that a divinity communicates with the faithful by incarnating itself in a person who then becomes his mouthpiece. The person is then possessed and he experiences a feeling of emptiness as though he were fainting. During the period, he becomes the vessel or the instrument of the divinity. People say that the spirit 'mounts' the person as a man mounts a horse. This is a common feature of the worship of the divinities. In the case of Ẹlégùn Ṣàngó, the person so possessed loses consciousness and does things which he would not have been capable of doing under normal circumstances – sitting on an iron spear point, passing a sharp-edged knife through his tongue, carrying a pot of live coals on his head, eating fire and similar actions, without getting hurt.

Such an 'Ẹlégùn' wears a cotton coat which is dyed red and to which are fastened many charms, cowry shells and miniature symbols of Ṣàngó. He dances to the drumming of the special drum called the 'bàtá' drum. In the midst of drumming, singing and dancing, he 'hears' the message of Ṣàngó and this he relates to the devotees. In most places, the Ẹlégùn are male and they usually plait their hair like women. But the Ẹlégùn in some places, for example in Ẹ̀gbá area, are female.

Before we leave our examination of Ṣàngó, we should point out that there is the counterpart of this divinity in Ilé-Ifẹ̀ where he is known as Ọ̀ràmfẹ̀. His priests make offerings to him when lightning strikes, and this seems to suggest that both Ọ̀ràmfẹ̀ and Jàkúta (apotheosised as Ṣàngó) are one and the same divinity and performing the same function: bringing down the wrath of Olódùmarè on the evil people in the community.

Òrìṣà-oko

Òrìṣà-oko is the patron divinity of the Yorùbá farmers. The real name of the person who is apotheisised and associated with successful farm work and the fertility of the land has been lost. But a Yorùbá legend says that he once lived as a chief in the town of Ìràwọ̀. He was sent away from the town and from the community because he suddenly became leprous. His kind wife decided to go with him.

While they were in this predicament, both of them struggled to keep body and soul together by engaging in hunting and in fruit collecting respectively. Suddenly, by accident, the wife discovered that some fruits, eaten and thrown away in the past, grew and yielded the same kind of fruits. She therefore started raising crops and getting food to provide for herself and her husband. As a result of eating the plant-products and the flesh of the animals and birds he hunted in addition to using the medical powers in the surrounding herbs, the man was cured of his leprosy. Both of them returned to Ìràwọ̀ and were gladly welcomed back by the people. Because of their noble-mindedness, they did not keep their newly-acquired agricultural science to themselves, but taught it to others. Very many people came to learn of them.

When they grew old and died, they were never forgotten by the people who found it difficult to believe that such people could be taken away from them. Thus they spoke of them as 'those who entered into the bosom of the earth' to continue another existence. Hence the common saying among the Yorùbá, 'Òrìṣà-okó wọlẹ̀ nÍràwọ̀' ('Òrìṣà-oko entered into the bosom of the earth in the town of Ìràwọ̀'). They associate with them the fertility of the land and successful farm-work. And that was how the 'chief' and his wife who once lived in the town of Ìràwọ̀ came to be deified.

There is some confusion among the Yorùbá as to which of the two is deified and called Òrìṣà-oko – is it the man or his wife? Is Òrìṣà-oko a male or a female divinity? From the account that we have just given, it will be clear that both of them were involved either in the actual 'discovery' or in the predicament that led to the discovery. We therefore have to see this as a joint effort – the mutual co-operation of the man and his wife. And we observe that among the Yorùbá, the Òrìṣà-oko priesthood is open to men and women but with women in preponderance. The priests and priestesses bear two vertical lines, one white and the other red, on their foreheads. The female worshippers, however, are more tenacious than their male counterpart, and they form themselves into a sort of guild. It is, invariably, among the women that we have the '*Agégùn Òrìṣà-oko*' – the devotees usually possessed by the divinity as we have the '*Elégùn-Ṣàngó*'. The '*Agégùn Òrìṣà-oko*' lives very close to the shrine of the divinity. And on many occasions, she acts as an arbiter in deciding disputes, especially where accusations of witchcraft are concerned.

Òrìṣà-oko is represented by an iron staff covered with cowries and has the honey bees as his own servants. It is understood that whenever a swarm of bees is flying overhead, Òrìṣà-oko devotees usually rush to collect cold water which they pour on the ground in the open air as a mark of homage to the divinity and they pray that all may be sweetness for them and bitterness for those who wish them ill.

Since many of the Yorùbá depend chiefly upon the fruits of the earth for their living, they came to accord Òrìṣà-oko a very important place in their pantheon. It is the practice among earnest devotees to make an annual 'pilgrimage' to Ìràwò to invoke the blessings of the divinity and to make offerings. But besides the central traditional spot in Ìràwò, shrines are established in different towns and villages in Yorubaland. In Ìbàdàn alone, there are more than seven shrines dedicated to the worship of Òrìṣà-oko, even though an area in the city known as '*Olórìṣà-oko*' (Olóóṣooko) claims to own the first shrine.

Òrìṣà-oko loves pangolin (*akika*), goat (*ewúré*), the fish called *eja aborí* and melon stew (*ọbẹ̀ ègúsí*) with pounded yam (*iyán*) and wine from guinea corn (*ọtí sẹ̀kẹ̀tẹ́*). These materials of sacrifice are provided in addition to the farm products which are ceremonially presented to Òrìṣà-oko before men and women can eat or sell them. During the worship of Òrìṣà-oko, there is a great deal of eating and drinking; specific items of food and drink, such as those enumerated above, are offered first to the divinity and later shared by the worshippers. For any of the necessary items to be absent will be tantamount to offering inadequate worship.

The usual ceremonial worship of Òrìṣà-oko at the annual festival is interesting and dramatic. A huge quantity of pounded yam (*iyán*) is placed in a large wooden tray around which the priests and priestesses together with the devotees sit. They beat the food (the pounded yam) with the palms of their hands singing joyfully and rhythmically:

A ó jiyán lónìí	We shall eat pounded yam today
Iyan!	Pounded yam!
A ó jiyán lónìí	We shall eat pounded yam today,
Iyan!	Pounded yam!
Iyán tó funfun lélé,	White, white pounded yam
Iyan!	Pounded yam!
Iyán a bìlèwu lórùn	Yams pounded into a delicious pulp,
Iyan!	Pounded yam!
A ó jiyán lónìí	We shall eat pounded yam today,
Sègbèdè á sè	There will be much rejoicing
Iyán o'.	O, Pounded yam!

After this dramatic exercise, the priest or priestess cuts a sizable portion of the *iyán* and dips it into the pot of *égúsí* stew in such a way that several roasted *ègúsí* balls will stick to it. He or she then places this slice of *iyán* before the divinity. It is only after this that the priests and priestesses and the people can eat and drink. According to the people's belief, no one who belongs to this covenant group can partake of the new yam until this ceremonial eating has taken place and part of the food has been ceremonially presented to the divinity. In some places, the ceremony lasts seven days. The devotees come to the shrine daily, bringing pounded yam, part of which they give to the divinity, and the rest shared in communal meals.

In some places in Yorubaland, similar offerings are made to some divinities which are associated with agriculture. There are (to cite a few instances) the Eje festival in Itebu Manùwà, the Ìjèsu in Ìlárá near Àkúrè and the Owè or Orò Olófin in Ilè-Olújìí. During these festivals, yams are ceremonially harvested and offered first to the divinities and ancestors believed to be responsible for bringing about good crops. It is after the ceremonial giving that all, in the midst of jubilation, will eat and drink. It is to be pointed out that in Ilè-Olújìí, it is not only new yams that are presented in this way but kola-nuts, which are very important products in the area, are also ceremonially presented to Orò-Olófin. As the Àwòrò (the chief priest) passes by, every farmer who has harvested kola-nuts during the season, brings some quantity of kola-nuts and throws them at the priest (representing Orò-Olófin) as he is hailed 'Ọlọ́fin ò!' It is believed that if anyone keeps kola-nuts at home and fails to offer some to Ọlọ̀fin, such an ungrateful person will suffer great loss that year. All this is to emphasise the fact that the Yorùbá farmers attribute success in farm-work to some divine beings who act as the functionaries of Olódùmarè in His theocratic world.

As the ancient Canaanites gave thanks to Ba'alim (lords of the land) who made their crops do well, and the Mende of Sierra-Leone offer rice to the god of the earth, the Ashanti of Ghana make offerings to Asase Ya (goddess of the earth), the Igbo of Anambra and Imo States of Nigeria sacrifice to Ala/Ale, and the Ijaw of the Rivers State in Southern Nigeria sacrifice to Amakiri, so also do the Yorùbá in appreciation of their success in agriculture, offer thanksgiving sacrifice, at the beginning of the harvest season, to Òrìsà-oko who is believed to be one of the functionaries of Olódùmarè in His maintenance and organisation of the world, particularly, with regard to the fertility of the soil and agricultural products.

Ayélálà [23]

Ayélálà, who has become a popular goddess feared and revered today by most people in Òkìtìpupa Division of Western Nigeria and beyond, was originally a slave, probably brought, according to tradition, from Èkìtì Division to Kíṣòṣò, a village in Òkìtìpupa Division. She was a devotee of several divinities. Tradition says that she had sixteen gods, the greatest of which was Òrìsà-ńlá. As a symbol of the cult of Òrìsà-ńlá, she bore on her head a tuft of hair.

Ayélálà was not her real name. The Ìlàjẹ and the Ìjó people who worship Ayélálà and who were our informants, keep as ritual top secret the names of the woman, of her mother, and of her home town. The name *Ayélálà*, as we shall see below, came to be given to her in consequence of her cry of dereliction when, as a sacrificial victim, she was at the point of death.

Among the Ìlàjẹ people, high moral standards used to be maintained. Among other things, adultery was regarded a heinous crime, especially if a commoner had an illicit relation with a nobleman's wife. Such an offence was punishable by death.

It happened that one Kékò (a commoner) cohabited with Chief Temẹ̀tànán's wife. When this became known, and Kékò knew that his life was at stake, he ran to Ìgbòbíní, a town belonging to the Ìjó Apoi people in Òkìtìpupa Division, to seek refuge. The Ìjó Apoi people gave him asylum and withstood the attack of the Ìlàjẹ people who wanted to bring Kékò to Mahin, their headquarters, to face justice. Thus the Ìlàjẹ and the Ìjó made attacks and counter-attacks on each other.

Men of good will from the two sides sought to bring about a reconciliation: Ìdógbè representing the Ìlàjẹ, and Agbélẹ̀kì representing the Ìjó made a desperate effort to stop the fight. The Ìlàjẹ gave an irrevocable condition, namely that if Kékò was not to be killed, a substitute must be found because blood must flow in consequence of the offence committed by Kékò. The Ìjó agreed to this and made a thorough search for a human victim. At last, the woman called Ayélála today was found and brought to an agreed rendezvous – now known as Oríta-Ayélála (Ayélála Junction) where she was to be sacrificed.

Before the sacrifice was offered, the two parties agreed on the terms of the covenant. Both parties were to become reconciled and to enter into a ritual kinship. They were to be faithful to each other and one another; they were not to plan evil against one another; stealing, sorcery and witchcraft should not be practised among these groups of people; any Ìlàjẹ or Ìjó who was wronged should call on Ayélála to avenge the wrong.

The terms of the covenant were spoken aloud to the victim and she was asked whether or not she would punish anyone disregarding the terms of the covenant. She answered in the affirmative.

It was the practice among the Yorùbá that a human sacrificial victim should pray emphasising that the cause for which he or she was offered might prosper. In accordance with this, the woman was asked to pray. But all that she uttered before she was sacrificed was, 'Ayé lála' which in Ìlàjẹ dialect means 'The world is great' or . . . 'incomprehensible'. This was the cry of dereliction showing that she was being put to death for the offence which someone else had committed. From then on, known as the woman who was sacrificed came to be known as Ayélála. And this is the name which the goddess bears today.

The process by which she became deified is not quite certain. But in all probability her deification was linked up with what was believed to be a fulfilment of an undertaking that she gave before her death that she would kill anyone who contravened any of the terms of the covenant.

Tradition says that soon after the covenant, one Ìjó man who broke one of the terms of the covenant died suddenly, and it was widely believed that it was Ayélála who killed him because of his breach of the covenant. This event, or others similar to it, began the belief in the power of Ayélála which eventually resulted in her deification.

Happenings which were believed to be prompt judgments of Ayélála on any violations of the covenant instilled fear into the peoples' minds and, consequently, fair play and justice became the order of the day. Even in uneventful things of day-to-day life, like the sharing of food and drinks, there was the belief that Ayélála was keeping watch. It is still the practice when two people (an Ìlàjẹ and an Ìjó) are eating or sharing anything for each of the party to 'Mine is bigger than yours' (*'Tèmí mà jù tèrẹ o'*) and his partner to answer reassuringly, 'The goddess will not kill' (*'Umalẹ́ é pa'*).[24] In other words, 'I have no grudge against you, therefore, there is nothing for the goddess to avenge'. It is firmly believed that cheating in any manner would readily be punished.

It was not long before a shrine was set up for her at Orìta Ayélála, and the worship firmly established. An essential fact to note here is that a human being has turned into a goddess. Just as Ṣàngó is very rarely thought of today as one who was once a human being, so it is with Ayélála. She is now almost always thought of only as a guardian of morality and an anti-wickedness goddess. Any breach of the covenant incurs her displeasure. Witches, thieves, perjurers and other evil-doers are believed to be under constant displeasure of the goddess and punished accordingly.

It is forbidden to mourn the death of one of Ayélála's victims. This is because it is believed that she is goddess in opposition to wickedness and has acted with justice: she (like Ṣàngó) represents the justice of Olódùmarè. Rather than weeping, the people congratulate the relatives of the victim on the removal of the evil doer by the goddess, the 'queen' of justice and ready 'reckoner' whose eyes see all the evil-doers.

Ayélála is believed to have allies among the other divinities for the purpose of executing judgment. Such divinities include Ṣọ̀pọ̀nnó (god of smallpox), Èmìnalẹ̀ or Ọ̀rọ̀ (god of paralysis), Ṣàngó and Èṣù, to mention but a few. The following story illustrates how the alliances work. There was a man who practised sorcery on his daughter, as a result of which she was at the point of death. When Ayélála saw the wickedness, she decided to kill the man. The clever sorcerer changed himself into an ant and got into a drum containing palm-oil, feeling quite safe since he knew that Ayélála would not touch palm-oil. But Ayélála outwitted him by asking *Ọba Olúwáiyé* also called Ṣọ̀pọ̀nnó (god of smallpox) who loves palm-oil, to drink the oil dry. This was done, and the 'ant' was taken and killed. In this way, the wicked sorcerer was killed by Ayélálá with the co-operation of Ṣòpònnó.

Thus it is believed that Ayélálá helps to keep the community clean and sane. And this she does by pointing out through afflictions or death wicked people in the community; and, in this way, she keeps in check those who are prone to malpractices. Wherever the belief in Ayélálá is very strongly held, people dread vices, such as stealing, lying, cheating, poisoning, using charms or bewitching others. In consequence of this, and in the days gone by, before the introduction of Western 'civilisation', people from Òkìtìpupa Division in general and the Ìlàje and the Ìjó in particular, were held in great esteem for their integrity and probity.

The main shrine of Ayélálá is located at Orita-Ayélálá, the very spot where the victim, later called Ayélálá, was sacrificed in the nineteenth century, before the abolition of human sacrifice. This is a very small island which is only a few inches above water level and on which the water routes from Mahin, Ìgbókòdá and Abòtò converge. Here is erected a small shed (formerly thatch-roofed but now corrugated iron-roofed) which, somehow, protects the altar from rain and sun.

On the altar can be found five cowries (ẹyọwó), a red tail-feather of the parrot (ìkóódẹ), a lump of native chalk (gbòrò ẹfun), some kola-nuts (obì), and some pieces of half-kobo (eépìnnì), all put into a white dish. There is also some gin in a bottle and a gong or bell (agogo). These objects are curtained off by a piece of white cloth.

Regular offerings include kola-nuts (obì), gin (ọtì), native chalk (ẹfun); others include chickens, goats and pigs. Definite amounts of money are always required for offering – this is what is traditionally called ẹgbèrún Ìlàjẹ and ẹgbèrún Ìjó.[25]

Live birds and animals which are offered to Ayélálá wander about in the sacred island, and nobody will be tempted to steal any of them. They belong to Ayélálá and it is she alone who gives them to whom she wishes. If, for example, one of the sacred birds perches on and remains on a visitor's canoe, this will be taken as a sign that Ayélálá wants the visitor to have the bird as a gift from her.

Besides the main shrine described above, Ayélálá shrines are found in many places; individuals who seek protection from Ayélálá have simple shrines at home. But there are also public shrines erected in the open, possibly overlooking a river. Alongside such shrines there is a long pole bearing a piece of white cloth, a symbol of purity, representing the purity of life required by Ayélála of the people in the community.

Personification of natural forces and phenomena

Besides the primordial divinities and the deified ancestors, the Yorùbá believe in the existence of a number of spirits which are associated with natural phenomena like the earth, rivers, mountains, trees and wind. They are not as distinctly characterised as the divinities that we have so far discussed. Some of them are considered good and others as evil.

The earth (Ilẹ̀)

The earth is venerated in Yorubaland because it is believed to be inhabited by a spirit. The Yorùbá attach great importance to the earth. In creation, the myth says, earth was spread on the face of the deep, and land appeared. Furthermore, Ọbàtálá used clay (as we indicated earlier) to mould man before Olódùmarè gave him breath. When a new-born baby comes into the world, the first landing place is the earth; when man grows old and dies, he is buried in the earth. The earth supplies food for human consumption, and so it keeps life going.

From the Yorùbá point of view, an element which has such manifold and useful functions must have a spirit dwelling there. Hence, the spirit of the earth is constantly being called upon to witness to the pact made between people; and it is believed that it can punish anybody who breaks the covenant.[26] Because of the power of the spirit, intercourse with a woman is forbidden on the bare ground. It angers the spirit, for it is an unclean act. The breaking of such a taboo normally involves the offender in a very elaborate purification rite. People say of such a culprit, 'Ó ba ilẹ̀ jẹ́' ('he spoils or desecrates the earth').

Since most of the Yorùbá depend on agriculture for their sustenance, and crops are grown in the soil, Ilẹ̀ (the earth) receives special sacrifice at the time of planting and harvesting, almost in the same way as Òrìṣà-oko does. And since the corpses of the ancestors are buried in the earth and there are powerful spirits dwelling therein, the Yorùbá have the habit of pouring the first drop of any drinks on the ground and of throwing some portion of food to the earth before they drink or eat in order that the spirits may drink and eat first. Furthermore,

where no special shrines are used, the blood of an immolated victim is
poured into a hole dug in the earth.

Rivers, lagoons and the sea

As there are spirits in the earth, so the Yorùbá believe that there are
spirits dwelling in the rivers, lagoons and the sea. These spirits are
revered principally by those who dwell near rivers, lagoons or the sea
and who believe that the spirits, if suitably provided, can in return
provide man's needs. They control abundance of fish, they prevent
the capsizing of canoes and river accidents; some of the spirits supply
children to the barren. *Yemoja*, for example, is believed to be the
goddess of waters generally and from her body, according to the
people's belief, all rivers, lagoons and the sea flow out. Today she is
associated with the Ògùn River and is given elaborate worship in those
areas through which it flows, particularly in Abéòkúta.

Here main symbols are river-worn pebbles and sixteen cowry shells
– the latter being employed also as a means of divination by the
devotees. There is, also at the shrine of Yemoja, a pot filled with the
'sacred' water from the River Ògùn which is given to barren women
begging for children from Yemoja and to the children that are born as
a result.

Female devotees wear small shining beads and make offerings of
ègbo (mashed maize), *iyán* (pounded yam), *èbe* (yam porridge), *ewúré*
(goats), *adìe* (hens), *pépéye* (ducks) and *eja* (fish). Her main taboo is
the dog (*ajá*).

Oya is the goddess of the River Niger, and legend says that she was
the first and favourite wife of Sàngó. She decided to end her life when
she felt disillusioned in consequence of the ignominious end of her
husband's career. This she did by entering into the bosom of the earth
in the town of Irá. It remains a puzzle as to how the Yorùbá came to
associate her with the Niger.

Whenever there is a heavy gale, with trees uprooted or heavy
branches broken off and the roofs of buildings blown off, the Yorùbá
believe that Oya, the wife of Sàngó, is at work. It is believed that she
precedes or accompanies her husband when there is a thunder-
storm.

Her symbols are the two horns of 'bush cows' or buffalo and some
celts, much like those of Sàngó.

Her worshippers wear maroon beads and offer Oya her favourite
items of food – she-goats (*ewúré*), hens (*àgbébò-adìe*), plantains

(Ògèdè) and mashed maize and beans (àdàlú); but she abhors rams.

Òṣun is the tutelary divinity of Òṣogbo and she is associated with the river that bears her name. She is believed to be a fertility goddess, giving the joy of child-birth to barren women and healing the sick by means of her medicinal waters.

Ẹ̀kọ (corn meal), àkàrà (bean-loaves), iyán (pounded yam) with èfọ́ọ Yánrin (Yánrin vegetable), among other things, are offered to Òṣun during the annual festival.[27] Her main taboos are snails and guinea-corn.

The people of Ẹ̀pé have the annual celebration of Ọkọṣi.[28] It is meant to propitiate the goddess of the lagoon that can make fishing a safe and profitable enterprise.

Similarly, the Ìjẹ̀bú and the Ìlàjẹ who dwell along the rivers, and the Ijaw of the Niger Delta, firmly believe that there are divine creatures living under water, and that they have wonderful towns of their own; the creatures are thought to be light in complexion and gorgeously attired in coral beads and costly garments. People refer to them as 'Mammy-Water'. Stories abound among the Ìlàjẹ of brave men and women who have gone under water for a number of days together, have lived among the water-creatures and have returned home with some dried fish. We have also met Ìlàjẹ old men who bear on their bodies the mark of matchet-cuts claimed to have been received from these water spirits.

We mention this here because many of these mythical relations are reflected in rites and festivals observed. For example, among the Ìlàjẹ, the Ìjẹ̀bú of the water-side and the Ìjọ́, these water-creatures are invoked from time to time from the waters and are brought to the land in the form of masquerades called Imọlẹ̀, Umalẹ̀, or Àgbó. This is the personification of the water spirits.

Olókun or Malókun – the lord of the sea or the divinity that is in the sea – is given prominent worship in Ugbò and Igbó-Egunrin in Òkìtìpupa Division, in Itebu-Mánúwà (an Ìlàjẹ town in Ìjẹ̀bú Province) and in some parts of the Lagos State and in Ilé-Ifẹ̀. Because the sea strikes some terror into the people, there is the belief that a wonderful spirit dwells therein. It is also generally believed that wealth and prosperity come from the sea. This brings to mind our interview with the Olúgbò of Ugbò, one of the paramount chiefs in Yorubaland, on the role of Malókun (Olókun) in the religious belief of the Ìlàjẹ people. He said, 'Malókun is the divinity we [referring to the

Ìlàjẹ] worship principally. He (the spirit or divinity in the sea) gives us our health, our food and our wealth'. Spontaneously, the king gave a song in praise of the Malókun:

Malókun bu owo wa,	Malókun, please, give plenty of money,
Jími tètè núwà o;[29]	That I may be wealthy quickly;
Ọba omí ju ọba òkè.	The sea king is greater than the land king.
Malókun ni mo bá dó	It is with Malókun I stay,
Jími tètè núwà;	That I may be wealthy quickly
Ọba omí ju ọba òkè.	The sea king is greater than the land king.

In this song, Olókun is pictured as a king that tabernacles under the waters and he is capable of giving wealth to human beings. He is greater than any of the earthly paramount chiefs. This is why worship is accorded him by those who dwell near the sea.

Native chalk (gbọ̀rọ̀ efun), gin and white ram (àgbò) are offered to him. Human sacrifice was not uncommon before the practice was abolished.

As the Olókun is worshipped, so also is the Ọlọ́sà (the spirit of the lagoon). Such a worship is given prominence in Lagos and other towns and villages close to the lagoon.

Mountains and hills

Solid elevated rocks and highlands are regarded as abodes of some spirits. The size of the hills and mountains must have struck fear into the hearts of men. Furthermore, myths abound of how these hills and highlands have offered protection to the people dwelling near them from the attacking enemies during the inter-tribal wars.[30] The durability of the rock is another fascinating aspect, hence the popular saying: 'Ọta ò kì íkú' (The rock never dies). The people believe that if they serve the spirit that dwells in such a high land, they will live long.

It should be noted that the worship of the spirit of the hill or mountain is believed to bring about fertility in both the farm crops and in human beings. Prominence is given to such worship in areas where there are highlands. For example, the Òkè-Ìbàdàn is worshipped in Ìbàdàn; the Olúmọ in Abẹòkúta; the Ọlọ́sùnta in Ìkẹ́rẹ́-Èkìtì; the Orósùn in Ìdànrè; and the Òkè-Ìrágbìjì in Ìrágbìjì.

Trees

Certain trees are believed to be out of the ordinary. For example, the Ìrókò tree (Chlorophora excelsa) is held to be sacred and is believed to

A shrine on the Olumọ rock at Abeokuta where the spirit of the hill is worshipped.

An Ọbatala shrine showing the pot containing ritual water.

Symbol of Èṣù at an entrance.

A sacred iroko tree at Ile-Igbo.

be inhabited by some powerful spirit. Men fear having the tree near their dwelling place for it is believed that the spirit that inhabits it makes terrible sounds at intervals. Furniture made of its wood can also make disturbing noises in the house and doors made of the wood can fling open of their own accord. The tree cannot be felled unless special rites are performed. Furthermore, important meetings of witches are believed to be held at the foot or top of the tree and this might account for the reason why it is one of the regular places where the sacrifice offered is placed.

Besides the Ìrókò, trees singled out as abodes of certain spirits include Ẹegun (silk cotton tree; *eriodendron orientale*), Àyàn (*African satinwood*) and Ọmọ (*Cordia millenii*). Many of these trees are huge, towering over and above other trees. They strike awe into men, who look like dwarfs in their presence. Similarly, trees that have abnormal growth, for example, a palm tree with three trunks, cannot but be regarded as unusual and such is considered a likely abode of spirits. Men revere such a tree and tie round it a red or white piece of cloth to mark it out as sacred. Offerings are brought to these 'sacred' trees from time to time, but particularly during annual festivals and whenever medicine-men want to take the roots or the barks of such trees.

Wind

The Yorùbá believe that spirits are innumerable in the air. Ọrọ (a spirit that causes paralysis) travels about invisibly, and if a man is unfortunate enough to meet it, he will be paralysed. Likewise, Àájà or Àjìjà (a spirit travelling by whirlwind) is believed to be capable of carrying off human beings into the forest where they are instructed in the science of medical cure. Some Yorùbá, especially those in Oǹdó state, refer to such a spirit as Bàbájìí. Many herbalists in Yorubaland claim to have been carried away in this manner for a number of months or even years together. Being instructed by the spirit, the men become very proficient in the art of healing and magic. Àládòkun of Ìkìrun is a very good example of this.

It is clear that there are some elements of animism in Yorùbá beliefs. But it would be wrong to call the whole religion animism. The whole purpose of belief in the existence of the spirits is to keep in favour with these invisible spirits, and thus to avoid misfortune and disaster. This is done by seeking the aid of an expert mediator who is able to divine and ascertain which spirits are offended, what the means of propitiation will be and how to maintain good relationship with them. The attitude of the Yorùbá towards these beings constitutes one phase of their religion.

It is absolutely impossible to discuss, or even mention, all the divinities and spirits in Yorubaland within the ambit of this study. That alone would require a whole book if not a number of books. But we hope that this highly selective discusion will give an insight into the complexity of the belief of the people. Many of these divinities have symbols through which they are worshipped, but the Yorùbá strongly believe that they are not worshipping the material symbols but the spirits of the symbols represented by them.

Furthermore, when we speak of the people's belief in many divinities and spirits, we are not thereby suggesting polytheism. In a truly polytheistic religion, all the divinities are of equal rank and there is no unifying and transcending Ultimate. But in the Yorùbá religion the Supreme Being is the Creator who has brought into being both the divinities and human beings, and He is regarded as the absolute Controller. We may learn of Òrìsà-ñlá getting drunk or moulding human figures, at times, falsely; we may have myths portraying Ògún or Sàngó as bloodthirsty and of fiery disposition, but such mean human passions are never attributed to the Supreme Being as conceived of by the Yorùbá. He is therefore neither of the rank and file of, nor of like passions as, the divinities and spirits. He is a 'Wholly Other'.

The divinities act only as permitted by Him and they give an account of their activities to Him from time to time. They only act as His functionaries and as mediators between Him and His people. Thus they exist for the purpose of bringing the Supreme Being closer to His creatures. In other words, the divinities and spirits do not and cannot occupy the place of the Supreme Being. They constitute a means to an end, not an end in themselves. This is to suggest that all worship which is channelled through the divinities and spirits goes on to the one Supreme Being who is the sole Controller and has the final say.

But we should acknowledge the fact that there is a possibility of making that which is supposed to be a means to an end, an end in itself. When, for example, the divinities become ends in themselves and there is no reference to the Supreme Being who is the co-ordinator of the activities and actions of the divinities, we have polytheism. A casual observer of worship at the shrine of a divinity may not hear the name of God loudly invoked as he hears that of the divinity being worshipped. This may give him the impression that worship is directed solely to the divinity. Furthermore, he may not find a sanctuary dedicated to the Supreme Being whereas he will find many dedicated to the divinities. This kind of situation presents a problem which we cannot ignore. One needs great caution to understand; and the person who can understand and interpret accurately the relationship between the Supreme Being and the divinities is the patient investigator who allows the people to speak for themselves. People who have made thorough investigations among the Yorùbá will maintain that the many divinities exist and act only at the will of the Supreme Being who co-ordinates the activities of these functionaries and intermediaries.

NOTES

1. Ìdòwú, *Olódùmarè*, p. 74.
2. Yemòwo is Obatala's consort.
3. Ìdòwú, *Olódùmarè*, pp. 74–75.
4. P. A. Talbot, *The People of Southern Nigeria*, vol. 2, Frank Cass, 1969, p. 30.
5. One Yoruba myth holds that heaven and earth were, in the beginning, contiguous; so it was easy to go from one to the other.
6. See: Ellis, p. 56; R. E. Dennett, *Nigerian Studies; or Religious and Political system of the Yoruba*, Macmillan, 1910; Talbot, *The People of Southern Nigeria*, 1926, p. 33; Lucas, *Religions of the Yorubas*, p. 71; Parrinder, *West African Religion*, p. 153, wavers between calling the oracle-divinity Òrúnmìlà or Ifá; W. R. Bascom, *Ifá Divination: Communications Between Gods and Men in West Africa*, Indiana University Press, 1969, p. ix, claims that Ifá is both a method of divination and a deity. Wande Abimbola, *Sixteen Great Poems of Ifa*, Unesco, 1975, p. 2, agrees that the personal name is Òrúnmìlà, but that Ifá is sometimes used to refer to the paraphernalia as well as the personal name.
7. Details of this will be examined in ch. 6.
8. See M. A. Fabunmi, *Ife Shrines*, Ife University Press, 1969, pp. 3 and 4.
9. See Ellis, p. 41, Farrow, p. 44; Lucas, *Religions of the Yorubas*, pp. 93ff; Parrinder, *West African Religion*, p. 34.
10. Lucas, *Religions of the Yorubas*, p. 93f.
11. Ìdòwú, *Olódùmarè*, pp. 25 and 26.
12. For details see: M. J. Walsh, 'Edi Festival!', *African Affairs*, xlvii, 189, 1948, pp. 231–238.

The popular Yorùbà playwright, Duro Ladipo, also stages this in his famous play, *'Moremi'*. The only mistake is that he calls the people Ìgbò instead of Ugbò.

13. W. Bascom. *The Yoruba of South Western Nigeria*, Winston, 1969, p. 79.
14. Dennett, *Nigerian Studies* p. 95.
15. J. O. Lucas, *Religions in West Africa*, Lagos, 1970, p. 74.
16. Ìdòwú, *Olódùmarè*, p. 83.
17. N. Q. King, *Religions of Africa*, Harper and Row, 1970, p. 19.
18. Parrinder, *West African Religion*, p. 56.
19. Euhemerus was a Sicilian writer (c. 315 B.C.) who developed the theory that some gods that are today worshipped were originally human beings who had contributed so immensely to civilisation and to mankind that they were promoted divinities by the devotees.
20. E. E. Evans-Pritchard, *Nuer Religion*, O.U.P., London, 1956, p. 52.
21. Lucas, *Religions in West Africa*, p. 116.
22. See ch. 6.
23. For further details about Ayélálá, see J. O. Awolalu, 'Aiyelala, A Guardian of Social Morality', *Orita*, ii, 2 December 1968, pp. 79–89.
24. Ayélálá is the Umalẹ (goddess) that is most popular in Okitipupa Division. When a person says he will invoke umalẹ, everybody knows that the person means Ayélálá.
25. Until the last century, the Yorùbá currency was the cowry. Thus when they speak of *egberun* they mean 1000 cowries which is 2.5 Kobo of the present Nigerian currency.
    Tradition requires two priests (one representing the Ilaje and the other, the Ìjọ) at any worship of Ayélálá; and each priest must have as his remuneration the sum of 1000 cowries. But in an elaborate sacrifice, each priest must have *egbaasanan*, i.e. 18000 cowries which is about 45 Kobo, in addition to sharing in the food and drink offered.
26. See P. Morton Williams, 'Ogboni Cult', *Africa*, xx, 1960, p. 364, where he argues that the Ogboni worship and control the sanctions of the Earth as a spirit. . . . Earth existed before the gods.
27. For details of the annual festival of Osun, see ch. 10: Social significance of sacrifice.
28. See M. A. Odukoya, 'Ọkọ̀sí Festival at Èpẹ́ Town', *Odu*, 7, 1959, p. 28.
29. This song is sung in the Ilàjẹ dialect, *Jimi tete n'uwa = Jeki ntete loro* (let me be wealthy quickly); Uwa=Oro=wealth.
30. For example, Oke Ibadan offered protection to the Ibadan people and Ọlọ́ṣunta to the Ìkẹ́rẹ́ people during the attacks of enemies.

Chapter Three

BELIEF IN THE ANCESTORS

No one can hope to appreciate the thoughts and feelings of the
black man who does not realise that to him the dead are not dead
but living . . .[1]

Talbot is quite correct in this observation. The Yorùbá, like any other
Africans, believe in the active existence of the deceased ancestors.
They know that death does not write *finis* to human life but that the
earthly life has been extended into the life beyond – into that place
which is believed to be the abode of the departed souls.

To say that the dead are not dead looks like a contradiction. To
describe them as 'living-dead' as Mbiti[2] has done, may give an idea of
what is implied but it does not necessarily remove the apparent
contradiction. The truth is that nearly every religion tends to give a
holistic view of man: in addition to the tangible physical component
parts of man, there is an element which is intangible and indestruct-
ible and which outlives the physical death. This is the soul.

With regard to the component parts of man, the Yorùbá hold the
view that man's physical form (*ara*) is moulded from clay by Òrìṣà-
ńlá. After this, Olódùmarè breathed His breath into man; this is called
èmí (spirit). But in addition to the body (*ara*) and the spirit (*èmí*), man
receives the soul. The soul is a very complex concept and it is a term
which is seldom used with precision. S. G. F. Brandon describes soul
as 'a non-physical entity in the human nature'.[3] Different religions
have different anthropologies and psychologies and we cannot go into
these different concepts of the soul. Our chief concern is to examine
the Yorùbá concept of this.

For lack of apt vocabulary, the early translators of the Yorùbá
Bible, translated *soul* as *ọkàn* or *èmí*. Strictly speaking, *ọkàn* is the
heart, and *èmí* is spirit. The heart is a tangible organ; but the soul is

intangible and is the essence of being. Hence Professor Ìdòwú suggests the Yorùbá term 'orì-inú' for the word *soul*. Literally, 'orì-inú' means 'internal head' or 'the inner person'. And this is the essence of personality. In the belief of the Yorùbá, it is this 'that rules, controls, and guides the life and activities of the person'.[4]

Thus, whenever a human being is to come to life, he is endowed with the spirit and the soul in addition to the physical body. When the physical body dies, the spirit and that immaterial essence called soul do not perish but go to Olódùmarè who is the Source and who disposes of the soul as He pleases. We shall take up this idea again when we discuss the post-mortem judgment.

We are conscious of the fact that the destiny of the soul has assumed different interpretations in different religious traditions – some speak of the immortality of the soul; some, of the merging of the soul with an Ultimate Reality; others see it as a reincarnation and yet others describe it as life continuing in another realm but similar to this world.[5] The Yorùbá religion emphasises both partial reincarnation and life continuing in the hereafter much in the same way as life here. The people view death not as an extinction but as a change from one life to another.

Literally, an ancestor is one from whom a person descends, either by the father or mother, at any distance of time; one's progenitor or forefather. But when the Yorùbá speak of the ancestors, they think of the departed spirits of their forbears with whom the living maintain filial and affectionate relationship. It is not every dead person that comes in for consideration. To qualify, such men and women must have lived well, attained an enviable old age before dying, must have left behind good children and good memory. Children and youths who die a premature death, barren women, and all who die a 'bad' death – e.g. killed by Ayélála or Ṣàngó or Ṣọpọ̀nnọ́ – are excluded from this respectable group.

A man's father, after death, becomes for him the most important figure in the spirit world. The father is seen as the one who links the individual to the lineage ancestors. But all the lineage of past generations who are in the spirit world are ancestors of the individual and he is linked to all of them. Though the ancestors include not only the male but also the female members of previous generations of the lineage, the male ancestors are far more important. To become a welcome ancestor a man has to live well, die well, and leave behind good children who will accord him proper funeral rites and continue to keep in touch with him by means of offerings and prayer. It will be useful at this stage to examine what the Yorùbá do to accord the deceased what is called a 'befitting burial'.

Treatment of the corpse

Circumstances surrounding the death of a person, the age and the social status of the dead are the important factors that dictate the way corpses are treated and funeral ceremonies are conducted. When a person who has lived to a respectable old age dies a 'good' death, the corpse is immediately wrapped up in a mat and messages concerning the death go out to the relations. All that hear come from far and near to pay their last respects to the deceased. It is usually an occasion when one gets to know the members of the larger family: uncles, aunts, nephews and nieces, first, second or third cousins all come together.

Meanwhile, arrangements are made to wash the corpse. Soap and sponge are provided, and the body is given a tepid bath. A woman's hair is plaited beautifully; and a man's hair is sometimes shaved completely, or combed and brushed properly. It is the normal practice that the first-born son should be present when the corpse of his father is washed, and he should be the first to pour water on it. This emphasises the importance attached to having a son as a successor. Great importance is attached to the washing of the corpse because it is believed that one has to be clean in order to be admitted into the abode of the ancestors. It is believed that if a corpse is not washed in this ceremonial way, it will have no place with the ancestors and will become a wandering ghost, called *iwin* or *ìṣèkú*.

After the bath, the corpse is dressed in beautiful and dignifying clothing. It is brought into the sitting room and laid on a well-decorated bed to lie in state. Music, dancing and feasting begin. There is also the firing of guns outside. The boom of a gun is a sign of respect for the deceased and a means of announcing to the general public that some great event has occurred.

Since there was no provision for mortuaries in the days of the ancient Yorùbá, and putrefaction could easily set in, they had long devised means of preserving the body in such a way that it could lie in state for two or more days without stinking. The idea was that the deceased must not be buried immediately but must be given the chance of stretching his back and having the last rest in his earthly abode. During the lying-in-state, the clothing for the deceased and the decorations around the bed on which he was lying would be changed, each succeeding set of dress outshining the previous ones. This was regarded as part of doing honour to the dead. Children and close relatives donated beautiful and costly garments which were to be taken away by the departed spirit into the next world.

In very early days, graves were dug inside the house and in particular rooms; but that practice has changed. Graves are now usually dug in the family compounds. To the Yorùbá, to bury somebody in the common cemeteries is to cast him out and to lose contact with him, because regular ancestral veneration which involves pouring libations, breaking kola-nuts and praying on the grave of the deceased would not be convenient and domestic.

On the day that the corpse is to be buried, many people gather together to pay their last respects. The burial usually takes place in the evening. The body is once again brought out and placed on a couch. Different dancing and singing groups come to perform and they are well-received and remunerated by the children and the relatives of the deceased. Just before sunset, the dancing stops and the corpse, wrapped in beautiful heavy clothing and a special mat, is conveyed in a solemn procession to the grave. It is carefully laid, with every part of the body well placed. Beautiful clothing, pieces of silver, money and all that the departed is expected to require in the next world are provided. In the days gone by, slaves and wives of a departed monarch were buried with him. But today, some of these ancient customs have changed. It is unimaginable now for human beings to be buried with a deceased chief. Yet, since some kind of substitute has to be provided, an animal is immolated and the blood is poured into the grave. It is believed that the sacrificed animal accompanies the deceased to the next world. Before the grave is covered, many of the people present, particularly the children and the close relatives of the deceased, pray loud and long as they shed tears and throw the earth on the corpse beseeching him to do one thing or another for the living that he is leaving behind. They also send messages to the ancestors that have gone before. This is a living evidence of the people's belief in the hereafter and in the power of the ancestors. The deceased is believed to be going on a journey into another sphere where he or she is now more powerful than formerly.

Thus among the Yorùbá, it was the practice for the corpse of a deceased to be carefully prepared: washed, dressed and buried in the grave dug in the family compound. A woman would be buried with her immediate needs – necklaces, ear-rings, clothing materials, food and utensils; a hunter with his weapons; a royal personage was accompanied by a retinue of attendants and servants who were put to death at the time of burial. We could infer from this practice that the dead were expected to enjoy in the after-life the same social and economic advantages which they had possessed in this world. This seems to suggest, also, that life there continues very much like life here. It is believed that the new ancestors will see the old and that there will be a reunion; this is why the living send messages to the former ancestors. The Yorùbá provide food for their departed ancestors and they make sure that they make regular offerings at their graves. The more the offerings, the better-placed are the ancestors and consequently the more favour will they bestow upon the living descendants.

Location of the hereafter

The difficult problem is to state precisely where the hereafter is located. When we turn to the elders, we receive different answers. Some believe that the dead have a long journey to make to get to their abode – there is a river to cross; there is a ferry-man to be paid; there are mountains to climb; there is a door-keeper to open the gate. This is why some people say that the newly-dead has to gather energy by partaking of the food and drink offered during the forty-day funeral ceremonies before embarking on the long journey. Others say that the abode of the dead is under the earth, and yet others maintain that the departed are in an invisible world which is separated from the living only by a very thin partition, and that they are very close to the living. Yet others say that the dead go to certain ancient villages and market centres in Yorubaland. Stories also abound concerning people who claimed to have fainted one time or another and who later gained consciousness and were privileged to give vivid accounts of what they experienced during the interval between when they fainted and when they regained consciousness. Such stories included their experience of crossing a river or knocking at a gate where a senior ancestor sent them back; and the moment they were sent back, they found themselves in the world of the living.

Stories have also been told of men who are reported dead going to dwell in another village or town and living a normal life, until they suddenly disappear when they learn that the local people have found them out. We have met people who have encountered such men. We have also listened to pupils who were at boarding school when their parents died at home. Such pupils have testified to the fact that their fathers or mothers called to visit them and to leave important instructions and messages with them. These men and women come in human form, not in the form of spirits at all!

All these views make it very difficult for us to make a categorical statement as to where the hereafter is located. Like the ancient people, the Yorùbá do not attempt to solve the ultimate problems confronting them by one coherent theory. They are happy to employ a variety of approaches and are not easily conscious of contradictions. They regard the theories as complementary one to another. But anyone who wants to draw a logical conclusion concerning the location of the hereafter will say that if it is the soul that lives on after death, and if Olódùmarè is its Source, it would have returned to the Source in the first instance to be disposed by the Supreme Being as He considers fit. We believe that when the dying person says, *'Mò ńre'lé'* ('I am going home'), he means that he is returning to the place from where he or she came to the feet of Olódùmarè.

Post-mortem judgment

This brings us to the question of judgment after death. We have earlier indicated that judgment goes on all the time, even here on earth. The anti-wickedness divinities (e.g. Ayélála or Ṣàngó) can and do single out individual wicked persons for punishment which may result in 'bad' death. But the final judgment rests with Olódùmarè to whom all return in the first instance and Who decides those who are good and those who are evil. The good are privileged to go into Ọrun rere (good heaven) otherwise referred to as ọrun baba ẹni (the heaven of one's father); but the evil are allocated to ọrun burúkú (bad heaven) or ọrun àpáàdì (the heaven of potsherds). Judgment is based upon the deeds of the individuals while here on earth.

The details of how the judgment is conducted are not given by the elders. But they have a very important saying: *'Ohun gbogbo tí a bá ṣe láyé, la óòkúnlẹ̀ rò lọ́run'* (All that we do on earth, we shall account for kneeling in heaven). This suggests that every soul returns to Olódùmarè, the presiding Judge in heaven, and in a humble position, gives an account of all that he or she has done on earth. There will be no way of holding back anything. One will have to account for *all*. It is only when one has been acquitted by Olódùmarè that one has the opportunity of going into the heaven of the fathers, reuniting with one's ancestors and continuing another existence. The idea is that the heaven of the fathers is divided into various countries, towns and villages where the different groups of people live together as on earth. At the end of the post-mortem judgment, the good person is allowed to go to the particular part occupied by his or her own people. Thus life goes on as it is here. The good wear good clothes, eat good food and can be reincarnated and reborn into the family. We shall return to this idea presently.

But if one is condemned, one goes to the heaven of potsherds where one suffers with the wicked. Such a soul is not allowed to reunite with the ancestors. When it is released at last, it does not have the chance of living the normal life, but it is condemned to wander about in lonely places, to eat useless or inedible food and sometimes to be reincarnated in lower animals or birds. This is why children say to their departing ancestors:

Má jòòkùn má	Don't eat millipedes,
Má jekòló;	Don't eat earthworms;
Ohun tí wón bá ńjẹ	But whatever good things they eat
lájùlé òrun	in heaven,
Ni kó ma-bá wón jẹ	Eat with them.

But the philosophers among the Yorùbá do not fail to remind people that if they do not want to eat millipedes and centipedes in the hereafter, they should behave well while still here on earth. Men and women are held responsible for their actions.

Reincarnation

The Yorùbá strongly believe that the departed ancestors have different ways of returning to the living. One of the commonest ways of doing this is for the soul to be reincarnated and to be born as a grandchild to a child of the departed parents. It is believed that the ancestors choose to do this in consequence of their love for the family and of the world. The world, according to the Yorùbá, is the best place in which to live. Hence, it has been said that the Yorùbá attitude is world-affirming, not renouncing. This is contrary to the view of some religious traditions which regard the world as a place of sorrow and suffering.[7] There is a strong desire on the part of the living to have their parents reincarnated as soon as possible after their death. Hence well-wishers pray: '*Bàbá/Ìyá á yà lówóò rẹ o*' ('May your father or mother turn to be a child for you'). And sometimes, in their enthusiasm, they pray saying: '*Bàbá/Ìyá á tètè yà o*' ('May father or mother be reincarnated soon'). The child who is lucky to give birth to the father or mother usually feels particularly happy. This is contrary to Mbiti's claim that the phenomenon (reincarnation) is not 'something that individuals look forward to, or hope for'.[8]

Normally, when a child is born, the Yorùbá consult the oracle to find out which ancestor has been reincarnated. But, it is usually assumed that if a child is born soon after the death of a father or grandfather, it is the soul of the immediately deceased that is back, and such a boy is automatically called *Babátúndé* (father has returned). Similarly, a daughter born after the death of a mother or grandmother is called *Ìyábò* or *Yétúndé* (mother has returned). It is not the practice to give Babátúndé or Yétúndé to more than one child after the death of a grandfather or mother. This means, therefore, that the same father or mother is not reincarnated a number of times or in a number of grandchildren, but only once and in a particular child. It is to be noted, also, that only good ancestors are reincarnated in their grandchildren. No family desires to have a reincarnation of an ancestor who died a 'bad' death lest the bad traits be repeated in the family. Bad ancestors, as we have pointed out, are reincarnated in lower animals or birds, and wander about in neglected and lonely places.

We have to point out here that this idea of reincarnation sounds paradoxical when we remember that the Yorùbá also believe that in spite of the child that is born, called Babátúndé or Ìyábò, the ancestral spirit still continues to live in the spirit-world where it is invoked from time to time. This is why we cannot describe what we have among the Yorùbá as full reincarnation but, at best, a *partial reincarnation*. The living are satisfied that they do see part of their departed ancestors in the newborn children, but at the same time, they are happy that they (the ancestors) are in the spirit-world where they have greater potentiality and can be of great help to their children on earth.

Relationship between the living and the ancestors

In the Yorùbá belief, the family is made up of both the living members and the ancestors. The ancestors constitute the closest link between the world of men and the spirit-world and they are believed to be keenly interested in the welfare of their living descendants. They exercise protective and disciplinary influences on their children. 'They are the guardians of family affairs, traditions, ethics and activities. Offences in these matters is ultimately an offence against the forefathers who, in that capacity, act as the invisible police of the families and communities'.[9] It is, therefore, believed that the ancestors can be of tremendous benefit to the children who keep them happy and who observe the family taboos; but can be detrimental to the disobedient and negligent children. The implication is that the ancestors expect their descendants to care for them by making offerings of food and drinks. They are regarded as presiding spiritually over the welfare of the family. The living have the confidence that they live in a world in which their ancestors are interested and over which they are watching.

It is believed that witches and sorcerers[10] cannot harm a man and bad medicine can have no effect on him unless his ancestors are 'sleeping' or neglecting him. It is a common thing to hear a man in difficulty saying to his ancestors, *'Bàbá mi, má sùn o'* ('My father, don't sleep'). This is an appeal to the departed father to be vigilant and helpful and never to neglect his child.

If a woman is having a protracted labour, usually the family head will consult an oracle; and if it is revealed that the ancestors are angry for one reason or another, he will bring offerings, as kola-nuts, gin, a goat and, perhaps, a cloth belonging to the woman in labour, and will say something like this:

Ah, my grandfathers! [names of the ancestors according to their age will be enumerated] I have come to you for help. Your little daughter, X, is the one travailing. Oracle reveals that she has broken the family taboo or that she has neglected you. She is a little girl, quite foolish. I, as the family head, am here to appeal to you to pardon her, please. She has brought a very big she-goat, several kola-nuts, a bottle of gin and a beautiful dress of hers. As soon as she is delivered safely, we shall bring this goat here to be slaughtered. Therefore, as you gave birth to those of us who are today remembering you, we implore you to release X from her pain and to let her deliver safely.

When the woman is delivered, she will come to fulfil her vow. This will be followed by a family feasting where the ancestors, though invisible, are believed to be present.

There is, therefore, a communion and a communication going on all the time between those that have gone into the life beyond and those that are here on earth. We need to point out to Laroche that the Yorùbá cannot be included among the Africans whose ancestors 'are wholly dissociated from the living and have no means of remaining in a habitual relationship with them'.[11] Laroche came to this conclusion on the assumption that the departed soul is deprived of the body and of its natural means of knowledge, that is to say, the senses. 'It is no longer possible', he maintains, 'for it to know by its own means what takes place in the world of the living'.

The Yorùbá never believe that their ancestors have lost their senses; rather the people strongly believe that the ancestors can see, hear, feel and have human emotions. But for the fact that the ancestors retain their senses and human feelings, men and women would not have bothered appealing to them. The ancestors are constantly being invoked, and they are 'aware of the actions and even thought of their descendants who, on their behalf, are the temporary caretakers of lineage and prosperity'.[12]

The Yorùbá, like any other African ethnic groups, believe that the ancestors are able to see what is happening on earth, and that they maintain the greatest interest in the affairs of mankind, and especially in those of the members of their family. They do not lose their senses of seeing, hearing or feeling as Laroche wants us to believe. To the Yorùbá, survival after death is not a matter for argument or speculation, it is an axiom of life. This important fact is underlined by Idowu when he claims:

> . . . the deceased are truly members of the families on earth; but they are no longer of the same fleshly order as those who are still actually living in the flesh on earth. They are closely related to this world; but are no longer ordinary mortals. Because they have crossed the borderland between this world and the supersensible world, entering and living in the latter, they have become freed from the restrictions imposed by the physical world. They can

now come to abide with their folk on earth invisibly, to aid or hinder them, to promote prosperity or cause adversity . . .[13]

Worship or veneration?

We shall now turn our attention to the problem raised by scholars as to whether we are to speak of an 'ancestor *cult*', 'ancestor *worship*' or 'ancestor *veneration*'. Professor Ìdòwú feels that ' "ancestor worship" is a wrong nomenclature for what in fact is no worship but a manifestation of an unbroken family relationship between the parent who has departed from this world and the offspring who are still here'.[14] J. H. Driberg is of the same opinion as Ìdòwú when the former said, 'What we have mistaken for a religious attitude is nothing more than a projection of [the African's] social behaviour. The attitude is a purely secular one'.[15] Objecting to such a view Edwin Smith said, 'Only on a narrow definition of religion can the ancestral cult be dismissed as purely secular. . . . If the essence of religion is a sense of dependence upon super-sensible powers who are able and willing to help, then we are in the presence of religion when Africans can commune with their kinsmen in the unseen world, who have enhanced powers associated with their new status and particularly as mediators between man and God.'[16]

When we look up the dictionary meanings of the words *cult, veneration and worship*, we discover that they are very close to each other. The word *cult* means *homage*; *worship*; a system of *religious belief and worship*. The word *worship* means *adoration*; *reverence*; *reverent honour* and *homage* paid to God or a sacred personage or to any object regarded as sacred; while *veneration* means the *highest degree of respect and reverence*; a feeling or sentiment excited by the dignity, wisdom and goodness of a person, or by the sacredness of his character.

If a person wants to avoid the expression 'ancestor worship' by using other expressions such as 'ancestor cult', 'cult of the ancestors' or 'veneration of the ancestors', we doubt if he is conveying to us anything different from that which is conveyed by the use of 'ancestor worship'. In the three key-words, emphasis is placed on *adoration, homage, honour* and *reverence*. From the dictionary meaning, as spelt out above, we understand that worship is accorded to God or a sacred personage or to any object regarded as sacred. The dictionary meaning of *sacred* is 'devoted or dedicated to a deity or to some religious purpose; entitled to veneration or religious respect by association with divinity or divine things'. We may then ask: 'Do not the ancestors serve a religious purpose?' 'Are the ancestors limited to things secular and social or are they associated with things sacred?' Our answers to these questions will go a long way to solving this tricky problem. It is true that the deceased are 'truly members of the families on earth; but they are no longer of the same fleshly order as those who are still actually living in the flesh on earth. . . . Because the ancestors are no longer in the world of ordinariness, the way they are approached must be different from the ordinary approach to them during the time of their earthly life.'[17]

We are convinced that the ancestors are included in the religious system of the Yorùbá and that they play the role of being the immediate intermediaries between men and the 'totally' supersensible world. We believe that they are not limited to things secular and social but that they have great concern for religious matters. From our observation of activities at the graves of the ancestors or wherever the ancestors are invoked, we are convinced that what is done is much more than a secular rite or sheer veneration. In the day-to-day secular life, when a son wants anything from his father, it is not the usual practice for him to take gin or kola-nuts to his father before making a request. It is true that if a man gives a gift to his son, the son will say 'Thank you, father'! But at the ancestral shrine, there is a system or ritual which engenders the feeling that one is standing before an aged, revered being who is interested in the supplicants and who is capable of supplying their needs. There is no doubt about it that the Yorùbá believe that the ancestors are nearer to them than the divinities. But this does not rule out the fact that there is invocation, there is adoration, there is the presentation of the immediate problem followed by petition. What more have we when we think of worship?

We share the view that 'there is a difference in the tone of prayers addressed to ancestors and the Supreme Being . . .'[18] and that the ancestors still bear the title of 'My father' or 'My mother',[19] but this does not rule out the fact that they are worshipped. The use of 'father' or 'mother' in addressing the ancestors does not reduce their sacred status but emphasises the love and affection that characterise the relationship between them and their living descendants. Addressing the object of worship by the familiar term of 'father' is not peculiar to African traditional religion. In the Christian tradition, God is known and addressed as Father through Jesus Christ. And in the present trend of events in the United States of America, the Women's Liberation Movement and the Christian Science Church want God to be seen as and called Father/Mother because, according to them, God combines the qualities of a father and a mother. To call Him Father/Mother does not reduce His status or prevent men from according Him proper worship; rather it underlines God's accessibility.

Comparisons may indeed sometimes be odious, but where the comparison may shed some light on the subject under consideration, it can be quite useful. The Christian Church (especially Roman Catholicism) faces this same problem when she attempts to distinguish between *worship* and *veneration* in connection with the saints and the cult of Mary in particular. Holy Mary is constantly being invoked to pray for sinners. And when one attends a Roman Catholic Church, one may find that there is more genuflection before the symbol of Mary or Peter or any of the other saints than before the symbol of Jesus. Yet people claim that they *worship* only God but *venerate* the saints.

We need to underline the fact that it is not every ancestor that is worshipped in Yorùbá traditional religion. Only those ancestors who have lived well on earth and have been 'justified' by Olódùmarè in consequence of the final post-mortem judgment go to '*òrun rere*' (good heaven or heaven of the fathers) and are permitted to reincarnate. It is such good ancestors that are invoked. They are invoked because it is believed that they are in the good book of Olódùmarè and they can be employed by the living in their appeal to the Supreme Being. It is to be noted, also, that the Yorùbá use the word '*bo*' (to worship) both when they speak of making offerings to their deceased ancestors and to the divinities. They say, for example, '*Mo féé bo bàbáà mi*' ('I want to worship my father') when they think of the ancestors, and '*Mo féé bo òrìsà*' ('I want to worship or make offerings to the divinities') when they think of the divinities. Furthermore, the things that are offered are similar to those things offered to the divinities. The offerings may be votive, thanksgiving or propitiatory in the same way as they are offered to the divinities.

It is left for us to mention that the spirit of the ancestors is materialised in the *Egúngún*. The Egúngún is an embodiment of the spirit of a deceased person who is believed to have returned from *òrun* (the spirit-world) to visit his children; hence he is called '*ará òrun*' (the citizen of heaven). In this materialised form, the Egúngún is attired in *agọ̀* – a special dress or outfit made from cloths of various colours and sewn together in such a way that it covers the wearers from head to foot – no part of the Egúngún must be visible. He wears an improvised pair of shoes to cover the feet and a netting veil over his face to facilitate his vision but also to hide his identity. He speaks in a guttural manner.

Many Egúngún wear different masks and charms which have become black with years of sacrificial blood. The belief is that a living person who puts on the family Egúngún attire (*agọ̀*) also puts on the spiritual powers of the ancestors whom he represents. In this materialised form, the Egúngún can speak to and pray for the living. He is accorded full honour and respect which should be given to such an august visitor from heaven! Women and the uninitiated are forbidden to come too close to him and men who meet him must remove their caps and shoes and prostrate themselves. In former days, it was death for the uninitiated to touch the Egúngún.

The spirit of a particular ancestor may be invoked to assume a material form and to appear singly and speak to the living children and widows, bringing them assurance of the spiritual care and blessings which they desire. There may be summoned the spirits of all the departed ancestors on festival occasions, when many Egúngún are seen in the streets of the cities, towns and villages going from house to house and from one street to another blessing the living and receiving offerings. Such an annual Egúngún festival can aptly be described as 'All Souls' festival of the Yorùbá. Different types of Egúngún, including the 'elder Egúngún', the 'trickster' Egúngún, the children of Egúngún and the Egúngún *alágọ̀* wearing the 'shroud' of a particular family, appear in the streets. They receive the people's gifts and they bless the givers in return. Such an annual festival in honour of the ancestors is, in many places, the principal event of the year, and it marks the beginning of the new yam season (and in some places, the beginning of the planting season). The ancestors who have farmed the land successfully in the past must partake of the farm products before anybody else. Details of such annual festivals we shall consider in a later chapter.

It is to be mentioned in connection with Egúngún, that whenever there are terrible calamities in a town or village, and there is the need to offer a propitiatory sacrifice, it is the usual practice for an Egúngún to convey such prescribed sacrifice to the appropriate place in the middle of the night. The idea behind this is that the ancestors are close to the divinities on the one hand and to their living children on the other, and that they can readily plead with the angry divinities on behalf of their erring and suffering children.

To some people, the ancestral cult will appear to be gross superstition. But this is not so. The fact of the matter is that the Yorùbá, like the other ethnic groups in Africa, employ it as a means of protesting against death. And we share Edwin Smith's view that 'the cult (of the ancestors) answers to what lies deep in human nature – the desire for survival, the refusal to acknowledge that death ends all'.[20]

We want to end this chapter by emphasising the fact that there is nothing wrong in employing different avenues of reaching the Supreme Being. The ancestors, divinities and spirits are means to an end; the end in view is Olódùmarè. But we should not fail to point out that it would be wrong to suggest, as some foreign investigators have tried to do, that ancestor worship is the religion of Africa. The essential fact to emphasise is that the Yorùbá, like other Africans, believe in the Supreme Being and have the strong desire to have constant contact with Him; they, therefore, employ the ancestors (who are the closest and most familiar to them in the spirit-world), the divinities and spirits as a means of reaching Him who is the Source of life and whose biddings never go unfulfilled.

NOTES

1. Talbot, *The People of Southern Nigeria*, 1926, p. 298.
2. J. S. Mbiti, *African Religions and Philosophy*, Heinemann, 1969, p. 83.
3. S. G. F. Brandon, ed., *Dictionary of Comparative Religion*, Charles Scribner, 1970, p. 587.
4. Ìdòwú, *Olódùmarè*, p. 70.
5. See E.R.E., vol. 2, pp. 725–753.
6. People avoid the inclusion of red cloth among gifts to the departed because it is believed that this would render the deceased leprous when he gets to the spirit world and would separate him from the respectable group.
7. The Buddhists, for example, regard the world as a place of suffering, and seek an escape from rebirth to *nirvana*.
8. J. S. Mbiti, *Concepts of God in Africa*, Praeger, 1970, p. 265.
9. Mbiti, *African Religions and Philosophy*, p. 83.
10. We shall examine witches and sorcerers in the next chapter.

11. Laroche, 'Traditional African Religions', in C. G. Baeta, ed., *Christianity in Tropical Africa*, O.U.P., 1968, p. 299.
12. A. Shorter, 'Conflicting Attitudes to Ancestor Veneration in Africa', *AFER*, xi, 1, 1969, p. 29.
13. E. B. Ìdòwú, *African Traditional Religion*, p. 184.
14. Ìdòwú, *Olódùmarè*, p. 192.
15. Quoted by E. Smith, ed., *African Ideas of God*, London, 1966, p. 25.
16. Smith, *African Ideas of God*, p. 26.
17. Ìdòwú, *African Traditional Religion*, pp. 184 and 185.
18. Smith, *African Ideas of God*, p. 26.
19. Ìdòwú, *Olódùmarè*, p. 92; cf. *African Traditional Religion*, p. 184.
20. Smith, *African Ideas of God*, p. 27.

Chapter Four

BELIEF IN MYSTERIOUS POWERS

A survey of the beliefs of the Yorùbá will not be complete without examining the people's belief in what we can call *mysterious powers*. These mystical, preternatural and esoteric powers are virtually inexplicable, but they cannot escape notice when they are manipulated by those who have access to them.

Foreign investigators of the peoples' religion tend to dismiss such powers as superstitions; others class them as *mumbo-jumbo* and the like. But we should realise that one man's superstition is another man's belief. Almost every Yorùbá who has grown up in a traditional society will understand what we mean by belief in mysterious and mystical powers which manifest themselves in different ways – in the form of incantations, medicine, magic, sorcery and witchcraft. Belief in these powers which can alter the course of nature is very real and prevalent among the Yorùbá.

Incantations

Incantations involve the chanting or uttering of words purporting to have magical power. Sometimes, the incantations go with some medicinal preparation which is carried in the form of a ring (*òrùka*), amulet (*ìfúnpá*), girdle (*igbàdí*), small gourd (*àdó*) or needle (*abéré*). We shall examine this more closely when we take up medicine and magic. But for the present, what we want to emphasise is that words coupled with charms have mysterious powers which are frequently used by the Yorùbá; such words have been uttered, by 'those who know how', to escape death, to vanish in the approach of an imminent danger, to escape a ghastly accident, to destroy an enemy or wild animal, to stupefy thieves, to shorten distance, and such like. Practical examples are too numerous to be enumerated but what we may do is to give a few illustrations of happenings in the community.

Before the advent of bicycles and motor-cars and lorries, old men and women depended upon trekking from place to place. The elders claimed that by the use of incantations, they used to shorten distances particularly in moments of extreme anxiety and need. This kind of preparation is called *kánàkò* (that which shortens the distance or the road). There is, also, the use of *egbé* (the carrier or remover). Men who know these incantations claim to be capable of disappearing from imminent danger and finding themselves wherever they command the charms to take them. It is said that soldiers who have this knowledge have vanished from the battle-front only to re-appear when circumstances are better. Hunters, who might have been destroyed by wild animals, have escaped death simply by disappearing and escaping death or by changing into something else, for example a fly. *Gbètu-gbètu* is another means commonly employed. This consists of an enchanted small gourd covered with red and white cloth which the owner keeps in his pocket or hangs around his neck. It is used mainly to dismiss enemies who have planned to waylay and attack a person. All that the wearer of the charm does is to say a word and whatever instruction he gives to these enemies will be carried out. He may ask them to run into the bush or to clear out of the way or to begin to cut or flog one another. Whatever he says will be done. This means was used a great deal by the politicians during the political upheavals in Nigeria when organised thuggery was the order of the day and politicians could be attacked by the thugs of the opposition party.

In the early history of Ọ̀yọ́, a story was told of a bitter encounter between Gbọ̀nká Èbìrì and Tìmì, two of the war champions until Ṣàngó, the Aláàfin of Ọ̀yọ́ who set them to fight against each other until one got rid of the other. In actual fact, Ṣàngó considered them thorns in his flesh and wanted to get rid of them both. The champions met in a gruesome encounter and fought not only with bows and arrows but also with words, i.e. incantations. It was recorded that after a series of exchange of incantations, Gbọ̀nká uttered the following incantation:

Ewé tí a bá já lọ́wọ́ ọ̀tún,	Leaves picked from the right side,
Ọ̀tún níígbé,	Are usually kept in the right hand;
Ewé tí a bá já lọ́wọ́ òsì	Leaves picked from the left side,
Òsì níígbé	Are usually kept in the left hand;

À-sùn-fọnfọn ni tígi àjà A supporting beam usually lies still;
Ìwọ, Tìmì! sísùn ni kóosùn! You, Timi, lie still and sleep!

The story concluded that, in consequence of this incantation and charm, Tìmì was overpowered by Gbọ̀nká and carried off bound to Ọ̀yọ́.

Another good illustration of the use of incantation was given by an experienced medicine-man and Babaláwo (Ifá Priest) who claimed that if a person is desperately in search of a job, some herbal preparation could be made for him (the job seeker), and he will use it as directed and by saying the following:

Ẹ bá mi wáṣẹ́	Help me look for a job,
Ẹ fọ̀rọ̀ mi lọ̀	Tell my problem to others;
Ẹ fetí ketí	Whisper to every ear,
Ẹ fọ̀rọ̀ mi lọ̀;	And proclaim my need;
Bí aláǹtakùn ilé bá tàwú,	When the home-spider makes his web
A fi lọgi ilé	He reports to the wood in the house;
Ẹ bá mi wáṣẹ́	Help me look for a job,
Ẹ fọ̀rọ̀ mi lọ̀;	Tell my problem to others;
Ẹ fetí ketí	Whisper to every ear,
Ẹ fọ̀rọ̀ mi lọ̀	And proclaim my need;
Bí aláǹtakùn okó bá tàwú	When the rural spider makes his web,
A fi lọgi igbó;	He reports to the forest-wood;
Ẹ bá mi wáṣẹ́	Help me look for a job,
Ẹ fọ̀rọ̀ mi lọ̀	Tell my need to others;
Ẹ fetí ketí	Whisper to every ear,
Ẹ fọ̀rọ̀ mi lọ̀	And proclaim my need;
Ẹnu òkéré lòkéré fi ńpọdẹ	With the squirrel's own squeaking he invites the hunter
Tí fi ípa á;	That kills him;
Ẹnu yín ni kí ẹ fi bá mi wáṣẹ́	People themselves should use influences
Tí ñ máa ṣe	To get me a job

According to the people's belief, whoever uses the preparation together with the incantations in the appropriate manner will surely secure a job.

About thirty years ago, there was a terrible clash between the Aládùúrà Church (the Prayer Group) and the priests in charge of the traditional Ìwò Festival in Ìlútitun, a town in Òkìtìpupa Division of the Oǹdó State of Nigeria. The Ìwò Festival is celebrated to honour the river spirits in the area, and it is believed that the spirits travel by the wind and whoever encounters them, will be paralysed. Women and the uninitiated men are normally expected to be behind closed doors when the river spirits are 'flowing' by. But, on this particular occasion, the members of the Aládùúrà Church decided to have an open air preaching procession in defiance of the traditional festival; thus a clash occurred. The results were disastrous. Very many of the members of the Aládùúrà Church were paralysed and a number of them died immediately. It was believed that they encountered the mysterious power of Òrọ̀ (the spirit which causes paralysis). What happened was that the priests of the Ìwò Festival carried 'power' both in their lips and on their bodies; they uttered words and the destruction was done.

At the annual Agẹmọ Festival in Ìjẹbú and the Egúngún Festival in different parts of Yorubaland, there is the free use of incantations. The Agẹmọ and the Egúngún masquerades display the use of charms and incantations and it is believed that they can bless effectively those who bring them gifts on their routes and can equally effectively curse those who spy on them or do things contrary to the traditional practice. There are many living evidences of the use of such mysterious powers.

Thus, by means of evil incantations men have been ordered to be paralysed or to run mad; and they have been so. Similarly, by means of good incantations, men have escaped imminent dangers and have acquired good jobs and important positions in society.

Besides incantations, other means of harnessing and using mysterious powers under consideration are to be found in medicine, sorcery and witchcraft.

Medicine

By medicine we mean any substance or substances that are used in treating or preventing disease or illness; in other words, medicine as conceived by the Yorùbá involves medicament as well as prophylactic. Thus, the professional skill of a medicine-man includes curing, alleviating and preventing diseases as well as restoring and preserving health. In many cases, he is a diviner, a priest as well as a manufacturer of charms. He has the means of ascertaining the causes of ailments, misfortunes and death. He employs different means including herbs, plants, leaves, roots, barks, animals, birds, skins, bones, rings, brooms, pieces of thread, needles and minerals, to do his 'business'. In almost all cases, he has some magical words to go with his preparation. And so, unavoidably, magic finds a place in the practice of medicine. 'In fact', observes Ìdòwú, 'the two can become so interlinked as to make it difficult to know where one ends and the other begins'.[1]

The truth is that the medicine-man does not see his medical preparation in isolation. His medicine is in the realm of religion, perhaps with some element of magic. In many cases, when he goes to collect leaves or barks or roots of trees for his medicinal preparation, he performs some rituals – he usually invokes the spirit in the tree or herb, he breaks kola-nuts and offers them to the spirit. Sometimes, he provides a small piece of white calico which he ties round a tree before he can take its bark or roots for medicinal preparation. At other times, he has to utter incantations as he digs for roots or picks leaves. On some occasions, he does not speak until he has taken back home his collection. In this way, the herbs or leaves or barks are treated as changed from the ordinary things into the 'sacred' and they carry some potency, some mysterious powers.

When the preparation has been completed, the medicine is believed to be charged with power. The person who is to wear a ring or an amulet, or he who is to apply a black 'powder' into the incised portion of his body, or use a soap to bathe does this accompanied by the use of incantations which imbue the medicinal preparation with power. Furthermore, the medicine-man makes offerings to the spirit of his medicine from time to time. He chews kola-nuts and alligator pepper and spits these on the medicine as he utters incantations and prays that its power may be retained. He sometimes offers blood in addition to gin, kola-nuts or alligator pepper. What we are stressing here is the fact that medicine, as conceived by the Yorùbá, is believed to have something *extra* – a mysterious power which can cure or prevent ailments but in some cases could be used to do harm to an enemy.

Because of the powers believed to be inherent in these medicinal preparations, anyone who uses them has to observe certain taboos. For example, some medicine must not be taken to a dirty place, for example, a latrine; or be worn by a man when he has intercourse with a woman or be touched by a woman who is menstruating. The power in such preparation will disappear and the medicine will be rendered useless. In some cases, food taboos have to be observed – one may not drink palm-wine or share one egg with another person or eat the okra stew, if the preparation is to retain its potency.

The medicine man tries to combine the power in the medicinal preparation with some other power which is invoked and without which the medicine will be worthless. Thus, when the Yorùbá speak of *Oògùn* (medicine), this usually embraces the normal medicinal preparation and charms. A medicine man goes about his task in a systematic and ritualistic manner – he invokes the tutelary spirit of Ọ̀sanyìn (the divinity controlling medicine), he pays homage to the spirits and the ancestors who have made the preparation before him, and he makes necessary offerings soliciting spiritual blessings on the preparation. All this is in the realm of religion. Then, he goes further to utter incantations which are magical in character. But some other observers may argue that the incantations are to be passed for prayer and that everything done is done in the realm of religion to make the medicine efficacious.

It should be pointed out that the mysterious power in a medicine may be used for good or evil end. It may be used, for example, for curing certain ailments, for gaining success in different enterprises (e.g. fishing, hunting, trading, burglary or protection against burglary and for warding off the attacks of enemies). It may also be used in rendering an enemy blind or impotent or causing him failure and untold hardship. While the good medicine man is loved and respected by all lovers of things beautiful, the wicked and bad medicine man is feared and hated by all. The bad medicine man is singled out and described as a sorcerer. He is believed to be notorious for his use of medical and magical powers in bringing harm, discomfort, failure and even death to people, especially those that he happens to hate. We shall understand this better when we turn our attention to an examination of the mysterious power of magic.

Magic

The *New Encyclopaedia Britannica* defines magic as 'a ritual performance or activity believed to influence human or natural events through access to an external mystical force beyond the ordinary human sphere.'² From this definition, we see that magic is a practical affair. It is a human art which involves the manipulation of certain objects which are believed to have power to cause a supernatural being to produce or prevent a particular result considered not obtainable by natural means. It is regarded as a means of handling the forces of nature, of bending them to man's will, of safeguarding his welfare and shaping his destiny.

Man as a creature knows his limitations – he knows that he has needs of a number of things which he cannot procure on his own. He is confronted with many problems in the universe and he seeks aid to be able to cope with them. He is convinced that there are supernatural resources in the universe for his benefit and that these resources can be obtained by two different means:

(a) By appealing to the transcendental Being to satisfy his needs;
(b) By devising a means of tapping the elemental forces which are already created in the universe by the Supreme Being, and which can be procured by those who know 'how'.

When man makes an appeal in order to get the required resources, theologians will say that he is practising religion; but when he devises a means of getting the resources, they will say that he is practising magic. In religion, man depends upon and submits to the transcendental Being for his basic needs, but magic operates on the principle that supernatural power can be controlled by some mechanical techniques. Hence religion has as its motto: 'Your will be done', while magic has as its own motto: 'My will be done'. But when we have said this, we want to underline the fact that we do not subscribe to the idea that magic uses coercion on the transcendental Being to get things done. No one can exert force on the Supreme Being. What magic does is to tap the resources which are already provided by the transcendental Being for the use of mankind – which resources are known only to those who have the esoteric knowledge. In both religion and magic, there is a power beyond man. Religion is *exoteric*, that is, it is open to all; but the tapping of the elemental forces of nature is *esoteric* in the sense that it is limited to those who have the knowledge. Magical practices are done by special experts and they constitute a class in the community. In fact, the magician

is a kind of scientist, in that he seeks to discover and use the laws of the universe, not only of intimate nature but also spiritual forces. He believes that there are powers that are hidden secrets that can be tapped, not necessarily that he can force these powers to a different purpose but that there are laws which may be set in motion by the knowledgeable, as an electrician uses the forces of nature to light his house.[3]

Religion and magic are so closely connected that it is difficult to say when one passes from one realm to another. In Yorùbá religion, 'the offices of the priest and of the magician are sometimes held by one and the same person, and ceremonies are sometimes performed with an admixture of religious and magical elements'.[4] In consequence of long traditions, the Yorùbá Traditional Religion, like the African Traditional Religion in general, has come to assume a set pattern. Things must be done in one way and not in any other way if worship is to be acceptable – songs must be sung in appropriate places, dancing steps must not be missed, one type of offering and not the other must be given for a particular occasion. Many of these rites and ceremonies have become so stereotyped and mechanical that they look magical in operation. In the Christian religion, certain things have to be done in a stereotyped manner if a desired goal is to be achieved. For example, some priests and prophets claim to know the names of the different angels of God that bear the pillars of the earth from hour to hour; and that if they are called by their holy names and in the right manner, they will readily respond to one's requests. Some Christians also claim that if the Psalms are recited with the appropriate, holy and esoteric names and if they are recited according to certain patterns, they will prove particularly effective. This is an attempt on the part of man to get a quick solution to problems. This desire is present in every religion; it is not peculiar to the African traditional religion.

The Yorùbá believe in the reality of the supersensible world, in the existence of powers causing and controlling the phenomena of nature and in the possibility of establishing contact with these mysterious powers. As we have indicated above, they employ both religion and magic to achieve their goal. The practitioners of magic use incantations, amulets, spells, enchanted rings, horns, small gourds, padlocks, alligator pepper and many other objects for the purpose of tapping and controlling the supernatural resources in the universe.

Magic has been employed in a practical way for good and for evil. For example, magical preparations have been used for personal protection against attacks by witches, adversaries or bad medicine or as a means of warding off evils. They have also served as a means of securing invulnerability from or protection against gun-shot or matchet cut. Magic has been used to bring rain to the crops or game to the nets; to win the love of a lover, to give skill in war, speed in travelling or to win in sporting activities. Besides personal protections, we have many examples of magical preparations for the public good. Many houses are protected by charms which are found hanging above the doorway or buried in the floor of the house or outside the building. Entrances to towns and villages are also protected by such magical preparations.

As we have good magical preparations so also do we have examples of evil magic. Dangerous burglars are equipped with magical preparations which enable them to burgle houses easily and without molestation; by the use of enchanted rings men have been rendered blind; charmed alligator pepper has been used to bring incurable diseases on victims of circumstance; the hair or nail parings, chewing sticks or articles of clothing of people have been used in preparing offensive charms against them.

Details of how the different kinds of magical preparations are made and used cannot be given here, but we shall attempt a brief description of one of these. One of the magical preparations which have been classified as both good and evil is the 'Mágùn' ('Do not mount'). It is a means of controlling sexual immorality, and thus making the marriage bed honourable. A Yorùbá man who discovers that his wife is unfaithful and is fond of running after other lovers, devises a magical preparation which makes it deadly for another man to have coitus with his wife. According to information gathered from those who know, this involves putting an enchanted string or a sprig of broom in the woman's path – possibly in the entrance to her room. She unknowingly crosses the enchanted string. Right from that moment, she bears a mysterious 'power' in her genitals. The husband who sets the trap does not approach her during the 'dangerous' period. If the woman goes to her lover and engages in intercourse, the adulterous man is automatically thrown off her and bounces three times consecutively after which he gives up the ghost. This is why people call this type of magical preparation 'Mágùn', meaning 'Do not mount' (another man's wife).

Sometimes, there are variations. Instead of the adulterous man falling off and bouncing three times and dying, he has his full share of the temporary enjoyment but discovers at the end that he cannot be separated from the woman. Their genitals are locked together, and both of them are caught in the very act and are exposed to the ridicule of the whole community. After much appeal to the husband, an antidote (èrò) is offered and the two are separated, but looking helpless and completely ashamed.

This will sound fantastic to readers who are strangers to the Yorubaland and to Africa, but it is the whole truth. It is a difficult (perhaps unpleasant) way of controlling extramarital sexual relations: but it injects sanity into the society in a very hard way. We should mention, however, that some clever men who want to engage in adulterous practices have procured anti-Mágùn rings which they wear to counteract the Mágùn trap. And sometimes a man who has set the trap, expecting that its task might have been done, may be caught in his own trap. We choose to elaborate on this type of magical practice because we regard it as a classical example of the mysterious power in the Yorùbá belief.

A magical act has almost always three elements:

(a) There are words to be uttered according to a formula or set order. Any slip, omission or alteration of wording deprives the magic of its power.

(b) There is a set of actions to be carried out. For example, if there is a plan to kill an enemy from a distance, the preparation may include the following actions: the sorcerer will procure water in a bowl and have ready a cudgel or matchet or a loaded gun; then he summons, by magical means, the spirit of the enemy to appear in the water in the bowl; then the sorcerer hits, cuts, or shoots the figure that appears. As a result of this, the person whose spirit has been so summoned will receive an actual wound or gun-shot wherever he may be.

Rain-making usually involves sprinkling of water on the ground or dipping of twigs in water and sprinkling water in an imitation of rainfall. Likewise, rain-preventing involves tying some seeds of alligator pepper and some other objects in a hand-kerchief or tying palm-fronds into knots and swinging these overhead swiftly as incantations are uttered.

Other acts may involve pulling out an enchanted needle stuck into an enchanted horn, or spitting ritually upon a magical preparation, or sticking needles into the effigy of an enemy to cause him incessant pain, or locking an enchanted padlock to make it impossible for an accuser to speak against one in the law court.

(c) The condition of the 'actor' is also of ritual significance. In all communities, the magician is hedged round by taboos – he must refrain from eating certain foods, from casual sexual indulgence and from other contaminating actions. Unless he observes these taboos rigidly his charms will lose their potency.

In consequence of belief in magical power, many Yorùbá are found wearing all kinds of charms – copper rings (*òrùkao bàbà*), amulets (*ìfúnpá*), preparations sewn up in leather girdle/belt (*oǹdè*). In homes, we sometimes find a broom hanging from the door post, a small gourd shining bright from which some liquid is apparently dropping, an enchanted chain partly buried in the ground or some cowries arranged in symetrical order on the floor. Some babies wear coils round their necks and waists; men and women have some black powder injected into their bodies through incisions (*gbéré*).

These and many others are living pointers to the people's belief in the mystical power of magic. Some of these preparations are protective measures, others are intended to bring good health, fortune or prosperity. But some others are employed for nefarious deeds and they make people live in constant fear.

While we may condemn evil magical preparations because they are antisocial, we advocate the exploring, the use and control of healthy magic to aid modern scientific inventions and improve the standard of living of the people. We do not share Ìdòwú's view that 'the aid of magic is sought by those who are not sure of their character or those who are positively wicked. . . .'[5] His suggestion would be acceptable if all magical preparations were evil. But from our survey of magic among the Yorùbá, we know that there are both good and evil magical preparations. There can be no wickedness, for example, in employing magical means to escape from imminent danger, or to ward off evil spirits, or to shorten distance, or to stupefy burglars and discourage them from their evil deeds, or to improve upon agricultural products and the like.

Witchcraft

What is witchcraft and who is a witch? According to the *Encyclopaedia*

Britannica, witchcraft is 'the art or craft of the wise, as the word "witch" is allied with "wit" (to know)'.[6] This was revised to 'the believed use of supernatural means for harmful, evil ends.'[7] Thus, a witch is a wise person supposed to possess supernatural powers in consequence of forming a league with the devil or evil spirits, and through such an evil alliance and co-operation the possession of the craft which enables her to perform supernatural acts which, in most cases, are destructive. Hence, witches are seen as the personification of evil, as innately wicked people who work harm against others. They are capable of their nefarious deeds through their possession of mysterious powers unknown and unavailable to ordinary people.

In his description of them, Ìdòwú says:

> Witches are human beings of very strong determined wills with diabolical bent; . . . (they) are the veritably wicked ones who derive sadistic satisfaction from bringing misfortune upon other people. . . .[8]

And Margaret Field (probably because her concern was with religion and medicine in Ghana) describes witchcraft as 'a bad medicine directed destructively against other people, but its distinctive feature is that there is no palpable apparatus connected with it, no rites, ceremonies, incantations, or invocations that the witch has to perform.'[9] According to Field, a witch is 'a person who is the abode of an evil entity. . . .'[10]

We must, at this point, distinguish between witchcraft and sorcery. A sorcerer uses charms, incantations, spells and magic knowingly and with premeditation. 'A witch', says Evans-Pritchard, 'performs no rite, utters no spell and possesses no medicine. An act of witchcraft is a psychic act'.[11]

In their own contribution to our understanding of the distinction between sorcery and witchcraft, Middleton and Winter say:

> Witchcraft is part of an individual's being, a part of his innermost self while sorcery is merely a technique which a person utilizes, Thus, in some society, a person's witchcraft can operate at times without his being consciously aware of the fact that it is doing so. This can never be the case with sorcery; recourse to it must always be on a deliberate, conscious, voluntary basis. . . .[12]

This suggests that the sorcerer makes magic to kill, but a witch has an inherent and intangible power for harming others. While a witch projects her evil thought directly from her mind, invisibly, and with-

A priest in white apparel.

An Ọbatala priestess holding an *aja* (bell) for invocation and blessing.

An Ifa priest (called Babalawo) using the Ọ̀pẹ̀lẹ̀ to divine.

A diviner using sixteen cowries.

and members of the society also make confession of their ill deeds. Accusations of witchcraft are made against real persons, not imaginary personalities; victims of witchcraft are real; those who confess to the heads of the anti-social secret organisation are also real persons. We do not have to be witches before we can sense the influences of witchcraft in any African community. 'We must get away from the psychologist's fallacy of thinking that simply because a particular person has not experienced something, that something must necessarily be unreal or untrue.'[16]

The main source of information concerning witchcraft is gathered from confessions made by the witches themselves. These confessions contribute largely to people's belief in the existence of witches. People ask: 'If X is not a witch, how could she claim to have done all these things that she claimed she had done?' A witch, for example, spontaneously declared that it was she who killed a number of relatives, who ate a number of infants, who caused the other woman to be barren; a wife confessed that she caused her husband's trading business to fail; another woman confessed that she had caused her husband to fail in his university studies; yet another confessed that she had taken away another woman's uterus and had buried it under a tree, thus making it impossible for her to bear a child; and yet another woman claimed to have 'stolen' a man's phallus, thus causing him impotence.

Modern scientists and psychologists will claim that the witches cannot do what they confess that they have done. These psychologists sometimes claim that such confessions are made under pressure or threat or when the witches are delirious and are not conscious of what they are saying. But a pre-scientific and naturalistic approach and interpretation will be that the confessions are not forced but quite natural. If the people making such confessions are delirious or unconscious, they will not talk sense. But there have been instances when what they claimed to have done was actually established. The woman who claimed to have buried the uterus of another woman under the earth and had planted a plantain stump over it, asked the witch doctor to go and dig a particular area, and when this was done, something like a small parcel tied round and round with red and black thread was recovered. And when the woman took it and loosed it ceremonially, the other woman soon afterwards experienced the joy of childbirth. Instances like this abound all over Africa. It may, also, be added that there are anti-wickedness divinities in Yorubaland (e.g. Ayélála) who

out cursing and invoking, a sorcerer manipulates [...]
materials to carry out his devilish 'business'.

In the mental and social attitudes of the Yorùbá, and [...]
in general, there is no belief more profoundly ingrain[...]
the existence of witches (àjẹ́). All strange disease[...]
untimely death, inability to gain promotions in offi[...]
examinations and business enterprise, disappointment[...]
renness in women, impotence in men, failure of crops an[...]
other evils are attributed to witchcraft.

Is witchcraft real? This is a very crucial question. '[...]
according to Evans-Pritchard, 'is an imaginary offence [...]
impossible. A witch cannot do what he is supposed to d[...]
fact no real existence.'[13] Like Evans-Pritchard, C. K. [...]
asserts, 'Witches and witchcraft do not, of course, exist; [...]
a purely imaginary crime.'[14] These two writers dismiss w[...]
imaginary and impossible. But Margaret Field, a remarka[...]
of witchcraft in Ghana, confessed that it was difficult to [...]
tigation into and understand witchcraft and that it was after[...]
four years of intensive study that she came to realise that '[...]
solid reality of witchcraft is, from the European point [...]
medical one.' Witches (according to the Europeans) are 'pe[...]
tally afflicted with the obsession that they have the power[...]
others by thinking them harm.' But Field's conviction was[...]
African point of view is based on a solid reality and not on a s[...]
ous and senselessly cruel fantasy.'[15] Field had many exar[...]
terrible deeds of the witches which she collected through inter[...]
of people who were either witches themselves or those who ha[...]
bewitched at one time or another. She conveyed a convicti[...]
witchcraft is a reality to the Africans.

Africans who are conscious of the belief of their people will [...]
foreign investigators who claim that witchcraft is an illusion o[...]
exists only in thought and not in reality. To the Yorùbá as well a[...]
ethnic groups in Africa, witchcraft is a reality. It is a belie[...]
prevalent among literates and illiterates, among the high and t[...]
in the society. Witchcraft is carried out secretly, and like any [...]
secret society, unless one belongs to that secret society one c[...]
make a categorical statement about it. However, men may get to [...]
about such a society if its activities are publicised, or if members [...]
society divulge top secrets. With regard to witchcraft, its activitie[...]
known in any African communities, evils of all sorts are attribut[...]

can and do single out wicked witches for punishment. It is the general belief that these divinities do not pick on innocent people; those singled out to be witches are, indeed, witches. When they make full confessions and promise not to engage in further evil deeds, they are usually spared.[17]

What we need to realise is that a person whose conscience is still functioning properly never feels comfortable whenever anything contrary to the will of God and of the norm of the society is done; this is because the conscience is disturbed. Confession naturally eases the conscience. Our attitude to the confessions made by the witches is quite clear: we believe that a woman who confesses that she has done one evil or another must be taken seriously. We believe that it is out of the abundance of the heart that the mouth speaks. If, for example, a woman confesses that she has caused the death of a neighbour's daughter or her own daughter, it must be that at one time or another she has wished that evil of some sort should befall the victim. In other words, she has borne malice; she does not wish her neighbour's daughter or her own daughter well. If any evil should befall such a girl against whom she bears malice, she (the witch) will confess that she has done it. We must bear in mind the fact that all evil thoughts come from the heart and that no one can discern what wickedness a wicked person harbours in his heart unless he makes a confession of it. It is no use dismissing such confessions as things without substance.

Furthermore, we should realise that man has what psychologists call the 'omnipotence of thought'; with this gift, a man wishes that certain things may happen, and they do happen as he wishes – the wishes may be good or evil. This is because man is created powerful; he is capable of building and reconstructing as well as demolishing and damaging. When he is doing the latter, he is acting contrary to the will of his Creator, and he cannot have the peace characteristic of those who do the will of God. Witches indulge in evil doing, hence they cannot have peace, that element which gives wholeness and totality to man. And one way in which one can have peace is to make confession of the past evil deeds and to resolve to do that which is right and acceptable.

Foreign investigators and writers on witchcraft in Africa should heed the advice of Middleton and Winter when they say:

The fact that most Europeans no longer hold these ideas [i.e. ideas about witchcraft], and the fact that they regard them as superstitions, products of ignorance and error, often hampers communication between Europeans and Africans. . . . These beliefs are social, not psychological, phenomena and must be analysed.[18]

Still here

We need to add that foreign investigators should be reminded that witchcraft survived in England till the eighteenth century, 1200 years after the introduction of Christianity. The number of witches put to death by the inquisitors and other persecutors in the sixteenth and seventeenth centuries is proof of the obstinate belief in witchcraft in Europe. In the United States of America, Margaret Jones was executed in Boston in 1648; and soon afterwards, Mary Parsons of Springfield was indicted for witchcraft, but actually executed for murdering her child. Mrs Anne Hibbins was hanged in Boston on 19 June 1656. In 1688 a girl in Boston accused an old washerwoman of bewitching her, and as a result the woman was hanged. Thus went the witchcraft craze in New England. Twenty persons and two dogs suspected of being witches' familiars were hanged as well. Whenever one mentions Salem today, one remembers witchcraft in the U.S.A.

As belief in witchcraft was deep-rooted and is still lingering in Europe and the United States of America (as we shall show below), so it is in Africa. Islam, Christianity and Western education do not necessarily rid a community of this belief. Among the Africans today, there are thousands of progressive Christians and Muslims, including persons of the highest intelligence, who still retain their belief in witchcraft; they do so in consequence of what they have heard and experienced concerning witchcraft.

Essential elements of witchcraft
Wherever witchcraft is practised, it has distinctive features. We shall now examine those features as they are presented in Yorubaland.

As we have pointed out earlier, witchcraft is intangible; it is not anything that can be handled or touched. Witchcraft is projected from the mind – it is psychic.

Witchcraft enjoins secrecy. The person who practises it hates being known or caught in the very act. Whenever she goes 'on active service' she disguises herself, using bird or animal familiars or dressing in a strange manner, for example, being draped in palm fronds rather than wearing normal dresses. Witches are mostly women but it is not altogether unknown for men to practise witchcraft too.

Another important feature of witchcraft is the organisation of regular nocturnal meetings. These meetings are called *Àjọ*. The witches are said to meet at night between midnight and 2.00 a.m. while their physical bodies remain on their beds at home. The gathering is not in any physical form. If an ordinary person happens to be passing by when witches are at their meeting, he may not be able to see them. Only those who have the power of 'vision', particularly the witch-doctors, can see them. They attend the meetings using various means of movement. Some, according to information, are said to turn upside down and walk with their feet in the air. Some somersault to increase speed, others fly naked after rubbing on their bodies some ointment which makes them invisible. Yet others walk to the meetings on spiders' webs; some ride on animals like cats, dogs, rats or on toads and even on human beings. Many others turn into owls and lizards and into insects and glow-worms. Meetings take place at the banks of rivers, at the foot or branches of big trees or at the road junctions or on mountains or hills. These meetings are held at different levels: local, divisional, regional, inter-regional, national and international. Communications are maintained between one level and the other.

It is at such meetings that witches plan how to get their victims and feed upon those already procured. Sucking the blood of the victim is the usual thing sought. When the essential organs are claimed to be eaten, it is not in any physical form. The eating causes a wasting disease to the victim's body. Children and adults alike are eaten by witches. It is said that they also eat the foetus in a pregnant mother's womb, thus causing a miscarriage.

The essential contribution at any meeting is in the form of a human victim. The more a witch can contribute, the higher she is rated in the assembly. If, for example, a witch is able to procure an eminent person in the family or in the town or village, she can easily become the chairman at important meetings. In order to achieve an enviable position in the council of witches, therefore, a witch contributes her daughter, son, father, mother or husband. Any witch who does not contribute towards the general 'pool' in the form of human victims will be reminded again and again of her negligence of duty. Such a negligence will rob her of her 'promotion' and may cost her her own life. So it is not at all impossible that witches may kill their fellow witches. It is to be noted that witches take delight in doing harm indiscriminately. A witch, for example, can kill her own daughter or her own husband. Hence the Yorùbá say, 'While a mad woman will do no harm to her daughter, a witch does kill indiscriminately, including her own daughter.' This suggests that an insane person is more rational than a witch.

It is generally believed that a woman is the head of the council of witches. Men may be present but they are always in the minority; this confirms the fact that witchcraft is the cult of women. It is among the men, however, that 'executioners' are appointed. Such men are known as the 'knife holders'. This means that the actual 'immolation' of the victims is done by the men-folk. Whoever is killed, is the responsibility of the whole group – it is a corporate responsibility. If, on the other hand, the whole assembly has agreed to release an afflicted person, however serious the illness may be, such a person will, indeed, be released, and will continue to enjoy life. In actual fact, it may be a member of the council of witches who will act as a medicine-man and who will prepare some medicine that will prove wonderfully efficacious. Furthermore, a substitute sacrifice may be prescribed by a knowledgeable priest, to be offered to the witches; and once the witches are satisfied with the offerings, they will 'release' the prospective victim.

Witchcraft is acquired in different ways. Some people are born witches; others inherit witchcraft from their mothers, that is, by heredity. It is said that some people pay for and procure it and others have witchcraft 'stuff' passed to them in food given by women who are witches. The most stubborn of the different types is the first one.

Finally, witches among the Yorùbá are believed to have a kind of bird which makes a peculiar chirping sound as it flies overhead in the dead of night on its journey to the àjo (the meeting place).Old people who may happen to be outside the house or still awake indoors when the chirping sound is heard, usually address the 'bird' saying: 'A kìíso pé kí ode òrìsà ó má de, bí kò bá ti de wára eni, Onàire o! (One cannot decree that the hunters for òrìsà (divinities) should not hunt, provided that they do not hunt one's immediate neighbour. Safe journey!) This is a way of appealing to the witches not to do any harm to the supplicant. It also shows that people believe that witches are terrible and that they constitute a source of fear for human beings. As hunters go on hunting expeditions, so witches go on their mission of hunting for human beings whom they may destroy.

Belief in witchcraft

There is the belief that this is God's world; that the Creator of the world is good; and that He wants man to have the best in life. If, therefore, there are noticeable elements of evil, there must be some factors responsible for such disruption in the orderly and smooth running of life. Thus, witchcraft is brought in to explain misfortune. When anxieties and stresses arise in social and domestic life, when things do not go according to plan, when there is barrenness or sterility, depression or misery, ghastly accident or premature death, failure in business, in academic or other pursuits, the Africans pick on witchcraft as the cause. In this way, things that otherwise would have been difficult to explain, easily find explanation.

Moreover, man is expected to love his fellow-men, and the society in which he lives has certain principles of morality. If a man does that which is unethical, he is described as evil; but if he does that which is ethical and acceptable, he is good. In an African context, a bad person is often referred to as a witch. Nadel puts this succinctly when he says:

> The woman who behaves as the Nupe think witches do, is one whose character belies the common precepts and ideals of conduct; she is ill-conditioned, eccentric, atypical . . . not the physical abnormality . . . which is merely a matter of ill-luck; . . . but the abnormality of social and moral deviants.[19]

In other words, anybody who does that which is contrary to the acceptable standard of the society, particularly where the person involved does that which is harmful to the good of the society, will be dubbed a 'witch'.

Sometimes, witchcraft is a product of suspicion. If, for example, a man's son goes to visit his aunt during holidays, and the boy is taken ill and dies, there is nothing to exempt the aunt whom he is visiting from the accusation of witchcraft. Everybody will suspect that she is a witch who has killed her nephew. Or, if someone becomes ill or is overtaken by any calamity soon after an argument in which threatening words were used, the chances are that his misfortune or mishap will be attributed to the person who used the threatening words. The Yorùbá will say:

Àjẹ́ ké lánàá	The witch-bird chirped last night;
Ọmọ́ kú lónìí;	And the child dies today;
Ta niò ṣàì mò pé	Who does not know that

Àjẹ́ àná ló pa ọmọ jẹ?   It was the chirping witch of the previous
night that has killed the child?

Witchcraft accusation may, sometimes, be a result of jealousy. If
the children of one of the wives of a man prosper while those of the
other wives (in a polygamous home) do not, this will be attributed to
witchcraft. Hence, accusations of witchcraft by women against each
other are very common; such accusations are, on many occasions,
based on suspicion or jealousy. Boasting invites jealousy. A well-to-do
or fortunate person who boasts of his prosperity or wealth will be
envied in a society where many are poor. It is believed that the evil
ones can change one's good status into a bad one; hence the Yorùbá
caution: *'Bí iṣu ẹní bá tú, a fọwọ́ bò ó jẹ'* ('If one's yam is good and
delicious, one eats it under the cover of one's hand'). This is to say that
one does not advertise one's prosperity. This is particularly important
in a society where the 'haves' are fewer than the 'have-nots'.

People who are exceptionally clever, successful or charming are
sometimes believed to be, and are called, witches. It is common, even
among schoolchildren, to nickname a boy who is usually top of his
class an *'àjẹ́'* (a witch) – this may be a figure of speech!

Sometimes, the inability to assess situations correctly leads to
attributing failure to witchcraft. A man who eats unripe fruit and
develops acute belly-ache, may attribute his ache to witchcraft rather
than to the eating of the fruit. Likewise, a man who lacks academic
ability beyond high school level, but who desires to get into a university, may blame his failure to gain admission on witchcraft rather
than on his natural limitations.

All this suggests that not every case of witchcraft accusation is a
genuine one. Witchcraft, viewed in this way, looks like an African
way of projecting a philosophy of life, an attempt to explain the
problem of failure, sorrow, pain or death. While we share the view
that the people sometimes 'cry wolf' when there is no wolf, we want to
underline the essential fact that there are genuine cases of witchcraft
practice in Yorubaland and in Africa as a whole.

It is rare to find an African who will agree to the suggestion
that 'witchcraft is an imaginary offence' or that 'witchcraft is impossible' as some foreigners have claimed; this is because many Africans,
in consequence of their various personal experiences, are convinced
that witchcraft is a reality and that it is a thoroughly evil and destructive force in the society.

The future of witchcraft
Some scholars have argued that Africans will be relieved of the fears of witchcraft only when they relinquish their beliefs in the reality of witches and cease to believe that others can harm them through the use of evil powers. Others claim that these beliefs will disappear with Western education, improved medical facilities and technology. But we share the view of Middleton and Winter who implore such scholars to exercise caution in this matter 'because Western education, of a secular type at any rate, while it deepens a schoolboy's understanding of how things operate as they do, does not provide any answer to the ultimate question of why misfortunes occur'.[20] We must realise that even nowadays, with all the influence of Western education and improved medical facilities, one still finds accusations of witchcraft between fellow-workers who are competing for the regard of their employer, between political opponents and even among educated children of the same father.

Furthermore, it is common practice among the Yorùbá that patients receiving treatment in modern hospitals still seek the traditional means of healing and of security even when they are taking advantage of the improved medical facilities. The practice is that the close relations of the patient usually go to consult the oracle to 'ascertain' the cause of trouble (as the medical doctor consults his medical text-book to ascertain the correct diagnosis); that is, they go to 'ascertain' which forces have brought about the ailment and what offerings should be given to placate the angry forces – almost always the oracle reveals that a witch or sorcerer is at work and prescribes sacrifice as well as medicine that should be used. Such medicine as is prescribed is usually brought into the hospital and given to the patient stealthily during visiting time when the doctor or the nurse is not around. The people strongly believe that unless the traditional medicine is given, the patient cannot recover.

At some other times, doctors in hospitals have confessed that certain cases cannot be handled effectively in the hospital because they baffle medical knowledge; such doctors have encouraged people to remove their patients home for treatment in the 'native way'. And, in many cases, when necessary 'appeal' is made to the evil forces, healing, which could not be effected in the hospital, has been effected simply by placating these evil forces and applying the 'prescribed' herbs. This suggests that the so-called improved medical facilities and

Western education cannot remove belief in witchcraft among the Yorùbá and the other ethnic groups in Africa.

Witchcraft belief seems to have an enduring attraction for people everywhere in the world. In his book, *Modern Witchcraft*, Frank Smyth gives an interesting and eye-opening account of a resuscitation of and a return to witchcraft among the so-called civilised nations of the world. Among these nations witchcraft is called the 'Cult of Wicca'. It is claimed that 'witch' is derived from the Middle English word *'wicca'* meaning 'wise'. These modern' witches claim that:

> Witchcraft is the true religion of Europe, usurped by Christianity but never completely killed by it. It is the worship of the creative forces of the universe, the recognition of the two halves which make up the whole, the bringing together of male and female, . . . black and white . . . It is also the means whereby mankind is able to tap the ancient forces of creation, the magical powers of centuries ago, translate them into physical terms, and use them for good or ill.[21]

According to this author, it is estimated that about 600 people attend 'coven' meetings in Scotland, Wales and England today, and a small growing number of Americans are also members of the 'wicca' cult. 'They number among their naked ranks school teachers, book keepers, policemen . . . local journalists and salesmen.'[22] We also gather from the same book that there is now discrimination in witchcraft. One man interviewed by Smyth in Highgate (London), said, 'I wouldn't admit coloured people to our meetings, simply because they have different traditions of witchcraft, and they wouldn't harmonise with us. I'm not biased of course, but that is the way it is. A foreigner could upset all our members and break the whole thing up.' And a woman sorcerer interviewed by the same man in London was more explicit; she said, 'I would never teach magic to a black or anyone else of an inferior race. They haven't the intelligence, and in the wrong hands magic can do untold harm'.[23]

While the man interviewed speaks of witchcraft, the woman speaks of magic. Neither of them seems to make a distinction between the two as we have tried to do. But, in both cases, there is that racial discrimination and a feeling that the coloured race (whichever group is so designated) is inferior to the white, even in things supernatural.

Our main interest is not a comparative study of witchcraft but simply to make some observations and to emphasise some essential facts:

(a) that witchcraft has been present from time immemorial; there seems to have been no time or place on earth where witchcraft and magic have not been practised;

(b) that some of the so-called civilised nations of the world who tend to ridicule the concept of witchcraft in Africa and who claim that the cult is an illusion, are not sincere as there is the evidence that they are resuscitating the cult in their own countries and in their own way;

(c) that witchcraft is almost universal and it is enduring.

The reason why man believes in terrors and evils and in mysterious powers is that terrors, evils and mysterious powers are there and very real. Man is sensibly conscious of the activities of these powers around him, and he refuses to be persuaded that they are imaginary. To the Yorùbá nothing happens by chance – something is caused by someone directly or indirectly by the use of power; and they, also, believe that there are individuals who have access to these mystical powers which can be employed either for good or evil purposes. This power is ultimately from a supernatural being, but in practice it is inherent in or comes from or through some physical objects, except in the case of witchcraft which is psychic.

SUMMARY OF PART ONE

Before we turn to the second part of this book, let us attempt a brief summary of our argument so far. The Yorùbá hold the following beliefs:

(1) The world was created and is maintained by the Supreme Being who has brought into being a number of divinities and spirits to act as His functionaries in His theocratic government of the world. These

divinities are of different categories, but they all serve the will of the Supreme Being.

(2) Death does not write 'the end' to human life but acts as a gateway to another life. In consequence of this, there is the belief in the hereafter and in the power and love of the ancestors.

(3) There are mysterious powers in the universe and these powers are experienced in the form of incantations, charms, sorcery, magic and witchcraft.

(4) There is orderliness in the administration of the world, and if disorderliness or disruption of harmony occurs, this should be attributed not only to man's neglect of the Supreme Being, the divinities and the ancestors, but also to the workers of iniquity, euphemistically referred to as Ọmọ Aráyé (children of the world) or Elénìní (implacable sadistic foe who plans evils against a person) or Àwọn ìyáàmi (my mothers). This last sobriquet is specifically used of the witches.

For him to enjoy full life and a total well-being, a Yorùbá man keeps in close touch with the Supreme Being who is the author of life and the determiner of destiny, by maintaining the various avenues of regular communication with the supernatural world. The different ways by which this is done are the subject of Part Two.

NOTES

1. Ìdòwú, *African Traditional Religion*, p. 199.
2. *New Encyclopaedia Britannica*, volume 6, 1974, p. 483.
3. Parrinder, *West African Religion*, pp. 157ff.
4. Lucas, *Religion of the Yorubas*, p. 267.
5. Ìdòwú, *African Traditional Religion*, p. 197.
6. *Encyclopaedia Britannica*, vol. 23, 1959, p. 686.
7. *Encyclopaedia Britannica*, vol. 10, 1974, p. 716.
8. E. B. Ìdòwú, 'The Challenge of Witchcraft', *Orita*, iv, 1, June, 1970, p. 9.
9. M. J. Field, *Religion and Medicine of the Ga People*, Oxford, 1937, p. 135.
10. M. J. Field, *Search for Security*, North-Western University Press, 1962, p. 35.
11. E. E. Evans-Pritchard, *Witchcraft, Oracles and Magic among the Azande*, Oxford, 1937, p. 21.
12. J. Middleton and E. H. Winter, eds., *Witchcraft and Sorcery in East Africa*, London, 1969, p. 12.

13. E. E. Evans-Pritchard, *Africa*, October, 1935, pp. 417–418.
14. C. K. Meek, *Law and Authority in a Nigerian Tribe* (Igbo), O.U.P., 1950, p. 79.
15. Field, *Religion and Medicine*, p. 136.
16. Ìdòwú, 'The Challenge of Witchcraft', p. 5.
17. See Awolalu, 'Aiyelala', p. 83.
18. Middleton and Winter, p. 1.
19. S. F. Nadel, *Nupe Religion*, Routledge and Kegan Paul, 1954, p. 171.
20. Middleton and Winter, p. 20.
21. Frank Smyth, *Modern Witchcraft*, Harper and Row, 1973, p. 17.
22. *Ibid*., p. 18.
23. *Ibid*., pp. 19ff.

Part Two

Sacrificial Rites

Chapter Five

ELEMENTS OF WORSHIP

In Part One of this book, we described the beliefs of the Yorùbá; in this second part we intend to show how the beliefs are put into action, starting with an examination of worship among the people.

What is worship?

Worship, in a secular sense, is sometimes defined as the title of honour used in addressing or speaking to a person of note – for example, a Court Judge or a Sherriff is addressed as 'His Worship' or 'Your Worship'. Worship may also be regarded as the respect, admiration or devotion for an object of esteem. Thus, subjects may and do 'worship' their kings or queens. In Greek, however, the word for worship is *therapeia*, which is translated as 'waiting on', 'service', 'attendance'. If, for example, a servant waits upon his master at table, such a servant may be said to be serving or 'worshipping' the master.

But the word 'worship' can also be looked at in a specifically religious sense; this, indeed, is the sense in which we want to look at it in this chapter. As a religious exercise worship is a means of honouring spiritual beings or an act of veneration paid by man to such spiritual beings. We agree with Evelyn Underhill who defines worship as the 'response of the creature to the Eternal'.[1] And like Underhill, J. Alan Kay defines worship as a 'response to the Eternal', and he expatiates upon those aspects of the Eternal to which man responds. According to him, 'worship is a man's response to the nature and action of God.'[2]

When these definitions (emphasising the religious aspects) are analysed, they show:

(a) that worship is truly offered by man to a Being or beings (by whatever name or names He is known and called) higher than himself;

(b) that the worshipper's response is evoked by his spontaneous or reflective discernment of the nature and action of the supernatural Power or Powers;

(c) that this response is conditioned by a person's conception of the divine being according to his mental level.

Where, for example, the Supreme Being is conceived as benevolent, bestowing good things upon man, there is a tendency on the part of man to give adoration, praise and thanksgiving. And if man happens to commit any wrong act against this benevolent Supreme Being, in spite of kindnesses bestowed, he has to show penitence. On the other hand, where the supernatural powers are considered malevolent and terrible, the 'worshipper' is generally filled with fear and will have to appease, in this instance, the offended or angry gods. In other words, worship depends upon and is conditioned by man's conception of God: it always has a theological basis. H. B. Alexander puts this point aptly when he said, 'Wherever men placate unseen foes or make offerings to hidden friends, and there are no human tribes so low in mind that these customs are not found among them, there worship is present and divinity recognised.'[3]

Worship is a religious exercise which involves the performance of devotional acts in honour of a deity or divinities. It presupposes a yearning for God and it is a means of glorifying the Source, the Sustainer and the End of life; it confirms man's acknowledgement of the Transcendent Being who is independent of the worshipper but upon whom the worshipper depends. Furthermore, the needs and limitations of ordinary human nature prompt men to seek a divine strength to sustain him in the fulfilment of his destiny here on earth. When man has lost the favour of the supernatural beings, it is through worship that he seeks to regain it.

Worship, therefore, testifies to the belief, creed, myths and philosophy of a people. In the life of the Yorùbá, worship is regarded as a matter of course. As indicated in Part I, the Yorùbá believe in the existence of the Supreme Being (who is the Creator and Preserver of the world) and in the divinities and spirits who act as His ministers and as intermediaries between Him and man. Worship is, therefore, accorded to the Supreme Being to whom man owes his own being and who is the Determiner of man's destiny. The Yorùbá respond to their spiritual world in different ways; hence they accord worship not only to the Supreme Being but also to His functionaries – the divinities and spirits. The people believe that if worship is given to these divine beings regularly and in the right manner, all will be well with man. On the other hand, failure to perform the customary rites and ceremonies, or the adoption of wrong modes of worship is regarded as fraught with serious consequences to the individual or to the community.

Characteristic features of worship

Worship, seen as a total response to the Ultimate Reality, is expressed by word as well as by deed. These words and deeds which take the form of rites and ceremonies, may include prostration, praying, invoking and hailing the spirits of the objects of worship, making offerings, sounding the bell or gong, singing, drumming and dancing, as occasions may demand. Worship may be private, offered by a single person in a house or shrine; or it may be corporate. In whatever form worship is undertaken, it is expected to be done in reverence and in an appropriate manner and mood, if the desired effect is to be achieved.

Every act of worship has distinct elements. Prominent among these are:

(i) Liturgy – which consists of ritual form and its content including prayer, music, and dancing;

(ii) Sacrifice – offerings for different purposes.

(iii) Cultic functionaries – the officiants and attendants at worship.

(iv) Sacred places – where worship is carried out – shrines, temples and altars.

Let us now examine each of these briefly:

Liturgy

When we speak of liturgy, with particular reference to the Yorùbá Traditional Religion, we are thinking of the prescribed form of public worship among the people. It may seem rather strange discussing liturgy in a religion which lacks written literature and depends mainly upon oral traditions. But lack of written literature is no barrier to our understanding of the people's approach to worship since the order of worship has been preserved for us, almost undisturbed, from generation to generation. The people have always had their cultic functionaries whose main concern is to preserve, among other things, the traditional conduct of worship. These people approach their task with awe and seriousness, always conscious of the fact that any omission in the normal order of service or any wrong word uttered or song not properly rendered during the service, could incur the displeasure of the deity and jeopardise the efficacy of worship. In consequence of this rigid observance of traditions by the people, it is fairly certain that the order of worship followed by them must have been more or less constant, as far as this is possible in a situation where things depend on what is stored up in human memory.

Among the Yorùbá, one observes that on social occasions, when drummers and musicians single out individuals at parties and sing their praises, such individuals as are singled out feel happy with themselves and are encouraged to dip their hands into the pockets to spend lavishly for the able musicians. Similarly, in almost all Yorùbá palaces, kings have *onì-kàkàkí* (buglers) who sing the *oríkì* (praise-names) of the kings and blow their bugles. Such praises gladden the souls of the kings that hear them. This secular practice is brought into the religious life of the people as this is noticeable in the way the Yorùbá sing the praises of their objects of worship. We shall illustrate with a few examples.

When the people come together to worship Ògún (god of iron, of the chase and of war), the priest praises or greets Ògún in the following manner:

Ògún ò!	Hail Ògún!
Ògún Oni'rè	Ògún, the lord of Ire!
Òkè ńlá kìléhìn Ìrè	The great mount that stands behind Ìrè.[4]
A-kó okolóko-gbéru-gbéru!	You who ravaged other people's farms.
Ògún pa sotúnun	Ògún killed on the right,
Ó b'òtún je,	And made the right a total destruction.
Ògún pa sosì,	Ògún killed on the left,
Ó bòsì je	And made the left a total destruction.
Ó pa olómú gògò sójú omi,	He slew the one with very prominent breasts on the waters,
Ó dá ìjà akàn àti eja;	Thus creating a bone of contention between the crabs and the fish;

Òṣìn Imálẹ̀!	Chief of the divinities!
Onílé kángun-kàngun òde ọrun,	The owner of many houses in heaven,
Ògún onílé owó, ọlọ́nà ọlà;	Ògún who owns the store of gold and the path of wealth.
O lomi sile fẹ̀jẹ̀ wẹ̀;	He who has water at home but prefers to bathe in blood;
Ògún a-wọ́n-léyin-ojú,	Ògún whose eyeballs are terrible to behold;
Ègbè lẹ́hìn ọmọ òrukàn,	He who gives support to the orphans.
Ògún ò!	Hail Ògún!

In the case of Ayélálá (an anti-wickedness goddess) the invocation and the praise-names are as follows:

Ìgbò ò (3 times)!	Ìgbò ò [a note of invocation and adoration]!
Yéyé ò (3 times)!	O Mother!
Òré Yèyé ò (3 times)!	O the very Mother!
Kawò ó, Kábíyèsílè!	Hail your Majesty!
Ọ̀kẹ́kélujẹ̀, Ọba obìnrin	The mighty and awesome Queen,
A-jí-fọtín wẹ̀ b'Òyìnbó,	She who early in the day bathes in gin like the whiteman;
A-jà-níjọ́-ọlọ́ràn-gbàgbé	She who takes vengeance when the evil-doer has forgotten,
A-jà-má-jẹ̀bi	She who can never be guilty when she takes action.
Ìgbò ò!	Ìgbò ò![5]

The praises of the divinities reveal, as in the above examples, not only the attributes of the divinities but also the beliefs of the devotees. The idea is that when the praise-names are given, or sung, the divinities will be moved to pay attention to the worshippers and thus heed their requests and wishes. Hence this aspect comes first in the order of public worship.

It is only after this eulogy that the people present their problems. This they do by stating why they have come before the divinity concerned. On joyful occasions, the people express gratitude to the divinities for protection, security and joy vouchsafed in the time past, and requests are made for the things desired. We shall see this in greater detail when we discuss elements of sacrificial rites later in this book.

Prayer

Prayer is a very important element in worship. It is a means by which man makes a devout supplication to, and enters into communion with, the object of worship. Adoration, praise and thanksgiving are offered to the Deity. The mind is fixed upon what the Supreme Being is and what He is able to do for man. His attributes and His acts of kindness are recalled and enumerated. It is practically impossible to worship without pouring out the mind before the divine being who is believed to be capable of granting man's requests. The more definite the conception of the supernatural powers, the more precise the prayers offered to them.

Among the Yorùbá, both formal and informal prayers are resorted to from time to time. The people firmly believe in the efficacy of prayer uttered by an individual person in private worship or by the priest at corporate worship. Prayer may be said whenever and wherever occasion demands, but formal worship takes place at a consecrated place. This we shall take up later when we discuss sacred places. For the present, let it be noted that while adoration, praise, thanksgiving and petition are very conspicuous in the prayer of the Yorùbá, little attention is paid to the confession of sins. This does not mean that the people do not have a sense of sin; the idea behind their action is that when they bring thank-offerings before their divinities they do so with joy and gratitude as they ask for a continuance of the benefits. But when there is a calamity, for example, if there is a drought, pestilence or infantile mortality, the people would readily conclude that something must be wrong somewhere. The oracle is normally consulted to know where the fault lies. When this is known, there is penitence on the part of the worshippers or individuals concerned. People acknowledge their sins of commission and omission and urge the divinities or the spirits to pardon. The propitiatory offering on such an occasion is usually a rite of purification. Thus we see that adoration, praise and thanksgiving characterise worship on happy occasions while the purificatory rite,[6] implying confession of sin as well as cleansing from sin and impurity, comes in when the worshippers feel the need to assuage the divine wrath.

Prayer is personal. It cannot be regimented because what a man prays for is conditioned by the circumstances that induce the prayer –

his economic distress, his sorrow and anguish, his failure and success, his pain and joy. When we observe the prayers of the Yorùbá, we discover that they are mainly petitionary. They entreat the divinities to grant a number of requests; and they believe that these requests can and will be granted only if it pleases the divinities to do so. Therefore, when prayers are said, the people respond, 'A ṣẹ', that is, 'May it be so'. The full meaning of the expression 'A ṣẹ' is 'May it please the divinities to give approval to these requests.' This emphasises the fact that the people believe that they cannot impose their wills on the divinities but that these divinities are capable of hearing prayers and of granting man's requests. Final sanction is the prerogative of the Supreme Being Himself. Hence the people say, 'Àṣẹ d'ọwọ́ Olódùmarè' ('Olódùmarè has the sanction').

Most of the people's requests stress their yearning for life. 'They consist usually of asking for protection from sickness and death, gifts of longevity, children, prosperity in enterprises, victory over enemies, protection from evil spirits . . . rectification of unhappy destinies, and abundant provision of material things. . . .'[7]

The people pray both in sorrowful and in joyful mood. These prayers are often spontaneous and informal but within a liturgical setting. Let us cite a few examples.

To every paramount chief in Ekiti, for instance, there is the greeting 'Ẹbọ á fín' ('May your sacrifice be acceptable or may you prosper'). To the people, this is very important prayer. The paramount chiefs are the leaders of the people as well as the representatives of the ancestors. It is when the offerings made by the chiefs (on behalf of their subjects) are acceptable that the people can have peace and harmony. So the subjects do not fail to say 'Ẹbọ á fín' to their rulers. The following greeting and prayer were recorded some time in 1968 when some chiefs came to greet the Ẹlẹ́kọ̀lé of Ìkọ̀lé in Ìkọ̀lé-Èkìtì during the Orò Èkù festival.

Kábíyèsí, Aláyé!	Hail, your majesty!
Ẹbọ á fín!	May (your) sacrifice be auspicious,
Wà á darúgbó, Ọlójà	May you live till old age, Ọlójà[8]
Ìgbà rẹ á sunwọ̀n,	May your time be prosperous.
Olórí á jẹ nìgbàa tìrẹ;	May there be good leaders in your time;
Àgàn á bímọ nígbàa tìrẹ	May the barren have issue in your time;
Ìlú á tòrò,	May the town be peaceful,

Ì lú á lágbà	May the town have elders,
Wé a rógun ọ̀tẹ̀,	May there be no rebellion,
Wo maa sẹ̀yí sàmọ́dún	May you live to see and celebrate another festival.

Here as we can see, both greeting and prayer go together. As the people greet their ruler so also do they pray for him, for his subjects and for the town as a whole.

On festival occasions, when priests or heads of families offer prayers, the same emphasis is laid on the essential needs of man. Further examples have to be given of actual prayers recorded in some of the places visited during our fieldwork.

I was privileged to witness the Èje Festival[9] in October 1969 at Ìtèbú Manùwà. At one stage of the celebration, an important rite took place in a grove called *Ugbówẹn* (the grove of fairies). There the following recorded prayer was offered to *Ọrọ̀ Léwe* by the presiding priest:

Ọdoọdún la ńrí Moràá;	It is every year we see Moràá;[10]
Ọdún tún kò;	The year is come round;
Ọmọ rẹ, Kabiyesi Ẹlẹ́rọ̀ ti Itebu, Ọba Manuwa,	Your son, His Highness, the Ẹlẹ́rọ̀ of Itebu, Ọba Ade Manuwa
Ní òun wáá dúpẹ́ lọwọ́ọ̀ re	Says he comes to express gratitude
Òun tún rí ọdún yìí	For the privilege of seeing another year.
Ó ní eja, ó ní obì	He has [i.e. offers] fish and kolanuts
Ó ní efun, ó ní ataare	He has chalk, he has alligator pepper,
Ó ní epo pupa.	He has palm oil.
Má jẹ̀ẹ́kí Ẹlẹ́rọ̀ pádéèrẹ lọ́dún yìí	Do not let the Ẹlẹ́rọ̀ meet you [i.e. be afflicted by paralysis]
Má jé kí ó kú ikú òjíjì.	Do not let him die a sudden death.
Jẹ́ Kí o dàgbà, ki o darúgbó.	Let him grow old and aged.
Jẹ́ Kí ọ̀rọ̀ọ rẹ̀ àti ti àwọn ará ìlú ó yéra wọn	Let there be understanding between him and the subjects.
Jẹ́ Kí gbogbo àwọn ijòyè ìlú rójú kí wón ràyè	Let all the chiefs have peace Let them have joy.
Kí ìlú kí ó kún	Let there be increase in population
Kí ó tòrò	And let the town have peace.
Kí àwọn àgàn bímo	Let the barren have children
Kí àwọn aboyún máṣe kú nínú ìrọbí	Let not the expectant mothers die in travail,

Kí wọn má baà rí	Lest they see your anger
ibínúà rẹ	
Gbogbo àwon ọmọ Ìtèbú	All the sons and daughters of Ìtèbú
gbá-à,	
Níbikíbi yòó wù kí	Wherever they may be,
wón wà,	
Kí wọn máṣe pàdéè rẹ	Let them not meet you [i.e. be
lọ́dún yìí	afflicted by you] this year.

It was a long prayer, it went on and on. This is only a part of the long piece, but it does illustrate that prayer brings together the people's requests.

Similarly, during the Orò Ọlọ́fin (Ọlọ́fin Festival) in Ìláwẹ̀, Èkìtì, I was able to witness the occasion of making offerings to Ọbàlùfọ̀n (the tutelary divinity of Ìláwẹ̀) symbolised by Ọṣùntá. On that particular occasion, Chief Èjìgbò, the Oba's representative brought the people's offerings to the chief priest. He knelt down before Ọṣùntá and prayed for everybody and for everything in the community. He prayed that a good *ọba* (king) might be chosen at no distant date to occupy the vacant stool;[11] that there might be understanding between chiefs and the townspeople; that women might have children; that the cocoa crop, the staple crop among the people, might flourish; that Ìláwẹ̀ children who were studying abroad might do well in their studies and return home successfully; that there might be no pestilence, and that the political trouble between Adó and Ìláwẹ̀, which was forty-four years old at that time, might be resolved.[12] The chief then prayed for himself that as he had brought the gift that year, he might be privileged to bring it again the coming year.

We see, then, that 'prayers are comprehensive and tend to include any spirit force that may give help. This may shock a monotheist, but the purpose is to call the varied powers to give health and well-being'.[13] Men generally seek augmentation and strengthening of life, hence they recognise and invoke the power of the divine beings.

Music and dancing
As the Yorùbá show their love of music and dancing in their day-to-day life, so also do they use these arts in worship; and, as the divinities have their praise-names which the priests and the worshippers recite at the beginning of any worship, so also are certain songs dedicated to the divinities sung in their honour as occasion demands.

For example, during the worship of Ṣàngó (god of thunder), especially during the annual festival, one hears songs such as the following:

Ọlọ́mọ kìlọ̀ fọ́mọ rẹ̀,	Let every one warn his child,
Ẹ má pèé Ṣàngó gbọ́mọ lọ	Lest Ṣàngó be accused of kidnapping.
Bí ó ṣoro,	When he (Ṣàngó) chooses to be ferocious,
A ṣọ 'gi dèniyàn	He turns a tree into a man;
Bí ó ṣoro	When he chooses to be ferocious,
A ṣèniyàn dẹranko	He turns a man into an animal.

Songs of this nature are very common during the worship of Ṣàngó;
they depict the ferocity and the power of the divinity. And to sing such
songs is to do honour to the memory of the fierce ruler who became
deified. Such songs are sung with excitement.

As a contrast to this, when we turn to songs sung in praise of
Ọbàtálá (Òrìṣà-ńlá) whose characteristics are gentleness and grace, we
feel the presence of peace rather than violence:

Ikú tí íbá ni ígbele	The powerful one! You who dwell with
Fọlá ran ni!	a person and make him prosperous.
Aláṣẹ!	The Chief Commander!
Ó ṣọ ẹnìkanṣoṣo digba èniyàn!	You who multiply only one into two hundred persons!
Ṣọ mí dìrún,	Multiply me into four hundred,
Ṣọ mí digba	Multiply me into two hundred,
Ṣọ mí dòtà-lé-légbèje èniyàn.	Multiply me into one thousand, four hundred and sixty persons.

Here Ọbàtálá is presented as an arch-divinity with authority and
power and the qualities not only of making persons prosperous but
also of multiplying them, that is of making them increase in number –
that is giving the blessing of childbirth. The song is an appeal to
Ọbàtálá to grant these blessings.

The following song by the devotees of Kórì is worthy of note not
only because it seems to us delightful, but also because its tone is
different from those cited above. Kórì is worshipped principally by
those women who long to have children. This divinity is symbolised
by cowries strung together and worn as necklaces by devotees. The
song goes thus:

Kórì o, aréwe yò	Kórì! You who delight in little children!
Je ñ rómo kàn gbé siré;	Bless me with a child to play with;
Gbé siré o, gbé siré	To play with, to play with;
Je ñ rómo kàn gbé siré o	Bless me with a child to play with.
Kórì o, Òrìsà èwe,	Kórì, children's tutelary divinity,
Bi ko si èwe,	If there are no little children,
Kórì ibá kú	Kórì would have been no more [i.e. would have been neglected].

There are many songs sung in connection with the worship of the different divinities in Yorubaland; we have cited the few examples above to illustrate the significance and the form of the songs many of which are sung on festival occasions. In some cases, a fixed number of songs has to be sung and in a particular order – the number varies from one to two hundred and one. Although the songs are not recorded, the officiating priests never forget the order in which they should be sung. The belief is that if the songs are not sung accordingly, the sacrifice will not be acceptable to the divinities.

Dancing is no less prominent during worship than songs. The dances take definite forms, depending upon the divinities to whom the offerings are made. These ritual dances are not mere emotional responses to the rhythm of music. They are symbolic, often re-enactments of something sacred. For example there is a Yorùbá statement, 'Oní-Sàngó tó jó tí kò tàpàá, àbùkù ara rè ni' (A Sàngó devotee, who dances without flinging his feet and legs, does discredit to himself). This statement is made because Sàngó in his lifetime was known to be a very graceful dancer, particularly to the rhythmic drumming of the *bàtàá* drums, and was always flinging his legs in a graceful manner. In consequence of this, his devotees must dance in imitation of him.

Similarly, in Ìláwè-Èkìtì, the Obàlùfòn devotees say, 'Òsì la ñjó ijó Obàlùfòn' ('It is towards the left that you move when you dance in honour of Obàlùfòn'). This is simply to show that the devotees do not dance anyhow, but are constrained to conform in their dance to certain forms and patterns.

The whole idea of ritual dance is succinctly put by Ìdòwú when he says:

Most of the dance, except where they are only expressions of religious conviviality, are of fixed patterns and must be done correctly – which foot goes forward first, which movements of the hands and body accompany it, which turns are taken next, and how many times each component of the pattern is to be repeated – all these must be carefully observed.[14]

Sacrifice

Sacrifice is a *sine qua non* in African traditional religion; so significant is its place, that we are devoting this second part of our study to it. We do not intend to elaborate the concept or the meaning of sacrifice at this point, but only wish to indicate that when we are considering the general subject of worship, reference to sacrifice is utterly unavoidable.

While prayer is a vocal or silent appeal to a divinity, with a view to achieving certain ends, sacrifice is an additional concrete method of serving the same purpose. Nobody comes forward to worship without bringing an offering, however simple, e.g. water for libation, kola-nuts or gin. The offerings may be given daily, weekly or as occasions demand. We shall elaborate these ideas in subsequent chapters.

Sacred people

By sacred people we mean those men and women who play conspicuous and leading roles during worship. In other words, they are the cultic functionaries. Their functions are sacred because worship led by them is directed towards the sacred or the holy. They are charged with the function of maintaining close and happy relations between the people and the divine beings. Such relations are regarded as demanding expert knowledge and technical training. This is because of the mystery surrounding the unseen world, in consequence of which man finds it unpredictable. Above all things, one must not risk offending the spiritual beings; if one approaches them too closely or carelessly, one may carry the infection of the taboo back among one's fellow men. In order to protect himself from all risk, and yet communicate at the same time with the sacred, man has found for himself the means of having an intermediary who will approach the divinities for him without running the risk of destruction, and is sufficiently 'human' to make intimate contact with man and not hurt him. Thus came into being the priest, whose primary function among the Yorùbá is that of a mediator. He is the person who stands between the object of worship and man.

Among the Yorùbá, there are different classes of cultic functionaries. They are:

(i) *Olórí Ẹbí* (family head)
(ii) *Ọba, Baálẹ̀, Ọlọ́jà* (town or village head)
(iii) *Àwòrò* (priests)
(iv) *Ẹlẹ́gùn* (the medium)
(v) *Olóògùn* (the medicine-man)

Olórí Ẹbí (family head)
By tradition, the family head is not only the political but also the charismatic leader among his people. Priesthood probably began with the family head by virtue of his charismatic position. Among the Yorùbá, the heads of the families are the superintendents at the family shrines. To every household there is attached an ancestral shrine where the spirits of the departed are invoked from time to time. Wherever an offering is to be made, the most senior member of the family usually leads the worship, of which offering forms an integral part. This is because by reason of his age and experience, he is the most familiar to the ancestors. He knows the order of invoking them, and it is believed that the more orderliness and correctness brought into worship, the more efficacious and acceptable the prayers will be.

These family heads, therefore, form a different category of priesthood. They are not full-time priests, but they do carry out priestly functions within a limited scope. When a child is born, it is the most senior member that will first carry the child in his arms and name him before any other person. He also performs other rites, such as giving the child the 'water of life', the oil, honey, sugar cane, fish, kola-nuts, bitter nuts, salt and other traditional and symbolic items associated with the naming ceremony of a child.

Similarly, when a girl reaches a marriageable age, and is leaving for her marital home, it is the head of the family who sits at the ancestral shrine and prays that it may be well with the woman in her husband's home. When there is a funeral ceremony, the family head gives necessary guidance. If a member of the family breaks a taboo, it is the family head who presides and gives, where applicable, the necessary offerings to the ancestors who are guardians of morality, and he also decides what punishment to give to the culprits. For example, among the Ìlàjẹ people in Òkìtìpupa Division, when an act of incest (which is a taboo) is committed, the offending couple are stripped naked and flogged by the elders as part of the propitiatory rites.

Ọba, Baálẹ̀, Ọlójà (town or village head)

As the family head presides over family worship, so also do the town or village heads preside over worship in their towns or villages. These paramount chiefs are regarded as sacred. It is believed that Olódù-marè gives the sceptre to Òrìṣà-ńlá who gives this to each ruler. The ruler, therefore, rules his subjects on behalf of Olódùmarè. Hence the chiefs are given respect parallel to the sort of reverence usually accorded the òrìṣà. By virtue of their position, the Ọba (kings) are styled 'Igbá kejì Òrìṣà' (next in rank to the divinities). In consequence of this, the ọba's body is sacrosanct, and any assault on his person is regarded as an act of sacrilege. 'A paramount Yorùbá clan-head', says Ìdòwú, 'is virtually a priest-king because he is regarded as "divine" in consequence of his sceptre which is derived from the divinity to whom he is vice-regent. The town belongs to him and so do all the cults'.[15]

To the paramount chief is given the right of performing certain religious ceremonies. In this way he plays the role of a priest; hence the Yorùbá say: 'Ọba ni olórí àwọn àwòrò' ('Ọba is the head of the priests'). It is also said, 'Gbogbo ọdún lọdún ọba' ('All religious festivals belong to the Ọba'). The idea is that the paramount chief embodies the unity of the ethnic group and offers sacrifice on its behalf as being its representative. When he does not actually perform the sacrifice or officiate during worship, his permission is sought for anything that is done. On great festival occasions, the townspeople normally congregate in the chief's palace or the market square to receive his blessing for the year. In actual fact, most festivals, especially those that have to do with making offerings at royal ancestral shrines, would not take place in the absence of the paramount chief.

Despite the fact that the priest of Ọ̀ṣun (Ọlọ́ṣun) does preside during the annual Ọ̀ṣun festival, the festival will be incomplete without the Ataọja of Òṣogbo being present physically to offer prayers and sacrifice at the traditional shrines. Similarly, although the Onírè who is the chief priest may be present, the Agẹmọ festival,[16] which is the most important festival in Ìjẹ̀bú, cannot take place unless the Awùjalẹ̀, the paramount head of the Ìjẹ̀bú, is also present. This caused some trouble some years ago when the Awùjalẹ̀ was on leave in the United Kingdom at the time the Agẹmọ festival was to take place.[17]

The regent, Chief T. A. Odùtọ́lá, the Ọ̀gbẹ́ni-Ọjà of Ìjẹbú-Òde, was not accepted as competent enough to represent the Awùjalẹ̀ before the Agẹmọ. The people say *'Agẹmọ ni elétùtù adé'* ('the Agẹmọ is the propitiator of the crown'). In other words, it is Agẹmọ which brings peace to the crown and to the people who are represented by the person wearing the crown. Hence, the most important aspect of the Agẹmọ festival is the face-to-face meeting of the Agẹmọ and the Awùjalẹ̀ when the latter receives blessings from the former on behalf of his subjects.

Another good example of the role of the paramount chiefs in religious matter is that of the Aláwẹ̀ of Ìláwẹ̀-Èkìtì. During the Orò Ọlọ́fin, it is the paramount chief who ceremonially presents the annual sacrificial cow (it used to be a human being) to the chief priest in Oke'pa. The ọba, in front of all the townspeople that come together for the ceremony, places his hand on the head of the cow and prays for himself, his chiefs and all his subjects. This is an important part of the ritual, and it is the ọba alone who can perform this rite. It is after the blessing that the cow is despatched through one of the chiefs (Chief Èjìgbò) to the officiating priests. As a result of this, there is a close link between the priests of the various divinities and the paramount chiefs who are, by virtue of their position, the political and religious heads among their people.

Àwòrò (priests in charge of the worship of divinities)
Each divinity in Yorubaland has his or her own priesthood. *Olóòṣà-ńlá* is the priest who presides at the shrine of Òrìṣà-ńlá; *Aláyélála* is the priest who presides at the worship of Ayelala; Oníṣàngó (otherwise called *Magbà*) presides at the worship of Ṣàngó; the *Alágbáà* is the priest who presides during Egungun worship. The priests who deliver the messages of Ọ̀rúnmìlà through Ifá are called *Babaláwo* (fathers who have the knowledge of the secret and mysterious things). They are in a class by themselves and are considered particularly important by the Yorùbá because through them, man learns what is necessary to be done to please Ọ̀rúnmìlà and the other divinities. To some extent, the Babaláwo give direction with regard to the worship of other divinities; and, in time of calamity, war or pestilence it is their business to declare what ought to be done to make the divinities propitious. They also ascertain what sacrifice is to be offered, how it is to be offered and whether or not that which is offered is adequate and acceptable. They are, therefore, the mouthpieces of the divinity and

whatever they say is believed to be the voice of Ọ̀rúnmìlà. We shall return to this in the next chapter.

These various priests officiate at the weekly celebrations. They become particularly prominent during great festival occasions like the annual sacrificial feasts, when the devotees come together to worship at the shrines. The priests really conduct the business of worship – acting as intermediaries between man and Deity; they offer man's sacrifice and lead his devotion; they also declare God's will and pleasure and reveal the unseen. They are guardians of the shrines and of the different objects of worship. They know the divinities well and direct worshippers on how to make an appropriate and correct approach to the divine beings.

Ẹlẹ́gùn (the medium)

In considering the various cultic functionaries, mention should be made of the fact that there are some men and women who become possessed during worship. This becomes very noticeable during religious festivals when drumming, singing and dancing combine to create an intense atmosphere which in turn creates an ecstatic emotion. It happens from time to time that one or two of the devotees are possessed; it is believed that it is the divinity worshipped who has descended upon them. Such a divinity manifests himself by speaking through the person so possessed.

When this happens, the 'possessed' person says and does things which he would not normally say or do. He becomes a changed person; he dances in a strange fashion; he becomes wild and uncontrollable in some cases.[18] In this state, he makes utterances, and people receive messages as coming from the divinity that is now personified in the medium. Through such a medium, messages are received from the spiritual realm and men are given knowledge of things that would otherwise be difficult or impossible to know.

Parrinder and Mbiti dwell much on the training of mediums in West Africa.[19] But it does not seem to us that there is any evidence of this sort of training among the Yorùbá. Those who are possessed among them find it difficult to explain how it all happens. It should be added, however, that it is not at every festival that men and women are possessed.

Olóògùn (the medicine-man)

We include the medicine-men among the cultic functionaries because in addition to their functions of curing the sick in body and mind by material and spiritual means (as indicated in the last chapter), many of them are also capable of ascertaining the causes of ailments and recommending offerings and how they are to be made. In this way, the medicine-men play the role of diviners, medical practitioners and priests. The Yorùbá call them *adáhunṣe*; they are believed to possess great knowledge of things unknown to the ordinary people. But it is not all medicine-men who are diviners. Similarly, diviners are not necessarily medicine-men.

From our survey so far, we can say that the cultic functionaries are the servants of the gods and they minister in the shrines dedicated to the various divinities. They give the divinities their daily, weekly, monthly or annual offerings and thus maintain relations between the community and the divine powers. In addition, they ascertain the wishes of the divinities and they reveal these to men. They pray for the people, help them to offer their sacrifice and advise them in time of trouble.

The priests, in particular, are ever conscious of the fact that they should approach their sacred task with care and awe; for, if they take the wrong step or say the wrong word, the worship led by them will not be acceptable, and their lives and those of the supplicants to whom they are ministering may be seriously jeopardised. In consideration of this, the priests realise the necessity of receiving some training for their task.

As the intermediaries and the guardians of the threshold between the world of men and the world of the spirits, the priests consider their training as of paramount importance. Among the Yorùbá, the youths train by studying under their elders. The normal practice is for clans, families or quarters in the town or village to worship certain divinities, and such groups of people produce an unbroken line of priesthood. In other words, priesthood is hereditary and traditional as far as the clan divinities are concerned. But, in some cases, where worship is not limited to any families or clans, individuals do go to the chief priests to get trained. For example, many men go to the Babaláwo (Ifá priest) to study Ifá divination. The apprentices devote a number of years to the study of Ifá divination during which time they observe strict discipline and abstain from certain foods and practices.

During apprenticeship as well as when officiating as a qualified person, the priest tries to remain pure. It is believed that his prayers will be most effective if he abstains from all forms of impurity. If he breaks a taboo or connives at sin, it is believed that the divinity to whom he is ministering can cause his death. The white apparel[20] that he wears is a sign of his purity. He sets up a shrine for the divinity and he visits this regularly.

Sacred places

As the principal divinities have their priesthood, so also do they have sacred places where worship is conducted. These places are called by different names depending upon where they are located and to what divinities they are dedicated. The Yorùbá refer to them mainly as 'Ojúbọ' (the place of worship). The place of worship may be for a divinity (òrìṣà) when it is referred to as 'Ojúbọ . . . òrìṣà or Ilé òrìṣà' (the place of worship or the house for the divinity). If it is the ancestral shrine, it will be called 'Ojúbọ bàbá or Ojú Eégún or Ojú orórì' (the place of worship of the ancestors). But if such a place of worship is in the grove, it will be referred to as 'Igbó'. For example, the grove dedicated to the worship of Agemo is referred to as Igbó Agẹmọ (the grove of Agemo) or Àgbàlá; the grove of Orò is Igbó Orò or Igbó Imalẹ̀. Similarly, the grove dedicated to the worship of Egungun is specifically referred to as Igbó Ìgbàlẹ̀ while that of Ifá is called Igbódù (Igbó odù). In Ilé-Ifẹ̀, we have the popular Iwinrin grove as we have Ugbowẹn in Ìtèbú-Manùwà.

There are innumerable shrines, temples and groves in Yorubaland – indeed there are as many shrines as there are divinities. There may be two, three or more shrines or temples dedicated to one divinity in the same town or village. This multiplicity of shrines stresses the fact that a shrine is not a permanent or only abode of a divinity; he can be invoked in one shrine just as in another. When he is invoked, it is believed that he will be present to meet with the worshippers, to receive their prayers and offerings and to bless them.

Shrines in Yorubaland are architecturally simple. They are sometimes accommodated in one of the rooms in a house, or situated in a screened-off portion of the sitting room, or in a corridor. In some cases separate houses or huts are erected. They are usually simple, rectangular thatch-roofed buildings with mud walls. They have open courtyards where spectators and supplicants can stay; there is also a portion for the drummers and singers. But the room containing the symbol of worship is usually cut off from the public eye, and it is so small that it is the officiating priest alone who can conveniently go in. Usually, the symbol is placed on a mud daïs. In some cases, the pillars supporting the shrine have some carvings and decorations, and the walls have drawings which, to an outsider, often look crude and meaningless.

In addition to the emblems of the divinities, there are, in the shrine, paraphernalia for worship – for example, gongs or bells, rattles, old swords, large pots, calabashes and old bottles. The equipment varies according to the nature of the divinities to whom the shrines are dedicated. The walls are painted according to the colour and symbols of the divinity. The sacred place is usually marked off by palm-fronds (màrìwò) which cover the entrance to the shrine or grove and warn the uninitiated to keep off. If the shrine is inside the house, sometimes white cloth (in the case of Òrìsà-ńlá) or purple cloth (in the case of Sàngó) is used to screen it off.

Besides the shrines shielded from the rain and the sun, there are others that are exposed. They are found in the market places or at road junctions, at main entrances to the towns or villages, by the riverside, by a tree or on a hill. For example, the main community shrine of Obalúwayé or Sòpònnó is always outside the village or town gate. A large agbada (a coverless earthenware vessel) is placed on a mound. Into this, people put palm-oil, palm-wine, and èko tútù (cold corn-meal). This divinity is to guard the gate and prevent smallpox from entering into the village.

In addition, there are water shrines erected at the banks of rivers, lakes or lagoons to worship river spirits, like Òsun, Yemoja, Olósà (the lagoon spirit) and the Olókun (the sea-spirit). Such shrines are common in riverine areas.

Rocks and hills are believed to be the symbol and, in fact, the residences of some divinities. These hills and mountains are considered to be a symbol of strength and durability; thus they remind man of his smallness and transitoriness. Usually stories are told of how such hills offered protection to the townspeople in the days of the intertribal wars. In consequence of this idea, many religious ceremonies are associated with large rocks and they serve as shrines. There are, for example, the Òkè-Ìbàdàn shrine in Ìbàdàn, the Òkè-Ìdànrè shrine in Ìdànrè, the Òkè Ìràgbìji shrine in Ìràgbìjí, and annual festivals are associated with these shrines.[21]

Sacred groves consist of narrow pathways leading to one or more clearings containing different apartments or graded court-yards. The first court-yard is open to women and the public. It is the portion nearest to the public road. The second apartment is accessible only to the initiated and the third apartment is entered only by the chief priests or the highly qualified initiates. In some cases, a small building is erected in this third apartment. The objects of worship are placed inside.

Usually at the main entrance to the grove is placed a barrier of palm fronds. In many cases the paths leading to the groves are allowed to become overgrown and are cleared annually when it is time for the festivals. These groves are held sacred and secret. The uninitiated, especially among strangers, are not allowed to go near. Songs are sung to scare people away. For example, when the Ìlàjẹ in Ìtẹ̀bú Mánùwà are going to Ugbowen during the Èje festival, they sing the following to scare people away:

Ugbólóre, Ugbólóre	Ugbólóre, [name of the grove]
Àjòjì kò wọ̀;	Must not be entered by strangers;
Àjòjì é mè yú o[22]	Strangers never go there;
Ugbólóre, Ugbólóre	Ugbólóre
Àjòjì kò wọ̀	Must not be entered by strangers.

Similarly, Ìrè people, the chief devotees of Ògún, keep away strangers from the Umeru grove which is sacred to Ògún. They say, '*Ìrè le fi igbó gbogbo han olójò, ṣugbọn a mu igbo Ògún sinra*' ('Ìrè people can afford to show some of their sacred groves to strangers; but the grove dedicated to Ògún is kept very secret').

We have been in some of these groves, which are situated in forests with huge and tall trees with many branches and thick foliage. These keep the sun from penetrating; such places can be dark and awesome even in the day-time. Because of the singular air of strangeness and quietness about them, they instil a sort of awe even in the minds of the worshippers.

Single trees are sometimes regarded as abodes of spirits, and worship is offered at the foot of such trees. The most popular of such tree is the Ìrókò (*Chlorophora excelsa*); others that normally mark sacred places are Pèrègún (*Dracaena fragrans*), Akòko (*Newboldia laevis*), Ìyéyè or Èkíkàn (*Spondias lutea*), Oṣẹ̀ (*Andansonia digitate*) and Àtòrì (*Glyphaea lateriflora*).

In the wake of Western civilisation, some of the shrines in Yorubaland are being modernised. The roofs of some shrines are now made of corrugated iron sheets instead of thatch. The Ọ̀ṣun shrine, for example, is being improved by Susane Wenger Alárápé, the European woman who has become a great admirer of the African Traditional Religion. The Ọ̀ṣun shrine in Òṣogbo is rapidly becoming a tourist centre. Furthermore, the temple of Ọ̀rúnmìlà, a huge edifice which is situated on Oké 'Tasẹ in Ilé-Ifẹ̀, is of modern architectural design, and when completed, will be as imposing as any of the existing Christian cathedrals in Nigeria.

Whatever form a sacred place takes, what is most important is the belief that such a place 'constitutes a break in the homogeneity of space; this break is symbolised by an opening by which passage from one cosmic region to another is made possible (from heaven to earth and *vice versa*; from earth to the underworld).'[23] In other words, such a sacred place provides a meeting place between the worshippers and the objects of worship. It forms a rallying point, a centre of interest.

At every shrine, there is an altar. It is usually covered or screened off and one is left to guess what is really there. This is the very place where sacrifice is offered, where libation of water, gin and wine is poured; it is on the altar that the blood of the sacrificed animal is sprinkled or poured; and it is on the altar that the portion offered is left for the divinity. Usually there is a stone, a piece of wood, a big jar, or a mound upon which the sacrifice is made. But sometimes, it is only a question of digging the earth and pouring the blood of the offering into the dug earth.

Altars are considered necessary because the need to have something visible and tangible on which to place a gift made to the invisible and intangible deity. There is also the need to ensure that things offered are placed in the appropriate places. Hence we have a heap of stones, or piles of iron, or a mound of consecrated earth or a large stone upon which the offering may fall. But, as indicated above, the earth is regarded sacred by the Yorùbá, and so, when it is dug and blood is allowed to flow into it, the blood is not flowing into a profane place but into that which is considered sacred. The sacredness of the earth is also noticed in the practice of libation (which involves the dropping of a little water or gin upon the earth) before man drinks.[24]

Mood of worshippers

Finally, we should describe briefly the usual mood of the supplicants during worship. Circumstances which lead to particular worship also dictate the mood of the worshippers.

In bad times, for example, if there is a scourge of *ṣòpònnó* (small-pox), the people will be gloomy as they are anxious to propitiate the divinity believed to be the cause of the scourge. The priest will tell the community what items to provide for the sacrifice: this is going to be a propitiatory sacrifice (*ẹbọ ètùtù*).[25] When the materials for the sacrifice have been procured and the time of worship fixed, then the people come together. The coming together is usually quiet and sombre because the people are in a pensive mood. There is no singing, no dancing or drumming. The priest makes the offering on behalf of the people and prays, begging the divinity to withdraw his wrath. The people say '*Á ṣe! Á ṣe!*' (May it be so) to every prayer. The kola-nut is cast to divine; it is only when the oracle speaks well that the priest orders the worshippers to hail the divinity. Except for such a salutation, there is no music, no mirth or sound of any type.

In contrast to this, when there is the annual thanksgiving sacrifice – for example, the new yam festival or the annual Ifá festival – the whole atmosphere will be characterised by plenty of drinking and eating, drumming and dancing, all in the midst of jubilation.

Thus we see that the mood of worshippers may be sorrowful or joyful. We may say that sacrifice offered to propitiate angry divinities, or to ward off evils, is usually an occasion of solemnity. But on festival occasions, when periodic sacrifice is offered, singing and dancing in the midst of eating and drinking figure prominently.

From our survey thus far, we can say that for worship to be meaningful, it has to be engendered by a belief in the power and position of the divine; it should have 'specialists' who know the approach to the sacred, and who can give necessary guidance to the devotees as to where, when and how worship is to be conducted.

NOTES

1. E. Underhill, *Worship*, London, 1936, p. 3.
2. J. Alan Kay, *The Nature of Christian Worship*, London, 1953, p. 7.
3. H. B. Alexander, 'Primitive Worship', *ERE*, Edinburgh, 4th impression 1959, p. 755.

4. This praise-name was recorded in Ìrè-Èkìtì; and so it is in the Èkìtì dialect of the Yoruba language. *Kí léhìn Ìrè* = *Èyí tí ó wà léhìn Ìrè* = that which stands behind or supports Ìrè.

5. For details concerning Ayélála, see ch. 2.
Reference to gin and the whiteman reflects the time Ayélála was 'inaugurated' – the beginning of the nineteenth century when the Europeans were introducing liquor and amunition to Yorubaland.

6. For purification rite, see Types of sacrifice in ch. 8.

7. Ìdòwú, *Olódùmarè*, p. 116.

8. Oloja is a title by which some village or town heads are known. Some other people have suggested that the name derives from the practice of establishing the main markets (oja) in towns and villages in front of or near the palace. So, the Oba is the owner of the market (Oloja). This may be the reason why market-places are changed when an Oba dies – an indication that the owner is no more.

9. The *Eje* Festival is the ceremonial occasion when the new yam is 'presented' to the ancestral spirits, to *Malokun* (the tutelary spirit in the sea) and to *Oro Lewe* (the spirit whose scourge is paralysis).

10. *Moraa* is the name of a seasonal plant – an annual plant which never fails to appear at the appropriate time or season.

11. This prayer was recorded in 1968 when the stool was vacant; hence the reference to the appointment of a new ruler.

12. This was the boundary dispute between Ado-Ekiti and Ilawe.

13. E. G. Parrinder, *Religion in Africa*, London, 1969, p. 71.

14. Ìdòwú, *Olódùmarè*, p. 115.

15. *Ibid.*, p. 132.

16. For details concerning *Agemo*, see Ogunba, 'Ritual Drama among the Ìjèbú'.

17. See *'Nigerian Tribune'*, 6 July 1967, p. 1.

18. See Elégùn Sàngó and Orisa-ako in ch. 2.

19. See Parrinder, *West African Religion*, p. 86ff; Mbiti, *African Religions and Philosophy*, pp. 173ff.

20. Most priests use white material for regalia, e.g. worshippers of Obàtálá, Obàlùfòn, Olókun and Orosun. This signifies purity. But Sàngó and Sòpònnó worshippers prefer purple or red, signifying the fierceness of these divinities.

21. See Mountains and Hills in ch. 2.

22. This song is in the Ìlàjè dialect of the Yorúbà language. *Ajoji e mẹ yu o* means '*Ajeji ko gbódò lọ*' (A stranger must not go there).

23. M. Eliade, *The Sacred and the Profane*, N.Y., 1959, p. 37.

24. See The Earth in ch. 2.

25. Types of Sacrifice in ch. 8.

Chapter Six

DIVINATION AND SACRIFICE

Definition and purpose of divination

'Man plans for foreseen contingencies, but is aware that much of the future is menacingly unknown. He has sought to penetrate this unknown by different means.'[1] Prominent among the means used is divination. *Chambers' Encyclopaedia* defines divination as 'the act of obtaining information about unknown happenings or future events from supernatural sources by means of signs and occult technique.' In other words, it is a means of seeking to discover the unknown and the future by manipulating some supernatural means and seeking guidance from supernatural sources. This is no guesswork, as suggested by Professor Armstrong who maintains that some of the problems investigated by divination are 'partly guessable unknowns'.[2] Furthermore, he locates the reason why men divine in the fact that the magical world scornfully rejects the answer 'we do not know'. It is the desire to know that which is obscure that leads men to divine. But Armstrong does not think that divination solves any problem; rather he sees it as 'a special case of *explicatio obscuri per obscurius*'[3] – a means of explaining the obscure by a more obscure means. In other words, he sees divination as being more obscure than the obscure situation to which a solution is sought. It seems to us that this is a negative way of looking at divination.

Divination is always associated with a situation which, from the point of view of the client or investigator, calls for a decision upon important plans or vital actions to be taken on important occasions. 'Typically', declared Park, 'divination is called for in cases of illness and death, in other life-crises; in the corroboration of a marriage-choice and in individual or collective moves involving some change in social alignments or, perhaps, economic condition; and in situation of loss, calamity or unresolved conflict, whether on a personal or a much larger scale.'⁴

Whatever happens, man wants to get the best out of life and he hates being limited in his effort to penetrate the future and to plan adequately. 'In nothing', said Yerkes, 'is man's finiteness more acutely recognised than in the realm of time. . . . He can devise vehicles and engines which will carry huge loads across land and water, but never has he been able to penetrate the future with certainty.⁵ This is why men divine. They want to know the Divine will and to be assured of longevity, prosperity, increase in life and success in enterprises. In addition, and this may be peculiar to the Africans, men believe that the world in which they live is influenced by certain forces – witches, sorcerers, the ancestral and other spirits. They also believe that it is wise and expedient to have these powers on their side and they are convinced that the oracle can reveal what these forces are planning and what men can do to forestall, propitiate and humour them. Thus, divination is a means by which divine will and directives are ascertained. It is also a guide as to how to approach the divine and the problems of life.

Men, all over the world, practise divination and devise various methods of doing this. The Assyro-Babylonians have their *Baru* (seer and diviner) who employ *hepatoscopy* (divination by observing the liver of a sacrificial sheep).⁶ The Buddhists in India practise astrology and they use lots and oracles as means of divination; every layman is equipped with a pocket divination manual called *mo-pe*.⁷ The Greeks had their oracular shrines of Jupiter at Dodona and of Apollo at Delphi;⁸ the Romans used the *Sortes*;⁹ the Japanese use *omoplatoscopy*, that is, divining by flaying the shoulder blade of a deer and subjecting the part to intense heating over fire.¹⁰ The Jews used Urim and Thummim (I Samuel 28:6).

Like other peoples of different religious faiths, the Yorùbá practise divination. They do this because they are anxious to know the behest of Deity and also the future with regard to themselves and to those close to them. They have the popular saying: *'Bi òní ti ri, òla kì írí bẹ̀ẹ̀; èyíyi ló mú kí Babaláwo máa dífá ọrọrún'* ('Because each day has its own peculiar problems, the Babaláwo (Ifa priest) has to cast his Ifa (to divine) every fifth day'). They also say, *'Ojúmọ́ kì ímọ́ kí Awo má ṣọ́dẹ wò; àgbẹ̀dẹ a gbọn àdá'* ('As there is never a morning when a blacksmith is not called upon to sharpen matchets for farmers, so there is never a morning when a Babaláwo does not consult his oracle').

Types of divination

The Yorùbá employ various systems of divination. Some of these we shall discuss very briefly; but the Ifa divination, which we consider the most important of the whole lot, will be examined in detail.

Dída Obì (casting the kola-nuts)

Kola-nuts are used by the Yorùbá as a means of divination; the kind of kola-nut used is the species called *obì àbàtà* (*Cola acuminata*) which must have four lobes (*awẹ́ mẹ́rin*). Two of the four lobes are known as *akọ* (male) and two are called *obí* (female) in consequence of the natural marks on them.

To divine, the diviner breaks the kola-nut into its four lobes; he holds them in his palm and asks a question – e.g. 'Is the journey I am about to take a safe one?' He then throws the lobes on the ground or into a plate. When the four pieces of kola-nut fall face up (i.e. with the concave sides facing up), the result is called *Èjìogbè*. When the four pieces fall face down, that is, with the convex sides facing up, the diviner calls this *Ọ̀yẹ̀kú*.[11] But when the two 'female' lobes show their concave sides facing up, this is called *Èdí méjì*. On the other hand, if the two which show the concave sides facing up are 'males' (*akọ méjì*), this is called *Ègúndá-Bèdé*. When three of the four lobes have their concave sides up and one of the three is a female and the remaining two are males, we have *Ègítán*. It is through permutation of this kind that the combination has a message which only the diviner can interpret. For example, if *Ọ̀bàrà-méjì* appears for the client, the diviner will say, among other things, 'You do not need to have any doubt about the project upon which you are about to embark. But you should care for your mother. If she is living, provide her with a pigeon to offer sacrifice to her *Orí* (i.e. her counterpart or the divinity controlling fate), but if she is dead, you must get six kola-nuts, a bottle of gin and a she-goat and make a sacrificial feast in her honour'.

Ẹ̀rìndínlógún

Ẹ̀rìndínlógún consists of sixteen cowries which the diviner holds together in his fists. These are shaken together as the diviner asks what action to take or what is the cause of the trouble being investigated. The sixteen cowries are then thrown on the ground, and they fall either on their concave or convex sides. For example, if two of the sixteen cowries fall with the concave sides up, we have *Èjì Òkò*. If they are cast, and six of the cowries fall with the convex sides up, then we have *Òdí-méjì*. Each of the sixteen falls has a message for the inquirer. This means of divination is used principally by the worshippers of Ṣàngó. The diviners who employ it refer to it as *Ìránṣẹ́ẹ Ṣàngó* (Ṣàngó's servant).

Ọ̀pẹ̀lẹ̀

This method of divination is less frequent than the *Obì*, but more frequent and less reliable than employing the *ikin* (sixteen sacred nuts) as we shall see below.

Ọ̀pẹ̀lẹ̀ consists of eight half-pods strung together on a cord or chain which is about three or four feet long. The half-pods are arranged in such a way that they are equidistant from one another; and when the chain is held in the middle, one has four half-pods hanging down on either side of the chain. Tassels are attached to the two ends of the chain – beads, cowries and coins are on one side and small bells and metals on the other.

To divine, the diviner holds the divining chain in the middle, swings it to the right and then to the left; forward and backward, invoking the spirit of Ọ̀rúnmìlà, paying homage to his (diviner's) predecessors in office, and casting the chain in such a way that the portion originally held by him is thrown away from himself and the two sides fall in parallel lines. Each half-pod can fall with either the concave or the convex side just as it is in the case of *obì*.[12] The fall of the eight half-pods depicts a particular *Odù* (i.e. verses of Ifá) and has a message for the inquirer which only the diviner can put across.

Ifá

This, as we have already mentioned, is by far the most renowned means of divination among the Yorùbá. The most important objects in Ifá divination are the sixteen specially-selected palm nuts called *Ikin*, the *ọpón Ifá* (the divining tray which may be rectangular, semi-circular or circular), the *Ìyẹ̀rosùn* (the divining power), the *Ìrófá* (a conical bell which is made of horn, ivory or wood) which is used in tapping on the divining tray at intervals to invoke the oracular spirit, especially at the beginning of the divination exercise, and finally the *Ìbò* (lots) consisting of a variety of objects – broken pottery, animal teeth, cowry shells, some large flat glossy brown seeds called *ṣẹsan*. The fragments of pottery or broken chinaware and teeth mean 'bad luck' or 'no'; the cowry shells and the *ṣẹsan* mean 'good luck' or 'yes'.

These materials, called ìbò, are used to decide which verses of the particular *odù* should be emphasised.

To divine, the Babaláwo (the priest specially trained in the mysteries of interpreting the messages of Ọrúnmìlà) sits on a mat or a piece of cloth, placing the divining tray in front of him; he spreads a thin layer of *Ìyẹ̀rosùn* (the divining powder) upon the divining board or tray; he brings out the *Ikin* (the sacred nuts) from the bag or bowl in which they are kept, and places them on the mat or on a piece of cloth on which he is sitting. He then invokes the oracular spirit, tapping on the tray with the *Ìrófá* as he sings the praise-names of the oracular divinity in the following manner:

Ọrúnmìlà Àjànà!	Ọrúnmìlà Àjànà!
Ifá Olókun,	The diviner for the Olókun (the sea god)
A-sọrọ̀-dayọ̀!	The one who prospers affairs!
Ẹlẹ́rìí ìpin,	The witness to individual's fate,
Ibìkejì Èdùmàrè!	Deputy to Olódùmarè!
Ká mọ̀ ọ́ ka là,	Whom to know is to be saved,
Ká mọ̀ ọ́ ka má tètè kú	Whom to know is not to die early;
Àmọ̀là Ifẹ̀ owòdáyé	The saviour of Ifẹ̀ from the pristine time;
Ọkùnrin dúdú Òkè Ìgètí;	The black man of Ìgètí-hill;
Olúwa mi à-jí-kí	My lord who is saluted first thing in the morning
Olúwaàmi, òkítíbìrí,	My lord, the averter,
Tí ńpojọ́ ikú dà;	Who changes the determined date of death;
Olúwà mi àmọ̀-ìmọ̀-tán;	My lord that cannot be fully apprehended;
A kò mọ̀ ọ́ tán ìbá ṣẹ;	Not to have full knowledge of you is to fail;
À bá mọ̀ ọ́ tán, ìbá ṣẹ	But to have full knowledge, is to be successful.

After the invocation of the spirit and the usual homage paid to his ancestors or predecessors in office, the diviner takes the sixteen[13] palm-nuts (Ikin) in his two hands and beats them together a number of times and attempts to take as many of the nuts as are possible with his right hand. If one nut is left in the left palm, he makes two short parallel lines (using the middle and the ring fingers of the right hand) in the *iyẹ̀-rosùn* on the tray; if two nuts remain, then he makes one straight line with the middle finger of the right hand. But if none is left or more than two are left then nothing is recorded for that round. The process is repeated eight times.[14] At the end of the eighth time, a meaningful figure of eight strokes in two columns of four is formed. They are arranged in two parallel columns of four, starting from the right to the left, and from the top to the bottom as follows:

$$
\begin{array}{cc}
2 & 1 \\
4 & 3 \\
6 & 5 \\
8 & 7
\end{array}
$$

The pattern that is formed is, so to speak, the 'signature' of Ọrúnmìlà, manifested in the sign of the *odù* figure whose name is declared by the diviner. The *ibò* is used at this stage to ascertain the message that is brought by the odù; this has to be done because there are many verses to one odù figure; the message may be evil or good. The diviner asks: 'Is it good luck?' If it is, then the cowry shell or *ṣẹṣan* is selected. 'Is it bad luck?' If it is, bone or broken pottery or chinaware is selected. We cannot go into details here of how Ifa divination is conducted – several books have been written on this.[15] But we should not fail to point out that there are sixteen principal odù, and each of the odù has a 'child', and the 'child' has a 'child' *ad infinitum*. Hence the Yorùbá speak of sixteen odù or 16 times 16 (256) odù or 16 times 16 times 16 (4,096) odù. Each of these figures has a name. The names of the first four odù and their signs are as follows:

(1) *Èjìogbè*		(2) *Ọyẹ̀kú méjì*		(3) *Ìwòrì méjì*		(4) *Òdí méjì*	
1	1	11	11	11	11	1	1
1	1	11	11	1	1	11	11
1	1	11	11	1	1	11	11
1	1	11	11	11	11	1	1

Each odù has several cantos of various lengths together with stories which elaborate the cantos. The exact number of cantos in each odù is unknown, and the best that a Babaláwo does is to memorise as many of them as possible because the more he knows, the deeper he is believed to have gone into the mystery of Ifá and the more respect he earns from his clients.

The odù verses are regarded as the messages of Ọrúnmìlà uttered through the Babaláwo who is his mouthpiece. Each one of the verses has its own characteristics. When one appears, the Babaláwo ascertains what message it has brought. Usually, Ifá speaks in parables;

hence the Yorùbá saying: 'Òwe ni Ifá ípa, ọmọ̀ràn ni ímọ̀ ọ́ (Ifá speaks always in parables; a wise man is he who knows or understands his speech). It is the Babaláwo who has the knowledge of Ifá and who can interpret these 'parables' meaningfully.

The parables deal with instances of how certain mythological figures – men and women, animals, birds or plants – were, in times past, confronted with one type of problem or another, how they reacted to the situations and what were the results of their actions. In other words, the stories or legends depict the experiences of the people who lived in the past and from whom inferences could be drawn to meet the demands of the present situation. 'By providing exemplifications in the form of what happened to mythological characters under similar circumstances, they give added point and meaning to verses which otherwise would be curt or obscure.'[16]

From these legends, one discovers that the commonest means by which the ancient people meet their difficulties and surmounted them was by constantly offering sacrifices. Those who refused to make sacrifice as directed, used to end in disaster. From such examples, the diviner draws his conclusion and gives guidance to the inquirer. The verses containing both the predictions and the sacrifices constitute the core of Ifá divination. 'The verses provide the key to the ultimate goal, that of determining the sacrifice required to solve the client's problem. Once the sacrifice has been offered, matters again rest in the hands of the god.'[17]

The relevance of divination to sacrifice

Ọrúnmìlà does not only possesses foreknowledge of future events but also prescribes remedies against any eventuality and pleads one's case before Olódùmarè. By means of divination, man knows what the gods desire; and almost always, divination ends in the prescription of sacrifice. Hence the Yorùbá saying: 'A kì ńdífá kámá yan ẹbọ' (One does not consult Ifá without prescribing a sacrifice'). If the situations are unpleasant, men will be required to offer sacrifice to change things for the better; and if they are pleasant, sacrifice will still be offered to retain and improve upon the good fortune.

To bring out the relevance of divination to sacrifice, especially among the Yorùbá, we will cite examples from the different odù verses illustrating how those who offered sacrifice in accordance with the directive of Ọ̀rúnmìlà flourished and those who acted contrary or did his biddings half-heartedly came into disaster.

EXAMPLES OF FULL OBEDIENCE

Jíkáléwi, awo òlógbò,	Jíkáléwi [Praise-name of the diviner]
Dífá fún ológbò,	Divined for the cat
Níjọ́ tí ó ńfi ojúmọ́-ojúmọ́	When daily his prey
Ńṣe òwò àmúbọ́	eluded him.
Wọn ní kí ó rú abẹ́rẹ́ méfà	He was asked to offer six needles,
Ẹyẹlé méfa, àti egbàáfà;	Six pigeons and thirty kobo [12,000 cowries]
Ó gbọ́, ó rú ẹbọ;	He obeyed and offered the sacrifice;
Láti ìgbà náà, ni ológbò	Thenceforth, the cat never missed
Kò tún mú àmúbọ́ mọ́	Any of his prey.

From the above mythological story, we see that the cat is used as the client who approaches the diviner. He approaches the diviner because of his past failures in capturing his prey. After the offering of the sacrifice, circumstances change for the better. The cat never misses his prey again.

When the diviner has recited the odù verse, he will draw his conclusion and will advise the client present. What Ifá is saying here is that the person on whose behalf Ifá is consulted, is one who has been experiencing failures in many ways. He should, therefore, offer sacrifice so that the circumstances might change for the better as they did for the cat in the odù verse.

Ẹ̀bìtì-jáwọ́-fàyà-lulẹ̀	Ẹ̀bìtì-jáwọ́-fàyà-lulẹ̀ [Praise-name of the diviner]
Ló dífá fún Oyèníran	Cast Ifá for Oyèníran
Tí ó ńsọkún aláìlóyún	Who was weeping for being barren
Tí ó sì ńgbàáwẹ̀ aláìrípọ̀n	And who was fasting for having no child to carry on her back.
Wọ́n ní kí ó rú ẹbọ,	She was asked to offer sacrifice
Wọ́n ní ọmọ kan ni yóò bí yìí,	For she would have a child
Wọ́n ní gbogbo ayé ni yọ́ọ̀ mọ̀ ọ́;	Who would be known the world over.

Kìjikìji rè yóò gba ayé kan;	His fame would spread throughout the world;
Ó gbọ́, ó sì rú igba abẹ́rẹ́,	She heeded the oracle and offered
Àgùtàn kan, àti àmù epo kan;	200 needles, one sheep and a pot of palm-oil;
Nígba tí Oyèníran máabí,	When Oyèníran was to have a
ó bí Ọjọ́	child, she gave birth to Ọjọ́ (the Sun).

Here again, we see Oyèníran, the mythological figure who was in great need of a child, offering the prescribed sacrifice in obedience to the oracle's instruction.

If such an odù appears on the divining board, the diviner will tell the client: 'Ifá says someone is bemoaning her having no child and that if the person can make the necessary sacrifice as will be prescribed by the diviner, all will be well with her as it was well with Oyèníran. The child that she will have will be very famous'.

EXAMPLES OF PARTIAL OBEDIENCE

In the following example, Lizard offered a partial sacrifice; he made the sacrifice which would enable him to procure a wife, but refused to make that sacrifice which would enable the wife to stay permanently with him. It runs thus:

Ìsánsán awo ídí-òpẹ	Isansan awo idi-ope
A dífá fún Alángbá,	Divined for Alángbá (Lizard)
Níjọ́ tọ́ máa ní obìnrin kan;	On the day he was going to take a wife;
Wọ́n ní kí ó rú ẹbọ àkùkọ méjì,	He was asked to offer two cocks
Wọ́n ní yóò fẹ́ obìnrin kan,	That he might win the woman's love;
Wọ́n ní tí ó bá fẹ́ obìnrin náà tán,	To avoid evil people luring away
Kí ó má baà rí ẹni tí	His wife soon after their marriage,
Yóò bá ti obìnrin náà sigbó	He should offer sacrifice.
Nítorí náà, kí ó rúbọ elénìní ilé	To ward off sadistic people.
Alángbá rú ẹbọ eyẹlé méjì,	Lizard offered two pigeons
Kí ó baàle rí obìnrin fẹ́	In order to get the woman,

Ṣùgbọ́n kò rú àkùkọ méjì   But he did not offer two cocks
Kí obìnrin náà baà lè pé lọ́dọ̀ọ rẹ̀ Which would make the woman stay

This recital speaks of two types of sacrifice which were meant to serve two different purposes. The two pigeons are for the purpose of securing a wife; Lizard was eager to get a wife, and so he readily made that sacrifice. But there was also the need to retain the woman's love. The diviner knew that there would be enemies of success in Lizard's home (elénìní ilé) who would feel displeased with his success (getting a wife), and who would lure her away by some mysterious means. But Lizard refused to make this second sacrifice; hence he had to face the unpleasant consequences of losing his wife soon after their marriage.

Our next example which depicts the result of both disobedience and obedience is the following:

Adéfolúkẹ́ ńṣawo re òde	Adéfolúkẹ́ was going on a divination tour
A dá a fún Ọ̀rúnmìlà	Divined for Ọ̀rúnmìlà
Níjọ́ tí ó ńṣe awo re àjọ̀,	On the day he was going on a divination tour;
Tí wọ́n sọ̀ fún un pé	He was told
Kí ó fi ewúrẹ bọ òkè ìpọ̀nrú rẹ̀;	To offer a she-goat to his guardian-spirit
Pé kí ọ̀nà àjòo rẹ̀ baàlè dára fún un,	In order that his trip might be successful.
Ọ̀rúnmìlà kò bọ òkè ìpọ́nrú rẹ̀	Ọ̀rúnmìlà refused to make the offering.
Títí ó fi lọ sọ́nà àjò náà	Yet he went on the journey
Nígbà ti ode ibi tí ó ńlọ ṣawo,	When he got to his destination
Kò sí ẹni tí ówá sọ́dọ̀ọ rẹ̀ láti ṣawo.	No one patronised him.
Nígbà tí ó rí i pé ebi ńpa òun,	When he could no longer bear his starvation.
Nígbà náà ni ó padà sílé	He returned home
Láti wa bọ òkè ìpọ̀nrú rẹ̀.	To make sacrifice to his guardian spirit.
Nígbà tí ó pa ewúrẹ́ náà,	Having immolated the goat,
Ó pín in fún àwọn àgbààgbà ìlú,	He distributed it to the elders in the town.
Wọ́n sì bẹ̀rẹ̀sí i fún un ní egbèwá-egbèwá	They started giving him 2000 cowries each.[18]
Ọ̀rúnmìlà di olówó níjọ́ náà	And Ọ̀rúnmìlà started getting rich.

In the above recital, Ọ̀rúnmìlà first refused to make the offering prescribed. In consequence of the refusal, his journey ended in a fiasco. Then he came to his right senses and decided to offer the sacrifice he had earlier refused. When he did, things turned out better; benefactors and clients came to him, and he quickly became rich.

If a client comes to a diviner and this odù verse appears on the divining tray, he (the enquirer) will be warned of the consequences of refusal to offer sacrifice as illustrated by Ọ̀rúnmìlà's plight in this example. If Ọ̀rúnmìlà, himself the divinity controlling the Ifá oracle, could offer sacrifice in order to get on well, then the present client has to do the same thing – not in disobeying but in implicit obedience to the directive of the oracle.

EXAMPLE OF TOTAL REFUSAL TO SACRIFICE

In the following example, two friends who refused to offer the prescribed sacrifice died on the same day as predicted.

Ikú tẹ́ ori ìgbá á,	Death steps on the garden egg,
Ìgbá á ṣe gbìrìà nílẹ̀;	And the garden-egg drops suddenly;
Alukunrin fàìwẹ̀, ó fàìkùn	Alukunrin (a bird) neither bathes nor rubs the body with oil
Ó ńdán ròjoròjo bí ọmọ aládìnín	Yet he shines like the son of *adin* (palm-kernel oil seller)
A daá fun Alápá-ilé,	Cast Ifá for Alápá-ilé,
A sì lu ikin fún Alápá́ oko	And beat *ikin* (divining nuts)[19] for Alápá-oko.
Ifá ní kí àwọn ọ̀rẹ́ méjèèjì rúbọ	Ifá asks both of them to make sacrifice.
Kí won má baà rí ikú àjọkú pọ̀	That they might not die simultaneously.
Ìgìrìpá òbúkọ kọ̀ọ̀kan	They are to offer a big goat
Ẹgbàafà àti aṣọ pupa tí wọ́n kégbẹ́ rà ni ẹbọ náà	12000 cowries and the red cloth which they had in common.
Àwọn méjèèjì gbọ́ ẹbọ, Wọ́n kò rú u	Both of them heard the prescribed sacrifice, but refused to offer.
Èṣù sì rán ìsàsí sí wọn	Èṣù caused them to misbehave,
Wọ̀n sì bẹ̀rẹ̀ sí íṣe àìsàn lójọ́ kan náà	And they fell ill the same day.

Nígbà tí Alápá-ilé rí i pé	When Alápá-ilé saw that the illness
àìsàn náà pọ̀,	was serious,
Ó sọ fún àwọn ará ilée rẹ̀ pé,	He told his people that
Bí òun bá kú,	If he died,
Kí wọn gbe òkú òun tọ Alápá	They should convey his corpse to
oko lọ	Alápá oko
Nítorí òun ni yóò mọ ètùtù	Who alone knew the funeral rites
òun ní ṣíṣe	to perform.
Nígbà tí Alápá-Oko rí i pé	And when Alápá Oko saw that
àìsàn òun ńpọ̀	his illness was serious,
Ó ní bí òun bá kú,	He told his people that when he
	died,
Kí wọ́n gbé òkú òun tọ Alápá-	They should convey his corpse to
ilé lọ	Alápá ilé
Nítorí òun ni yóò mọ ètùtù òun	Who alone knew what rites to
ní ṣíṣe	perform.
Kò pẹ́ lẹ́hìn èyí,	Soon after this,
Àwọn méjèèjì kú	Both of them died;
Ọjọ̀ kan náà ni wọ́n sì kú.	It was on the same day they died.

These two friends died because they failed to heed the warning of the oracle. The purpose of these myths, then, is to emphasise the significance of divination with respect to sacrifice. We agree with Bascom when he says:

> The theme of success gained by sacrificing, and of failure as result of refusing to do so, whether implicit or explicit, and whether stated concisely or documented at some length, runs throughout the verses. There is no verse in which a person is said to have prospered without making a sacrifice.[20]

The Yorùbá hold these myths to be true, and the people will prefer erring on the side of truth; they believe strongly in the statement:

Rírú ẹbọ ní ígbeni,	Offering sacrifice brings blessing
	to the offerer,
Àìrú kì ígbé ènìyàn	Refusing to do so spells disaster.

From the examples quoted and examined above, we see that the odù recitals act as guides for the daily life and conduct of the Yorùbá. Since instances of such recitals abound among the people, and since they are familiar with the mythological stories, it is difficult, if not impossible, to prevent them from offering the prescribed sacrifice once they go to the Babaláwo to obtain information about happenings unknown to them. This is so because the people believe in what Ifá says for he is the mouth-piece not only of Ọrúnmìlà but also of the spirits and divinities as well as Deity whose wishes are revealed to men by this means.

Ifá divination is freely used to determine the problem confronting an enquirer and to secure a favourable solution to the problem, while sacrifice is used to ensure that predictions of good fortune come to pass, and those of ill fortune averted. Thus, both divination and sacrifice are inseparably linked. The former suggests a theoretical solution to the problem presented before the diviner, and the latter a practical response to the directive of the oracle.

NOTES

1. D. H. Smith in Brandon, ed., *A Dictionary of Comparative Religion*, p. 243.
2. *Current Anthropology*, iv, 5, December, 1963, pp. 495ff.
3. *Ibid.*, p. 505.
4. G. K. Park, 'Divination and its social contexts', *Journal of the Royal Anthropological Institute (J.R.A.I.)*, vol. 93, part 2, July/Dec., 1963, p. 195.
5. R. K. Yerkes, *Sacrifice in Greek and Roman Religion and Early Judaism*, London, 1900, p. 29.
6. For details, see L. W. King, 'Divination among the Assyro-Babylonian', *ERE*, vol. 4, 1911, p. 784.
7. For details, see L. A. Waddel, 'Divination' (Buddhist), *ERE*, vol. 4, pp. 786ff.
8. For details, see H. J. Rose, 'Divination' (Greeks), *ERE*, vol. 4, p. 798.
9. For details, see G. Wissowa, 'Divination', (Romans), *ERE*, vol. 4, p. 821.
10. For details, see M. Revon, 'Divination' (Japanese), *ERE*, vol. 4, p. 801.
11. Reading of the omen portrayed by the kola-nut varies slightly from place to place. The one we are describing here obtains among the Yoruba in Okitipupa Division. For more details about kola-nut divination, see Ìdòwú, *Olódùmarè*, pp. 136ff. and R. Price, *Ifa – Yoruba Divination and sacrifice*, Ife University Press (I.U.P.), 1964, p. 7.
12. Parrinder is mistaken in saying: 'four of them (the half-pods) are convex and four concave'. (*Religion in an African City*, p. 32). The truth is that each of the eight half-pods has the convex and the concave sides can fall either way when cast.

13. The seventeenth nut (called *Oduso*) is set apart before divination; it is *never* beaten.
14. The figure produced at the end of the eighth round is what can be got by casting the ọ̀pẹ̀lẹ̀ once. Hence ọ̀pẹ̀lẹ̀ is easier to manipulate.
15. See Bascom, *Ifa Divination*; Price, *Ifa Yoruba Divination*; Wande Abimbola, *Ijinle Ohun Enu Ifa*; Judith Gleason, *A Recitation of Ifa*, New York 1973; Wande Abimbola, *Sixteen Great Poems of Ifa*, 1975.
16. Bascom, *Ifa Divination*, p. 122.
17. *Ibid.*, p. 120.
18. Before the coming of the British into the Yorubaland the currency used was the cowry. 2000 cowries = 6d = present 5 kobo in Nigeria. This would be about 7.5 cents in American currency.
19. 'To beat *Ikin*' is another expression for divining by means of the sixteen sacred palm-nuts.
20. W. R. Bascom, 'The Sanctions of Ifa Divination', *J.R.A.I.*, lxxi, 1941, pp. 43ff.

Chapter Seven

MEANING AND PURPOSES
OF SACRIFICE

General meaning of sacrifice

Technically, the word sacrifice is a religious term; but when used in a general sense, it also has a secular meaning. We here consider the general or secular usage briefly before examining the religious meaning.

In a general or non-religious sense, sacrifice means forgoing for a particular cause that which is precious; denying oneself certain benefits and advantages for a particular purpose. A few illustrations will no doubt make this point clear.

Some parents, particularly in African society, deny themselves certain pleasures and comforts in order to be able to pay their children's school fees. They forgo buying costly dresses and even sell valuable belongings to provide the opportunity of a sound education for their children. Such parents could claim that they have 'sacrificed' their comfort and pleasure to have their children educated.

Similarly, there are teachers who, after the normal school hours, stay behind to coach their pupils in their lessons in order that such pupils may do well in their examinations. They ask for no remuneration either from the parents or from the school. It would be correct to say that such teachers 'sacrifice' their time, comfort and energy to help their needy pupils.

During the civil war in Nigeria, the military government made appeals to Nigerians to make 'sacrifice' by way of donating generously to the 'Armed Forces Comfort Fund'. And, in response to this appeal, many salary earners did forgo certain percentages of their salaries; the market-women and businessmen donated articles of food and clothing; those who had books donated them to afford the people in the war-affected areas much needed reading material; young men volunteered to enlist in the army; some men and women joined the Red Cross to bring relief to the wounded and the sick. All these various gestures can be referred to as 'sacrifice' since the different donors and volunteers were clearly denying themselves certain things.

From these examples, it is clear that something precious is given away for a definite purpose. All this is done, however, at the man-to-man level. The parents who sell their belongings to get their children educated do so mainly to improve the lot of their children. The teacher who sacrifices his time helping the less fortunate ones does so, perhaps, out of sheer concern for the children. Men who enlist in the army and go to the battlefield to fight, may have the noble aim of preserving the territorial integrity of their nation.

Whatever the purpose may be, it is obvious that something is renounced in order that a certain end may be achieved. What is 'sacrificed', whether material or spiritual, is often costly. Sacrifice, therefore, involves cost. What a man gives – whether he gives time, his clothes, his food, his money or his life – is part of himself.

This general sense of the word *sacrifice*, as illustrated above, has become so popular that many suppose it to be the basic or core meaning of the term. But this is not so. The secular sense of the word, as shown above, is only an extension of the core meaning or a metaphorical use of 'sacrifice'. In this metaphorical sense, sacrifice may be defined as the 'giving up' of a thing for the sake of another that is higher or more urgent; it may also refer to that which is given up for a cause or for something else.

We must remark at this stage that when the Yorùbá speak or think of sacrifice, it is *never* in this metaphorical or general sense but always in a religious sense as we shall try to make clear later in our present study. Having examined the secular use of the word, it seems appropriate to consider here again its religious meaning and connotation.

Religious connotation of sacrifice

The *Encyclopaedia of Religion and Ethics* defines sacrifice as 'a rite in the course of which something is forfeited or destroyed, its object being to establish relations between a source of spiritual strength and one in need of such strength, for the benefit of the latter.'[1]

James has tried to define sacrifice in terms of its purposes; according to him, sacrifice involves the destruction of a victim 'for the purpose of maintaining or restoring a right relationship of man to the sacred order. It may effect a bond of union with the divinity to whom it is offered or constitute a piacular expiation to 'cover', 'wipe out', neutralize or carry away evil guilt contracted wittingly or unwittingly.'[2]

In one sense one cay say that sacrifice is an act of making an offering (of animal or vegetable life, of food, drink or of any objects) to a deity or spiritual being. In another sense, sacrifice can be seen as something consecrated and offered to God or a divinity. In other words, an offering of any kind laid on an altar or otherwise presented to a deity or divinities for definite purposes is a sacrifice.

From our own observation of sacrificial practices among the Yorùbá we can say that:

(a) sacrifice is a religious act; (b) as a religious act, it generally takes the form of rendering something to a supernatural being or beings; (c) the practice varies from religion to religion in details but essentially similar; (d) it has various intents and purposes. These various ends which are meant to be achieved will be discussed below.

Sacrifice is a universal religious phenomenon. Ringgren says:

> All over the world, and throughout history, whenever mankind has worshipped divine being, we encounter the practice of sacrifice. The Babylonian sufferer who gives a lamb to the gods to ransom himself from the sin he supposes to be the cause of his suffering; the Mexican Aztec who kills a young man and offers his heart to the sun-god in order to secure the vital forces of the sun for his land; the Moabite king Mesha who offers his son to his national god in order to win a victory over the attacking Israel (2 Kings 3:27); all these and thousands of others, are examples of the world-wide religious practice we refer to as sacrifice.[3]

Similarly, in his book, *Man and His Religion*, Prideaux cites examples of sacrifice offered at different times by different people and for different purposes. He quoted the example of North American Indians who, in order to quell a storm, procured a dog, tied its legs and cast it overboard into the sea. In like manner, when the sea was constantly rough in Guinea, and men were losing their lives and were afraid to go into the sea, the people appealed to their king to do something to calm the wrath of the goddess of the sea. In response to this appeal, the people provided a jar of palm oil, a bag of rice and corn, a jar of pitto, a bottle of brandy, a piece of painted calico and several other things and these were presented to the god of the sea. In this way, the anger of the god of the sea was assuaged.[4]

Such practical examples of sacrifice are not uncommon among the Yorùbá, whose diviners constantly recommended *ẹbọ* (sacrifice) and *rírú ẹbọ* (offering sacrifice), and whose priests give guidance in the way of making the *ẹbọ*. Thus, when the Yorùbá speak of *ẹbọ* or *rú ẹbọ* (offer sacrifice), it is always in a religious sense. As observed earlier, the Yorùbá believe in the existence of the Supreme Being who is the Creator of heaven and earth and in a number of divinities and spirits who are under the control and supervision of the Supreme Being. These divinities and spirits are higher and more powerful than men, they can be of great help to those who are loyal worshippers and who observe the family taboos and the ethics of the community; but can be detrimental to those who are negligent. In addition, the Yorùbá believe in the existence and the power of the forces of evil – sorcery and witchcraft – which are believed capable of reversing man's good fortune and making life unpleasant for him. In consequence of this kind of belief, sacrifice among the Yorùbá has its positive as well as its negative side.

On the positive side, it is believed that life should be preserved, and its preservation and continuation depend upon the favour of the beings which have the power to sustain or destroy it. As a result of this, there is a strong desire on the part of the Yorùbá to maintain communion with them. They know that they depend upon these spiritual powers for material prosperity, for good health, increase in crops, in cattle and in the family; they consider it expedient to show their gratitude to the givers of the good things. This is why thanks, which are due to the benefactors, are given in the form of thanksgiving sacrifice which is prominent on annual festival occasions.

Like many other peoples, the Yorùbá attribute qualities similar to humans to the divinities and spirits to whom offerings are made. It is believed that they can feel, sense, see, hear and share emotions; they have appetites, wants, and taboos similar to those of human beings. To come before such deities, man has to bring those things that are believed to be liked by them. It is also believed that when a man does this regularly and in the right manner, he will have favour with the supernatural beings who can give him his heart's desires, such as peace, cohesion and joy in addition to the material blessings.

On the negative side, sacrifice is offered to counteract the powers of destruction, for example witches and sorcerers who are wantonly wicked and who hate seeing men make progress in life. Because of such beliefs, the Yorùbá come to associate mishaps that befall them, the losses they sustain, the pains they experience and the sudden and premature deaths with the machinations of enemies who use their nefarious deeds to harm men and make life uncomfortable.

Purposes of sacrifice

Behind the offering of any sacrifice, there is usually a definite purpose. There is no aimlessness in making an offering, and we assert that no one ever makes a sacrifice without having a goal in view.

While scholars readily agree that sacrifice is an important element in religion, they find it difficult, if not impossible, to agree on the purposes of sacrifice. E. B. Tylor says, sacrifice serves as a means of 'bribing' the gods or of paying homage to them in the same way as men pay homage to their over-lords.[5] Van der Leeuw[6] sees it as a gift to enable the receiver (the god) to give something in return or as a means of teasing the gods to act as favourably as possible to those who give them gifts; Robertson Smith sees it as a means of cementing a communion between man and the supernatural being or beings. F. B. Jevons, like Robertson Smith, emphasises the communal aspect of sacrifice as this is noticeable in totemism.[7] Westermarch sees sacrifice as a means of providing food for the gods to encourage them to be kind to men, to bestow blessings upon men, to avert dangers or prevent epidemics, and he sees human sacrifice as a method of 'life insurance'.[8] E. O. James regards sacrifice as a means of giving life to have life.[9]

The various theories propounded by the different scholars attempt to spell out the purposes of sacrifice, but we do not consider it necessary to regard one theory alone as correct; each theory has an element of truth in it. When we examine sacrificial practices among the Yorùbá, we discover that we cannot speak of one purpose of sacrifice – the purposes are multiple. In order to establish these purposes, we can cite examples of observed sacrificial practices.

(1) Before the foundation of his house was laid, a man immolated a goat and poured its blood into a small hole dug in the ground. The severed head of the victim was carefully wrapped in a piece of white cloth and buried. Over the spot, a tree was planted, and sacrifice was brought annually to the foot of the tree. When we asked why this sacrifice was made, we were told that the oracle had revealed that there was a powerful spirit on the plot of ground and that it was

disturbed and aggrieved because of the building that was being erected. If the anger of the disturbed and aggrieved spirit was not assuaged by means of a prescribed sacrifice, the owner of the building or his first son might lose his life. So the offering was made to propitiate the angry spirit.

(2) A child was ill. His father, on the advice and guidance of the oracle, prepared some water in which special leaves had been crushed. In the dead of night, he took his sick child together with the concoction and a few days' old chick. At a road junction (*oríta*), the child was bathed with the concoction. Following this, the father held the chick by the legs and swung it over his child's head three times uttering some prayer and incantations to the effect that the chick might die in the place of his child. After swinging the chick three times over the child's head, he dashed it violently on the ground and it died immediately. Then the father and child, not looking back according to instruction, hastened back home. On investigation, we gathered that the man who took this action did so because he had been told by the diviner that his child's sickness was caused by the witches (*àjé*). In order to appease them, therefore, and make them release the child, the man had to give another life for the child's life. Thus, the chick offered was a substitute for the man's child; the chick died, as it were, the child's death.

(3) We observed that a farmer, before cultivating his land, gathered together his farm implements. Over them he poured a libation of cold water and palm-wine. Then he broke open the tip of the pointed end of a snail, and allowed the fluid from it to drip over the implements. He took a kola-nut and broke it into its four lobes which he cast to divine. We gathered from the man later that he made the offering to Ògún (the powerful divinity of iron and of war) to seek his aid in his farm operation for the year. On further investigation, the man said that he, like the other Yorùbá, believed in the power of Ògún; if man refuses to do him honour, he can cause ghastly accidents to occur and this can hamper the progress of the farm operation.[10]

(4) On one occasion, we visited a *babaláwo* (Ifá Priest). Soon after our arrival at the priest's house, a woman came in, bringing a number of things including some palm-oil, kola-nuts, some loaves of corn-meal (*èko tútù*) and a goat. She had probably made a prior appointment with the *babaláwo* because she received attention promptly. A broken pot was provided, and some corn-meal brought by the woman was broken into small bits and put into the pot. Some oil was poured

over the crushed corn-meal. The woman then held the animal in her
hand and prayed, enumerating all the good things she desired. The
animal was immolated and the blood was poured into the pot. The
babaláwo cast his *òpèlè*[11] to ascertain whether or not the sacrifice was
adequate and acceptable and to know where the offering was to be
placed. The directive was, accordingly, given by the oracle. On
inquiring from the priest the purpose of that sacrifice, we were told
that the oracle had revealed that the woman enquirer was suffering
from the evil machinations of the mysterious powers. In order to
change the unfortunate situation into an auspicious one, offerings had
to be made to these workers of evil. The blood, the oil, the cold
corn-meal were, therefore, offered purposely to make these powers
favourably disposed to the woman offering the sacrifice.

(5) On instructions received from the oracle, a man provided a bowl
of cold water, some salt, a pigeon (*eyelé*) and a kola-nut. He washed
the kola-nut in a bowl of water and then held it in his hand, touching
his head with it as he prayed that his *Orí* (his counterpart or the
divinity controlling fate) should bring him good things in life. Next,
he took the pigeon, touched his head with it and prayed as he had done
with the kola-nut. Having completed this, he wrung off the head of
the pigeon and smeared his own head with the blood of the pigeon.
Every one of the invited guests touched the salt in the plate with his
share of the kola-nut and prayed that his life may be preserved and as
tasteful as salt. The bird was then prepared, cooked and eaten by the
man and his invited guests. This offering testifies to an important
aspect of the belief of the Yorùbá, namely, that the fortune or fate of a
person is symbolised by *Orí* (head) and that *Orí* which is also the
divinity controlling man's fate, is responsible for the distribution of
fortune. Offering is, therefore, made to him so that the offerer may
find favour with the divinity and be endowed with good fortune.
Hence they sing to the praise of Orí the following song:

Bí o bá máa lówó,	If you want to have money
Bèèrè lówó orî re;	Inquire of your head;
Bí o bá máa sòwò,	If you want to start trading,
Bèèrè lówó orí re wò;	Inquire of your head first;
Bí o bá máa kólé,	If you want to build a house,
Bèèrè lówó orî re,	Inquire of your head,
Bí o bá máa láya o,	If you want to take a wife,
Bèèrè lówó orî rè wò	Inquire of your head first

Orí, máṣe pẹkùn dé	Head, please do not shut the gate
Lọ́dọ̀ rẹ ni mo ṁbọ̀,	It is to you I am coming,
Wá ṣayéè mi di rere	Come and make my life prosperous.

(6) A man turned to the side of a wall in a room where his late father was buried. There he poured libations of water and gin as he invoked the ancestors to be present and to hear his supplication and grant his requests. He broke one of the kola-nuts which he had for the offering and cast it to divine. On discovering that the oracle had spoken well, he and the invited guests ate kola-nuts, drank palm-wine, sang the praises of the ancestors and made merry. On investigation, we were told that this is an affirmation of the belief of the Yorùbá in the existence of the departed ancestors. As the living drink and eat together, so also do they invite the invisible spirits of the ancestors to partake of the offered food and drink in order that they may be well-disposed to the living. This kind of sacrifice serves as a means of communion between the living and the 'living dead'.

(7) It was harvest-time in a village where most of the villagers were farmers. Before the farm products were eaten, they were given first, in a ritualistic and ceremonial manner, to some divinities and ancestral spirits who, it is believed, made the crops do well. It was only after this ceremony that the people were free to eat and drink and to make merry. The sacrifice, on that occasion, was a means of expressing gratitude to the spiritual beings for the benefits received from them.

(8) It is a common practice among devotees of some divinities to vow before their divinities saying: 'If such and such a thing can be done for me, I will bring such and such a gift.' Whenever such blessings as have been asked for are received, men come before the divinities with offerings. This also constitutes another purpose of sacrifice.

From the foregoing, we can rightly say that sacrifice meets certain basic needs and aspirations of men. It is utilised, among other things, as a means of: (a) expressing gratitude to the spiritual beings; (b) fulfilling a vow; (c) establishing a communion between man and the spiritual beings; (d) averting the anger of the divinities and spirits; (e) warding off the attack and evil machinations of enemies; (f) purifying a person or a community when a taboo has been broken or sin committed; (g) preventing or expelling epidemics; (h) strengthening the worshippers against malign influences.

The purposes meant to be served are reflected in the types of sacrifice offered and these we shall examine in the next chapter.

NOTES

1. *ERE*, vol. 11, p. 1.
2. E. O. James, *Sacrifice and Sacrament*, London, 1962, p. 13.
3. H. Ringgren, *Sacrifice in the Bible*, Lutterworth Press, London, 1962, p. 7.
4. S. P. T. Prideaux, *Man and His Religion*, London, 1930, pp. 35ff.
5. E. B. Tylor, *Religion in Primitive Culture*, Harper, New York, vol. 2, 1958, pp. 461ff.
6. Van der Leeuw, *Religion in Essence and Manifestation*, Harper and Row, New York, vol. 2, 1963, pp. 351ff.
7. F. B. Jevons, *Introduction to the History of Religion*, London, 1921, p. 154. cf. R. Money-Kyrle, *The Meaning of Sacrifice*, London, 1965, p. 169.
8. E. A. Westermarck, *Early Beliefs and their social influence*, Macmillan, London, 1932, p. 98f.
9. E. O. James, *Origins of Sacrifice*, London, 1933, pp. 256ff.
10. See *Ogun* in ch. 2.
11. See ch. 6.

Chapter Eight
TYPES OF SACRIFICE

Broadly speaking, there are two categories of sacrifice among the Yorùbá: those which are feasts, partaken of first by the supernatural beings and then by the community of worshippers; and those which are intended to avert calamity and atone for the offences which provoke such sacrifices. While the first category of sacrifice is offered in the midst of joy and jubilation, the second category is joyless and fearful.

For purposes of elucidation, however, these two categories will be sub-divided into: thanksgiving, votive, propitiatory, preventive, sub-stitutionary and foundation sacrifice. We shall now examine each of these as observed among the Yorùbá.

Ẹbọ ọpẹ́ àti ìdàpọ̀ (thanksgiving and communion sacrifice)

This type of sacrifice serves as a means of expressing thanks to, and of holding communion with, the Supernatural Being or the divinities. The Yorùbá sacrifice of thanksgiving is almost always accompanied by feasting; the worshippers and the divinity (though the latter is invisible) share a common meal. In this way, beneficial relation is established.

In daily life, the Yorùbá show that they do appreciate kindness shown to them. This is depicted in their saying:

Bí a bá ṣe ni lóore,	For the benefits received,
Ọpẹ́ là ńdá.	One must be grateful.

They have yet another common saying:

Ẹni tí a ṣe lóore,	One upon whom we bestow kindness,

Tí kò dúpé̩,	But will not express gratitude,
Burú ju o̩ló̩̩sà	Is worse than a robber
Tí ó kó ni lé̩rù lo̩	Who carries away our belongings.

Such common sayings give us an insight into the people's way of thinking and we can understand why thanksgiving sacrifice is given prominence among them. When they receive their heart's desires, they know that the blessings have come from the supernatural beings. When there is a bumper harvest, when hunting or fishing expedition is successful, when victory is won over enemies, when there is an escape from an accident, when a new child is born, all these instances necessitate the bringing of offerings to express gratitude to the divinity or divinities. As they praise their benefactors, so also do they praise and thank the benevolent divinities whom they believe to be the determiners of their good fortune.

Most of the joyous periodic festivals among the Yorùbá involve thankofferings. By periodic festivals we mean those festivals which are observed at regular intervals – biennially, annually and, in a less elaborate manner, monthly, weekly and even daily. But strictly speaking, by periodic festivals we have in mind biennial or annual festivals which bring together a large number of people, who come before their divinities to express thanks for the turn of the year and for the benefits received during the period.

Among the Yorùbá, many of these festival occasions involve bringing of thanksgiving sacrifice to the many divinities acknowledged and worshipped by the people, and believed to be the dispensers of blessings. We shall cite a few examples of the divinities and festivals.

The new yam festival figures prominently among the Yorùbá, whose main occupation is farming. Surprisingly, the festival is even observed by the Ìlàjȩ whose main occupation is fishing. Among the latter, the festival goes by the name *Èje*. One remarkable thing is that the new yam festival takes different forms in different places; however, they all have in common the giving of the new yams first to one divinity or another before human beings partake of them. Furthermore, it is also to be noted that the devotees of certain divinities are forbidden to take new yam until it has ritually been offered to the divinities and partaken of by the people.

Èje festival is an annual event in Ìtèbúu-Mánúwà during which the E̩lé̩rò̩ of Ìtèbú-Mánúwà gives yam to Malókun (god of the sea), to the ancestors and to other local spirits and divinities believed to be

Ritual washing of a sacred object before the formal worship of Ọrọ̀ Léwe.

Crowd during an Egúngún festival at Olupọna.

Entrance to the Malokun (goddess of the sea) shrine at Ugbo.

Offerings of yams at an Orişa-oko shrine during an annual festival. The symbol of the divinity is overhung with cowries.

responsible for making the crops do well on the farm. Thus, when the harvest time comes, the first crop from the farm must be ceremonially brought home and presented to Malókun and the ancestors in gratitude for the fertility of the soil and for the preservation of the life of the people.

In preparation for the festival, the Ugbówẹn (the grove believed to house many spirits) is cleared, the Malókun shrine is kept clean and decorated with palm-fronds. On the day preceding the fixed date, the chief priest and some assistants go to the farm to bring yams from *ebè ńlá* (big yam-heaps) specially dedicated for this purpose in the Ọba's special farm. The yam is ceremonially brought into the Malókun shrine. When the yam arrives at the shrine, the *Àríbèjí*[1] (the Oro which is peculiar to the Ìlàjẹ and whose 'voice' is like the sound of a mighty ocean) booms out, announcing the arrival of the new yam and indicating joy at witnessing a new year. Everybody then comes out rejoicing and shouting *'Ìgbódò rè é, Pòókè ẹ'* . . . *'Ìgbódò rè é, Pòókè ẹ!'* ('Here is the new yam! Congratulations!'). People congratulate one another and the priest prays that the year may be peaceful and successful, and that the year's celebration may usher in an era of joy, prosperity and longevity. The yams are left at the shrine overnight while the people keep a vigil around the shrine singing the praises of the gods. They sing and ask the ancestral spirits and other spirits to come and take gin and kola-nuts and pray that the next day's celebration may be acceptable. The following is one of the songs recorded on the occasion:

Ogúngún wa,	Our ancestors,
Yànà wá nèní,	Please, call today
Jẹ́ wá mẹmu;	And drink palm-wine;
Ogúngún Bàbá,	Ancestors! Fathers!
Yànà wá o	Please come
Jẹ wá gbobì pa,	That you may accept and split the kola-nut
Ogúngún wa,	Our ancestors,
Yànà wa.[2]	Please, call.

The next day, the Ọba and his chiefs together with the priests fast from morning till the evening in order that their prayers may be acceptable. Early in the morning, the Ọba, dressed in white, takes some white kola-nuts and a white pigeon. He prays for himself, his subjects and the strangers in the town that all may be well. He also prays for the chief priest who in return prays for the Ọba. This ceremony takes place in the Ọba's palace. It is after this that the chief priest goes into the shrine to present the new yam formally to the Malòkun and the ancestral spirits. One of the yams is divided longitudinally into two and used for divining. This is one of the rare occasions when yam, rather than the kola-nuts, is used for divination. The two pieces of yams are cast. If they fall with one face up and one face down, the people hail the omen because it augurs well for the year; but if the two fall face-downward, it signifies a bad omen and it should be further investigated. When the omen is propitious, there is great rejoicing round the town.

Later in the day, a piece of new yam is also taken to the grove where a similar ceremony is performed by the priests. Here the yam is also ceremonially given to the spirits believed to be present. Like the previous occasion, the yam is divided into two and cast to divine; when the yam 'speaks' well (that is, when the oracle is favourable), the people rejoice and sing:

Orò fẹn, orò gbà,	The sacrifice is acceptable,
O fẹ́n ún ba wa, Ẹlẹ́rò;	It is acceptable for our father, the Ẹlẹ́rò,
A ira mo rò;	We, celebrants, believe;
Orò fẹ́n o, orò gbà,	The ceremony is all right and acceptable,
Ó fẹ́n ghun dede ùlú	It is acceptable for the whole town;
A ira mo ro[3]	We, celebrants, believe.

In a more jubilant manner the people sing on their way from the grove as follows:

Awa yú ríre,	We went well,
Awa bọ̀ ríre,	And have returned well;
Awa yú o,	We went,
Awa bọ̀ ríre[3]	And have returned well.

When the priests and the men return from the grove, the Ọba dressed still in white meets them near his palace and in the midst of jubilation, accompanied by all his subjects, dances round the town. He calls at sixteen shrines where he pays homage to different divinities. It is after this dancing and the offerings to the divinities that the Ọba and the priests break their fast. They are satisfied that they can now eat since the divinities have had their share. All the offerings are in the form of thanksgiving.

In Ilẹ-Olújĭí near Oǹdó, the new yam festival is called *Owè* or *Orò*

Ọlọfin.[4] Celebration takes place in August before the annual Ògún festival. As in Ìtèbúu-Manúwa, the chief priest, accompanied by an assistant priest, goes to the farm to bring yams from special heaps. These heaps are special in the sense that the yams planted in them are carefully watched and tended for the festival. The idea is that even if the rain does not fall in good time to water the farm crops in general, provision is made to water the heaps in order that new yams must be available at the scheduled and traditional time.

When the yams are brought from the farm, they are taken to the central market place near the Ọba's palace, and the people are informed through a signal that the new yams have been brought. All the townspeople come out in jubilation to hail the new yams. One noticeable thing in Ilè-Olújìí is that new kola-nuts are also offered together with new yams. This is because kola-nuts and yams are the chief products of the area; the idea is that the most important products of the farm must be offered ceremonially to the divinities before they are used by human beings. Everyone who has harvested kola-nuts during the season brings some quantity of kola-nuts and throws them at the priest as he is hailed 'Ọlọfin o'! It is believed that if anyone keeps kola-nuts at home and fails to offer some to Ọlọfin, such kola-nuts will be destroyed by maggots and such a person will suffer some loss that year. This is to encourage the people to be grateful to the spiritual beings who have caused the crops to do well.

One of the yams brought from the farm by the priest is sliced into three parts – one part is taken to the Olújìí ancestral shrine, the second to *Ìdí-Ògún* (Ògún shrine) and the third to *Ìdí-Ọlọfin* (Ọlọfin shrine). At each of these shrines, the *Àwòrò* (priest) thanks the divinity associated with the particular shrine for the preservation of the people and for the abundance of crops, and he prays that the people who witness the year's celebration may also live to see many more of such celebrations. The Àwòrò then runs seven times between the market place and the Ọlọfin's shrine, each time paying homage to Ọlọfin. The new yam having been offered to the divinities, is now ritually eaten by the chief priest and seven other priests.

Following this, the Jẹgun (who is the paramount chief of the town) offers yams to the ancestors, and all family heads do likewise. It is only after this ceremonial 'feeding' of the spiritual beings that men can eat of the farm products.

In the whole of Yorubaland, Ìlárá, near Àkùrẹ́, is famous for its Ọdún Ìjẹṣu (the new yam festival). The festival opens the gate for other traditional ceremonies in the town; this is why Ìlárá has the sobriquet '*Ọmọ a kórò méje ṣe lóòjọ́*' ('The descendants of those who observe seven ceremonies on the same day'). All the ceremonies put together lend colour and dignity to the grandeur of the new yam festival which lasts three days.

On the first day of the celebration, family heads, accompanied by their wives and other members of the family, go to their farms to harvest yams. On instruction, each of the most senior wives in the family holds two big kola-nuts which she presents to her husband at the appointed place and time in the farm. Each man selects the biggest of the yams harvested and brings it to a rendezvous. He then takes the kola-nuts from his wife, holds them in his two hands and touches the yam with them in a reverent manner as he prays, thanking the goddess of the earth (here called Imalè Ìjẹṣu) for making the land fertile and for sparing his life to celebrate another harvest thanksgiving. He also prays that the yearly celebration may be acceptable. He breaks one of the two kola-nuts and casts it to divine. When the omen is propitious, the men hail the result and rejoice. The remaining kola-nut is shared by the people who are present. The big yam, called '*Adeko*' (one that guards the farm) is not to be removed from the farm but is left on the spot where the ceremony has been performed. It rots away and returns to the earth from where it came. It is a way of offering the whole yam to the earth spirit as a mark of gratitude.

On the following day, the Ọba (the paramount ruler), together with the elders of Ìgbẹ̀hìn, goes to *Oko-ọba* (Ọba's farm)[5] to dig up yams. The Ọba removes his upper garment (*agbádá*) and solemnly digs the yam. People say '*Ọbá lọ soko ídásu*' (the Ọba is gone to the farm to dig up yams). After *ìdásu* (digging up of the yam), the new yams are hailed and this is followed by drumming and dancing. The Ọba and his entourage are met and joined by other people who then dance round the town in jubilation. Meanwhile, some of the yams harvested are taken to *Ọlọ́tìn*, the chief priest of *Imalè Ìjẹṣu* (also called *Imalè Iná* or *Imalè Ìlárá*), on the top of the hill near the town. He offers the yams to the divinity. The offering is followed by *Òbèrèmàyè*, a kind of music and dancing in which the whole townspeople are involved. People are gaily dressed; members of the same association or age-group wear the same kind of dress.

After this, the Ọba enters into his palace and remains indoors until after seven days. People say '*Ọbá wọlé ìfúnta*' ('the king goes in for meditation after the blessing ceremony)'. During the period of his confinement, he prays that the offering may be acceptable and that past sins may be overlooked. Then follows the *Àgògó* music, the most beautiful of the ceremonies. People dance to the beating of *abèbè* (fans) as they sing:

Alárá jẹun kàbí e tíì jẹ?	Has the Alárá eaten or not?
Àgògó Olóyè, Agogo!	Àgògó Olóyè Agogo (chorus)
Ọdún yìí á yabo kàbí é níí yabo?	Will this year be blessed or not?
Àgògó Olóyè, Agogo.	Àgògó Olóyè, Agogo.

Special bamboo torches are lit all over the town at night and the people continue jubilation. At about two o'clock in the morning, the chief priest bears the symbol of *Imalè Ìlárá* and moves round the town blessing the people. All the people who had made vows the previous year come out to fulfil their promises. The devotees who accompany the *Imalè* receive the gifts as the priest blesses them all.

The third day is marked by *Ìrèkékè* dance. Young girls who have just attained the age of puberty cover their breasts and the lower parts of their bodies and hold aloft some cuts of the sugarcane given them by their fiancés, and they dance round singing:

Ìrèkékè,	Ìrèkékè,
Ayé ye ye,	Aye yeye;
Mo lọ sọjà,	I go to the market,
Mo gba àìkú	And obtain immortality;
Mo gbọmọ tuntun tòhún bọ̀,	I bring back from there a new baby;
Ìrèkékè.	Ìrèkékè.

Then, in another song, they send a message to the *Imalè* (the divinity) as they sing:

Má gbèhìn gbé o	Do not forget,
Kó o má gbàgbée wa;	Do not forget us;
Ilé dọwọ̀ọ́ rẹ.	Our homes are entrusted to your care.

We see that the new yam festival, wherever it is observed, is marked by expression of gratitude to the divinity believed to have made yams thrive or grow well on the farm. It is also a period of jubilation and of communion between the townspeople and the divinities.

Most of these annual festivals are agrarian and are designed to thank the supernatural powers who are believed to bring about increase in crops, as well as for the preservation of life in general. All benevolent divinities deserve and are given praise. Some of them such as Ọ̀ṣun, Yemọja, Ọbàtálá and Ọbàlùfọ̀n are believed to be capable of providing children for the barren; others, like Ògún, are believed to be able to provide good jobs for the devotees and to protect them from accidents; yet others, like Orò and Àríbèjí, purify the town and village. Each of these divinities has elaborate annual festivals which emphasise thanksgiving.

Ẹbọ Èjẹ́ (votive sacrifice)

As sacrifice is used as a means of expressing thanks to the supernatural beings, so also is it used to fulfil vows. This, in a sense, is a sort of thanksgiving sacrifice. It is a common practice among the Yorùbá (as indicated in the last chapter) for devotees of some divinities to go before their divinities to pour out their minds and to promise that if their needs are met, they will give specified offerings in return. Vows could be made at any time but especially when a person is under some strain, and when the times seem troublesome and human aid is of no avail. The Yorùbá believe that whatever promise is made must be fulfilled; especially so when the promise is made by man or woman before a divinity. To fail to fulfil the promise is to incur the displeasure of the divinity and to lose the benefits already received and many more.

There is the popular story among the Yorùbá, particularly in Ilé-Ifè, of Mọrèmi who promised to offer her only son, Olúorogbo, to the river goddess, Èsìnmìrìn, if her requests were granted. This happened in the days when the Ugbò people, who claimed to be the original inhabitants of Ilé-Ifè, were driven away by the newcomers under Odùduwà. The Ugbò people, dissatisfied with their lot, decided to pester the lives of the Ifè people. They dressed in twigs and grasses and constantly raided the Ifè people.

Whenever the Ugbó 'masqueraders' came, the Ifè people would take to their heels. It was indeed a period of humiliation for the Ifè people. In that time of dismay and discomfiture, a courageous and cunning woman, called Mọrèmi, volunteered to risk being captured by the invaders in order that she might learn the secrets of the Ugbò people's continuous successes in their raids of the Ifẹ̀ people. But before then, she had gone to the goddess Èṣìnmìrìn and vowed to offer her only son if her enterprise proved successful.

In their next raid of Ifẹ̀, the Ugbò people captured Mọrèmi, and she was taken to the court of the Olúgbò of Ugbò where, as the ruler's favourite wife, she learnt the secrets of the people. She later escaped and returned to Ifẹ̀. She instructed her people to prepare flaming brands (ògùṣọ̀) and burn the Ugbò invaders for, according to her, the garments worn by the invaders were made of grasses and twigs which could easily be set on fire. This technique proved successful and the Ugbò people were routed in their next raid on Ifẹ̀. Everybody in Ifẹ̀ acknowledged the wisdom and bravery of Mọrèmi. But Mọrèmi had to fulfil the promise of offering her only son as sacrifice to Èṣìnmìrìn. She was reluctant to redeem her promise and tried offering other things instead – goats, sheep and even cows – but these were not acceptable to Èṣìnmìrìn. She had to offer her only son. Today, Mọrèmi and Olúorogbo are regarded as heroine and hero respectively in Ilé-Ifẹ̀.

This is just one of the many stories that emphasise the importance of fulfilling promises made before the supernatural beings. It is to be added that at most of the annual festivals among the Yorùbá worshippers, women especially, are seen and heard making all sorts of vows before the divinity: for example, at the annual Olua festival[7] in Osi-Èkìtì, men and women come to make requests, specifically for the gift of children. Everyone in need kneels down before the symbol of Olúa and asks for whatever she desires, adding at the same time what she will offer if her requests are granted. Invariably, year after year, men and women come to fulfil their vows bringing such items as fowls, goats, kola-nuts, pigeons, salt and other items according to the vow and the demand of the divinity. It is usually a busy time for the priests who make sure that the gifts of every devotee are presented before the ceremony is over. In many cases, if children are asked for and the blessing is received during the course of the year, they are brought to the shrine of the divinity as a mark of gratitude and as a dedication to the benevolent divinity.

Similarly, the striking sight may be seen at the Òkè-Ìbàdàn festival of a large number of women bringing gifts of goats, chickens, and items of food to Bẹẹrẹ, the abode of Abọ̀kè (the chief priest). Usually, these are women who have asked for the gift of children and have been blessed and have come to redeem their promises.

The same thing happens at the annual Ọṣun festival in Òṣògbo. Women pray for the gift of children at the top of their voices and loudly promise what they will offer to Ọ̀ṣun if their requests are granted. We have seen a number of such women coming to the priest to make their offerings.

Both the thanksgiving and the votive types of sacrifice are occasions of great joy when the devotees appear before the divinities to express their thanks for the gifts received. They are also occasions of communion with the supernatural beings. Such sacrifices are offered in the midst of dancing and music, eating and drinking.

Ẹbọ Ètùtù (propitiatory sacrifice)

Failure of crops, famine, outbreak of plague and disease, protracted illness and sudden death or similar calamities are attributed to the anger of the gods, the machinations of evil spirits or to some ritual error or defilement committed by men. Efforts are made to locate the causes of the trouble and to remove them, calm the wrath of the divinities or spirits and win back their favour. The chief means employed by the Yorùbá is the propitiatory sacrifice – a sacrifice that is believed to be capable of propitiating the anger of the gods and spirits and of purifying individuals and the community.

As earlier indicated, the Yorùbá believe that the divinities have feelings like human beings and can, therefore, be angry. For example, it is believed that if a divinity whose function is to control the fertility of the soil is offended, the land may not yield her increase. Or, if a woman acts contrary to the directive of a divinity controlling childbirth such a woman may become barren. Furthermore, certain divinities and spirits have specific taboos which their devotees must observe. For example, both Ṣàngó and Ayélálá hate stealing, witchcraft, bad medicine and other vicious practices. When such things are done, a terrible visitation is made by either of these two divinities, or any other anti-wickedness divinity. For example, when there is a visitation by Ṣàngó, he hurls a stone which damages windows, doors, houses, and even human beings. When this happens, the Magbà (chief priest of Ṣàngó) has to be notified. It is he and his assistant priests who can perform the necessary propitiatory rite. The belief is that if the rite is not performed, there will be no peace in that home. Hence the priest has to come and ascertain what offences have been committed and what can be done to propitiate the divinity. Among other things, the offenders will forfeit all their belongings to the priests. In addition, members of their families are asked to supply a number of things as materials of sacrifice, including a ram, plenty of oil, plenty of food, plenty of *pito* (drink from guinea-corn) and palm-wine. In addition, special leaves believed to bring about calmness and peace are fetched by the priests. In the midst of ritual drumming of the *bàtá* (special Ṣàngó drum), singing and ecstatic movements by the priests, the stones believed to have been hurled by Ṣàngó are searched for and dug out of the earth.

It is remarkable that everyone who visits the scene of the accident, rather than being sad and sympathetic, has to shout 'Kabiyesi' (the greeting accorded a Yorùbá Ọba) because Ṣàngó, once a king but now deified, has come to visit those affected. The people so visited are greeted '*Ẹ kú àfojúbà*' or '*A báa yín yọ̀*' ('We congratulate you on this visitation'). The idea is that the divinity has visited to purify the society and individuals in the society. This is regarded as a royal and just punishment. Whatever offerings are made are meant to propitiate the anger of Ṣàngó.

The same thing happens when a man is visited by Ayélála or by Sòpònnó. These anti-wickedness divinities are believed to be out to discourage evil practices among people. They symbolise the wrath of the Supreme Being and their visitation can only be minimised by propitiatory sacrifice and the desire to change for the better.

At times, the oracles reveal to the people what offences have been committed by the community as a whole. Propitiatory sacrifice, in which purificatory rite figures prominently, is performed. Such a sacrifice can be a very expensive undertaking, 'as the prescription may involve up to two hundred each of several articles, animate or inanimate, or up to a total of two hundred and one of several articles put together. With an individual, it may be as little as a fowl or a pigeon, or as much as a four-footed animal with some other articles added to it'.[7]

There are many examples of such ritual cleansing in Yorubaland. For example, among the Ìjẹ̀bú people, *Ẹ̀ẹ̀bì* festival is a rite for the general spiritual cleansing of the community. A kind of symbolic action accompanies the rite. At noon on the appointed day, every adult in the community gets an *òfọ̀nràn* (burning firebrand) and with this he or she chases evil spirits and calamity out of every corner of the house into the streets and from the streets into the bush and from the bush into an appointed flowing stream. This is done in an exciting manner because the people believe that misery and woe, calamity and the machinations of enemies are driven away from the community and sunk into the river so that the community can, once more, enjoy peace. In their excitement, and as they chase evils out of the village, the people sing or shout:

Oṣo yóò!	Woe to wizards!
Àjẹ́ yòó!	Woe to witches!
Ọni fọ kónúrún ma ṣè é, yóò!	Woe upon those who will not allow others to prosper!
Ọni fọ kọlọ́mọ́ má bi i, yóò![8]	Woe upon those who will not allow women to be delivered of their babies!

When people get to the stream, they push the firebrands into it and leave them to be carried away by the flowing stream. As the firebrands sink into the river and are carried away, so evil spirits, losses and sickness are believed to be carried away from the community. On their way from the street, people seek for and collect *Wọ́rọ̀* leaves (special leaves associated with calmness and peace); and with jubilation, like those who have defeated their enemies, they carry aloft the *Wọ́rọ̀* leaves as they sing:

Ewée Wọ́rọ̀ rèé o!	Here is the Wọ́rọ̀ leaf!
Gbágbátẹ̀!	Hail! Hail!
Ó dé! Ó dé!	It is come! It is come!
Gbá gbá tẹ̀!	Hail! Hail!
Ewée Wọ́rọ̀ olórí;	The Wọ́rọ̀, chief of the leaves!
Gbá gbá tẹ̀!	Hail! Hail!
É i rèn iwòriwò wọlú;	It never enters into the town naked!
Gbá gbá tẹ̀!	Hail! Hail!

In jubilation and high spirits all return to the shrine of *Ẹ̀ẹ̀bì* where *Wọ́rọ̀* leaves, brought from the river bank, *Ọ̀dúndún* (kalanchoe), palm-oil, snails, and a male goat are offered to *Ẹ̀ẹ̀bì*. It is remarkable to note that all the materials of sacrifice have soothing or calming effect. The idea is that once evils have been swept away in this dramatic way, peace will come back and remain in the town.

It is not only among the Ìjẹbú that this type of purificatory rite is observed. Among the Ìjọ́ Apoi people of Igbóbini in Òkìtìpupa division, during the annual *Bòábù* festival, there is the practice of getting fresh twigs and palm-fronds from the nearby Bòábù grove to sweep every corner of the house and town. All the things swept together with the twigs are thrown into the river which, the people believe, carries away the uncleanness and unpleasantness from the community. During this rite, the chief celebrants cover their bodies and faces with charcoal as marks of repentance. They beat each other gently with the twigs as if dusting away evil hidden in the body. During the procession, the chief priest has to roll about on the ground nine times as if saying, 'I am sorry for the sins of the people'. This is a solemn propitiatory and purificatory rite.[9]

In Ilé-Ifẹ̀ during the *Edì* festival, there is a chasing out of evil by means of firebrand (*òfònràn*) such as we have witnessed and described among the Ìjèbú and the Ìjọ́ Apoi. The people shout at the top of their voices *'Ògúná yòyò'*! ('Hot firebrand!') as they seize lighted torches and wave them over their heads begging that all their human miseries, diseases, sores and death be driven away, and also praying that they may live to celebrate the feast the following year. To crown the ritual cleansing, a human scapegoat (*Teele*) carries away the sins of the people.[10]

As part of the purificatory rite in some places, individuals who are believed to have committed some immoral acts during the year are singled out for ridicule. This is called *èfè* (ridicule or jest). For example, at the annual celebration of Ondòfóyì, the goddess believed to be the founder and mother of all the indigenous people of Ìmálà (Ẹ̀gbádò), there is the night performance during which evil doers are exposed and ridiculed. By so doing, it is believed that the goddess is propitiated since men themselves have ridiculed the offenders.

It can be very disturbing to read the works of outsiders who claim to be an authority on African religion and allege that Africans have no sense of sin. One such example is J. K. Parratt who claims that the sense of sin among the Yorùbá, if any, is nothing comparable with 'the developed ethical conception of sin which is to be found in both the Old Testament and the New Testament'.[11] If Parratt and others like him had suppressed their preconceived notions, and made a thorough and unbiased investigation of practice among the Yorùbá, they would have been persuaded that the Yorùbá, like other Africans, are as conscious of sin as the Jews of the Old Testament with whom Parratt was trying to compare them. 'The Yorùbá know the distinction between ritual errors which are calculated to be offences against the divinities, derelictions of filial duties which may arouse the anger of the aggrieved ancestors, and the breach of the Deity's behests which is purely a moral issue'.[12]

One is deeply impressed, however, by the way Westermann assesses the sense of sin and the removal of evil as observed among the Africans. 'The Africans know about sin and evil, their confession and their removal. . . On the Gold Coast the evil or sin is expelled from a town before the new harvest is allowed to be brought into it. The purging is done by cleaning every house, courtyard, and street and by throwing the rubbish far away into the bush'.[13] Later Westermann claims that the many taboos which a man has to observe are not to be regarded as things mechanical which do not touch the heart, but that 'the avoidance is a sacred law respected by the community. In breaking it, you offend a divine power, you expose yourself to danger, and you place yourself outside the community of the righteous'.[14] Westermann's statement is important here for our understanding of the religion of the Yorùbá who tenaciously believe that moral values are based upon the recognition of the divine will, and that sin in the community must be expelled if perfect peace is to be enjoyed.

In connection with propitiatory sacrifice, we should add that offerings made in consequence of persecution by witches, resulting in misfortunes, illness or premature death, figure prominently among the Yorùbá. There is the belief that a series of calamities may befall a man, not necessarily that he has wronged or neglected a divinity or an ancestral spirit, but because the evil ones who use their nefarious powers to harm others plan evils against him. Whenever a diviner points out that there is an evil force at work, sacrifice is usually prescribed to propitiate the miserable misanthropists called witches and sorcerers.

It is to be noted that when a propitiatory sacrifice is offered, there is neither eating nor drinking such as one will experience during the thanksgiving or communion sacrifice; there is no sharing with the spirits propitiated and there is no mirth. It is an offering that is quickly disposed of – a sacrifice of appeasement (ẹbọ ètùtù).

Ẹbọ Ojúkòríbi (preventive sacrifice)

It is strongly believed by the Yorùbá that as sacrifice removes evils from the community or from an individual, so also does it keep off evil or misfortune. In consequence of this belief, precautionary measures are taken to prevent imminent danger and disaster. People get to know the dangers ahead by means of oracles.[15] For example, before a man takes a wife (or a woman a husband), before a person undertakes a journey or begins an enterprise, he or she consults the oracle which gives him or her guidance as to what the future looks like, what dangers lie ahead and what can be done to change unpleasant circumstances. Once a person goes by the directive of the oracle, it is believed, he will easily avoid getting into trouble; but when the order or the directive of the oracle is defied, the consequences can be grave. The following episode illustrates how Ọ̀rúnmìlà once ignored the warning of the oracle and got into trouble.

Once upon a time, Ọ̀rúnmìlà wanted to go to Èjìgbòmẹ̀fọ̀n market to buy a horse. Before he went, he requested his sixteen children to consult the oracle concerning his proposed journey. His eldest child, Èjìogbè, was the one who divined. He told his father point blank that he must offer ẹgbàáfà (12,000 cowries, i.e., 30 kobo of the present Nigerian currency) as sacrifice in order that he might get a good horse and prevent any calamity. But Ọ̀rúnmìlà, disregarding the directive given by the oracle, went to the market without making the offering.

When he got there, he saw a well-fed and good-looking horse, not knowing that it was a stag that had been changed to a horse by Èṣù.[16] Ọ̀rúnmìlà bought the 'horse'. On his way home, he met one of his old friends who stopped to admire the horse. To the disappointment and discomfiture of Ọ̀rúnmìlà and his friend, the animal suddenly changed into a stag and escaped into the nearby bush. Ọ̀rúnmìlà pursued it crying:

Igbó nigbó Irúnmalẹ̀,	The forest is the forest of divinities,
Ẹ bá nmẹ́sin!	Kindly help me catch the horse!
Igbó nigbó Irúnmalẹ̀,	The forest is the forest of divinities,
Ẹ bá nmẹ́sin!	Kindly help me catch the horse!

The animal ran into the field and Ọ̀rúnmìlà pursued it crying:

Ọ̀dàn, ọ̀dàn eruku	You field, dusty field,
Ẹ bá nmẹ́sin;	Help me catch the horse;
Ọ̀dan, ọ̀dan eruku,	You field, dusty field,
Ẹ bá nmẹ́sin!	Help me catch the horse!

Thus Ọrúnmìlà chased the animal across valley and hill until he and the stag landed themselves in a pit. After much suffering Ọrúnmìlà was pulled out of the pit by a kind woman called Poróyè who came that way by accident. As the woman was pulling out Ọrúnmìlà from the pit, he was holding on to the leg of the stag; but before he could be pulled out completely, the leg he was holding got torn off from the main body of the animal which fell into the pit. Thus Ọrúnmìlà suffered untold hardship and humiliation as a result of his refusal to offer the prescribed preventive sacrifice.

It should be mentioned in connection with this sacrifice that whenever a Yorùbá community learn that an epidemic (for example, smallpox) is raging in a nearby village, they offer sacrifice to prevent the scourge from entering into their village. This type of sacrifice includes digging up the main entrance to the village and burying there a sacrificial animal, or knocking the life out of a fowl and hanging it whole on top of a pole which is stuck to the ground at the entrance to the village. All these precautionary measures are taken as means of preventing any calamities or evils.

Ẹbọ Ayèpínùn (substitutionary sacrifice)

This form of sacrifice has an element of propitiation as well as of prevention and substitution in the sense that something (rather than the person who should have suffered privation, discomfort or even death) is offered to propitiate a thirsty divinity or spirit who plans evil against man. The sacrifice also saves the person who offers it from premature death.

As we pointed out when discussing propitiatory sacrifice, witches and sorcerers may plan death for a person. When this is made known by means of divination, the person who would have died, procures an animal for sacrifice. With the head of the animal, he touches his own head as he prays that the animal may die in his place and that the enemies should take the animal and leave him (the supplicant) to enjoy his life. Such an animal is treated in specific ways: sometimes, the victim is treated like a corpse and may be wrapped in a piece of white cloth and buried at an appointed place; or it may be immolated and the head and entrails with plenty of palm-oil put into an earthen pot (agbada) and carried to a road-junction or near a stream or at the foot of an Ìrókò tree, depending upon the directive of the oracle. The animal slaughtered takes the place of the supplicant. Hence this type of sacrifice is also called 'bámidíyà' ('Be a substitute for my suffering').

The Yorùbá believe that some children, especially girls, had entered into an unpleasant covenant with mischievous spirits before they were born; and prominent in their agreement is the vow to die (that is to return to their 'companions') at a covenanted time – possibly as soon as they get to the world, or when they are about to be married or when they have got two children, or as soon as they have a male child. Such children are known as elérèé or elégbé.

> Whenever anyone believed to be of this company is born, the parents take every care to prevent his returning . . . the oracle usually prescribes a sacrifice whereby a substitute may be offered as a satisfaction for a breach of the covenant, and that is believed to have the effect of preventing the person from being carried away by his 'companions'.[17]

The sacrifice offered in this connection is substitutionary. What is offered is usually in conformity with the wishes of the invisible companions. Sometimes, the companions require a she-goat which is taken into the forest and tied on to a tree from where they (the companions) will come to take it away. Sometimes, in addition to the animal, some beads or wearing apparel of the girl are sent along with the sacrificial animal. The ceremony of 'separation' is carried out in the bush or an appointed place and it usually involves the invocation of orò (the bull-roarer) which is dreaded by these spirits – thus it scares them and enhances a permanent separation of the 'affected' girl from her 'companions'. This type of sacrifice is aptly called 'Ayèpínùn' (that which alters the agreement). The victim dies instead of the girl who should have died in consequence of the 'covenant'. The victim, so to speak, redeems the girl; this is why the sacrifice is also known as 'Ẹbọ Ìràpadà' (the sacrifice offered to 'buy back' or to redeem).

Ẹbọ Ìpilẹ̀ (foundation sacrifice)

We cannot complete this survey of the different types of sacrifice without discussing the many purposes served by the foundation sacrifice. In some respect, it is preventive; in another, it is propitiatory, and yet in another, it is thanksgiving. Hence it is difficult to classify it under one of the categories earlier discussed.

If, for example, a Yorùbá man wants to build a house, he normally finds out by means of oracle if the proposed site is safe for human habitation. If there is any bad spirit dwelling on the spot, it is propitiated by means of sacrifice. At the same time, once the anger of the spirit has been assuaged, it is expected that there will be no further cause for anxiety. In other words, future calamity is prevented in consequence of the propitiatory sacrifice offered. But when the building has been completed, there is also the so-called 'house-warming' ceremony when friends, families and admirers come to rejoice with the owner of the house. This is an occasion for joy and thanksgiving.

Furthermore, foundation sacrifice is based upon the idea that all new enterprises undertaken by a man – setting out on a journey, beginning a new career, taking a wife, laying the foundation of a house, building a new bridge, or cultivating a virgin land – are to be committed to the care of the Supreme Being or other spiritual beings, if such enterprises are to be successful because (to use the language of the Psalmist), 'The earth is the Lord's, and the fulness thereof' (Psalm 24:1).

But, besides committing all to the care of the Supreme Being in order that such enterprises may be blessed, there is also the idea of propitiating the spirits associated with these new places. This is aptly put by James when he said,

> When fresh ground is broken, a new house is erected, trees are cut down or the products of the soil gathered, a fresh outpouring of vital energy liberated through a sacrificial offering is required as a protection against the spiritual beings associated with the place or object that is disturbed.[18]

NOTES

1. Orò and Àríbèjí are secret cults employed by the Yorùbà to purify the society. While the former is known to every Yorùbà community, the latter (believed to be more powerful than the former) is restricted to Okitipupa Division where it is mainly used by the Ìlàjè, and those who are closely related to them, to purify the community and to mark important festivals – e.g. the New Yam festival known as Èje.
2. This song is in Ìlàjè dialect of the Yorùbà language.

3. These two songs are also in the Ìlàjẹ dialect of the Yorùbà language.
4. *Orò-Ọlọ́fin* is the festival in honour of Ọlọ́fin. Tradition says that Ọlọ́fin was the progenitor of the Ile-Oluji people and that he came from Ile-Ifẹ, the traditional home of the Yorùbà, to settle in Ile-Oluji.
5. This is not a farm in the true sense of the word, but a sacred plot having three big heaps in which special yam has been planted.
6. This is the most popular annual festival in Òsí-Ekiti. The divinity is notable for providing children for the barren. In consequence of this, many people from different walks of life converge in Òsí annually to ask for Olua's blessings and to fulfil promises made the previous year.
7. Ìdòwú, *Olódùmarè*, p. 123.
8. These songs are recorded in the Ìjẹbú dialect of the Yorùbà language.
9. For details, see E. I. Alagoa, *African Notes*, v, 1, 1968, pp. 18ff.
10. For further details, see ch. 9 (pp. 179–80).
11. J. K. Parratt, 'Religious change in Yoruba Society', *Journal of Religion in Africa*, vol. II, 1969, p. 118.
12. Ìdòwú, *Olódùmarè*, p. 148.
13. D. Westermann, *Africa and Christianity*, O.U.P., London, 1937, p. 96.
14. *Ibid.*, p. 97.
15. See ch. 5.
16. See ch. 2 for the role of Esu in Yorùbà belief.
17. Ìdòwú, *Olódùmarè*, p. 123.
18. E. O. James, *The Beginnings of Religion*, London, n.d. p. 97.

Chapter Nine

ELEMENTS OF
SACRIFICIAL RITES

Victims and materials of sacrifice

Before a man comes forward for the rite of sacrifice, he must make sure that he has procured the required materials and victims of sacrifice as dictated either by an oracle or by the prevailing circumstances of convention. Where, for example, a sacrifice is to be offered to a well-known divinity, convention rather than an oracle dictates what things are to be offered. This is because such periodic sacrifice has come to assume a fixed form in consequence of regular and constant observance. If an oracle is consulted on such occasions, this is merely to find out if other forms of offering, in addition to the conventional ones, are required for the whole worship to be fully acceptable. But where the offerings are to be made to the ancestral and other spirits, or where sacrifice is demanded by circumstances, what to offer will depend solely on the direction of the oracle. If the offering is in fulfilment of a vow, what the supplicant is to provide will depend upon the vow made. And even then the person making the vow must make sure that he vows to bring to the particular divinity what is normally acceptable to him (the divinity), and usually what the offerer himself thinks that he can afford.

Victims and materials of sacrifice vary from one circumstance to another and from one divinity to another. But, on the whole, things offered are those which are used by human beings in their day-to-day life. They range from the smallest living and non-living things to a big domestic animal like a cow. The materials for sacrifice are thus drawn from both the animal world and the plant kingdom. The Yorùbá do not have different names for the sacrifice of animals and the sacrifice of plant or other things. All sacrificial acts, whether they involve the offering of plants or animals, are known in Yorùbá by the single term ẹbọ. A man may be able to offer his dress (aṣọ) as a sacrifice just as he may be asked to offer a goat (ewúrẹ́). Both materials of sacrifice will be referred to as ẹbọ. This is why Mbiti's distinction[1] between *sacrifice* and *offerings*, used by the Hebrews, is not applicable to the Yorùbá. Materials used for sacrifice can be classified as follows:

Food-crops: kola-nut (obì), bitter-kola (orógbó), yams (iṣu), plantains (ògèdè), corn-meal (ẹ̀kọ), maize (àgbàdo), coconuts (àgbọn), sugar-cane (ìrèké).

Birds: hens (obi adìẹ), chickens (òròmadìẹ), cocks (àkùkọ), ducks (pépéyẹ), pigeons (eyẹlé).

Animals: she-goats (ewúrẹ́), he-goats (òbúkọ), sheep (àgùtàn), rams (àgbò), pigs (ẹlẹ́dẹ̀), cows (ẹranlá).

Liquid: cold water (omi tútù), palm-wine (ẹmu), gin (ọtí), palm-oil (epo-pupa).

Others: articles of garments or pieces of cloth, money (including cowries), fish, especially mud-fish (eja àrò).

It is from this great diversity of materials that selection is made for the purposes of sacrifice. From convention and experience the Yorùbá know what the traditional 'tastes' of the divinities are and they make sure that they meet these 'tastes'. They are thus guided in their choices or selection of what to offer. They believe that anything short of the tastes of the divinities will render the sacrifice unacceptable. Traditionally, it is believed that:

(a) Ògún (god of iron) is very fond of dogs, palm-wine, roasted yams, oil, snails, tortoises and, in some cases, rams.

(b) Ọ̀rúnmìlà (god of divination) loves rats and mud-fish.

(c) Ọbàtálá or Òrìṣà-ńlá (the arch-divinity) is fond of snails fried in shea-butter, cooked white maize (ègbo), white kola-nut (obi-ifin), or bitter-kola (orógbó).

(d) Ṣàngó (god of thunder) prefers a ram to any other thing. The bitter-kola (orógbó) is his special nut.

(e) Òṣun (the spirit dwelling in the Ọ̀ṣun river) loves Ẹ̀fọ-Yánrin (a kind of vegetable), goats and fowls.

(f) Èṣù (the 'Messenger') is fond of black fowls, cowries and half-kobo, and palm-oil.

(g) *Ṣọ̀pọ̀nnọ́* (the spirit whose scourge is the smallpox) is fond of cocks, palm-wine, palm-oil, cooked maize and cold corn-meal (*ẹ̀kọ tútù*).

(h) *Òrìṣà-oko* (the divinity controlling planting and harvesting) loves pangolin (*akika*), goats, fish and melon-stew (*ọbẹ̀ ègúnsí*) with pounded yam and wine from guinea-corn (*ọtí ṣẹ̀kẹ̀tẹ́*).

As the Yorùbá offer fixed materials and victims to the divinities so they also bear in mind their taboos. For example, Òrìṣà-ńlá has aversion for palm-wine; his worshippers are, therefore, forbidden to drink it. Èṣù loves palm-oil but detests palm-kernel oil (*àdín*); to bring the latter to him is to incur his displeasure. *Ẹ̀fọ Yánrin* is the favourite food of Ọ̀ṣun while *Ẹ̀fọ́-òdú* is abhorrent to her. Similarly, Ṣọ̀pọ̀nnọ́ (or Ọbalúwaiyé) abhors fried maize but loves palm-oil and cocks.

Worshippers are expected to know the likes and dislikes of their different divinities. For a man to agree to be a devotee of a particular deity means that he must be ready to supply the offerings involved. Hence the Yorùbá saying,

'*Òrìṣà-oko kò ju gbà bọ̀rọ̀, ẹni tí yóò si gbá Ṣàngó ko tójú ogun géndé*'.

This means 'Òrìṣà-oko is not a deity to be accepted with levity, and whosoever accepts Ṣàngó as his deity must have at least twenty stalwarts as his supporters.' This statement implies that the acceptance and worship of any deity demands some obligation and effort on the part of the worshippers. For example, during the annual festival of Òrìṣà-oko, there is a good deal of eating and drinking and specific items of food and drink offered first to the divinity and later shared by the devotees, should be provided. For any of the necessary items to be wanting will be tantamount to offering inadequate worship. In the case of Ṣàngó, apart from providing the necessary victims and materials of sacrifice, there is the absolute need for strong men to be in attendance and help to hold down the *Ẹlégùn* (the medium) when he is possessed and in a state of ecstasy, as he may be very violent.

It must be emphasised that a man who is to make an offering must obtain all the necessary victims and equipment for the purpose. If an alternative choice is to be made, the oracle will have to be consulted to ascertain whether or not the alternative is acceptable. The prescribed materials or victims must be provided because each of them is symbolical. A man does not offer sacrifice perfunctorily; every aspect of the ceremony is, to the offerer, full of meaning.

Convention dictates what to offer not only at the worship of particular divinities, but also on some other festival occasions like the *Agẹmọ*, the *Obìnrin Òjòwú, Egúngún, Èje, Ọ̀ṣun*, to mention but a few. For example, wherever Egúngún is worshipped, one expects to find *ọ̀lẹ̀lẹ̀* and *àkàrà* (items of food prepared from beans). Other items may be added, but these two items are *sine qua non*. At the annual Obìnrin Òjòwú Festival in Ìjẹ̀bú, a large number of dogs is usually slaughtered at the Òjòwú shrine. Dogs which are not 'protected', that is, those that do not have the palm-frond (*màrìwò*) tied round their necks, are killed indiscriminately. It is an indication that the goddess has a partiality for dogs. The *Èje* Festival, which is observed by the Ìlàjẹ in honour of the sea-god (Malòkun) is not celebrated unless there are new yams (*ẹgbodò*), turtle (*àlùkélùké*), alligator (*ẹlégungùn*) or white ram (*àgbò funfun*). There are alternatives in this last example because the emphasis is on eating the new yams with delicious dishes prepared with any of the animals or reptiles for human consumption. Furthermore, the *Agẹmọ* Festival in Ìjẹ̀bú will not be considered complete unless a dwarf cow (*eranlá*) is supplied by the Awùjalẹ̀ to the Pósà of Imọ̀sàn who is the priest. Similarly, *Orò Ọlófin* in Ìláwẹ̀ has no meaning until the 'special' gift tied in the *omù* leaves (a kind of fern) together with the sacrificial *ẹranlá* (cow) is taken by chief Èjìgbò, representing the Ọba and the townspeople, to Ọba-Nipa, the chief priest of Obàlùfòn. We cannot but add that the annual *Òkè* worship (the worship of the hill spirit) in Ìkọ̀lé does not take place until the special *Esuru Olókè*[2] is provided. This, for example, is the only place where I have come across the use of *Èsúrú* (Dioscurea dumetorum) as the chief sacrificial material.

Symbolic meanings of materials and victims of sacrifice

When discussing the materials and victims of sacrifice, we must point out that many, if not all, of these materials and victims have symbolic meanings. *Ìgbín* (snail) which is also called *èrò* (that which softens or soothes) is linked with gentleness, calmness and peace. It is offered on those occasions when the emphasis is on peace. Since Ògún is believed to be fiery, things offered to calm his anger include snail (*ìgbín*) and palm-oil (*epo*). Before a child is circumcised, for example, the body fluid of the snail is sprinkled on him especially on the part to be cut; after the circumcision, the knife that has been used is put in a plate in which there is plenty of palm-oil. Furthermore, the slow, cautious and steady movement of snails which enables them to avoid readily getting into trouble, fascinates man. And so, when *ìgbín* is offered, the supplicant is praying that his life may be smooth and free of all types of danger.

FOWL (ADÌẸ)

As domestic pets, hens and cocks are easily available for sacrifice. People use fowls very regularly as victims of sacrifice not only because they are easily available but also because certain parts of these creatures have distinct meanings for those who offer them. For example, the chest-feathers of a hen are believed to give protection when ceremonially used. There is the common saying which illustrates this: '*Bí adìẹ bá sọkún ìyẹ́, ìhùrìhù a bò ó; àyà ni adìẹ fi ḿbo ọmọ*' (If a hen cries for feathers [that is, lacks feathers], the young feathers will cover it up; a hen protects its young ones with its chest [that is, with its feathers]).

This statement suggests that even though the hen may be lacking something, it always has a device for making good its deficiency. In other words its blemishes and secrets are always hidden under the feathers. This is why it is believed that if a fowl is immolated and the blood together with the chest-feathers is applied to the symbol of the object of worship, the worshipper is praying that his own hardship will not be so great as to be known to all around.

PIGEON (ẸYẸLÉ)

The pigeon is another important domestic pet used for sacrifice, especially the sacrifice that emphasises good luck and longevity. The bird is noted for its serenity in flight, its neatness of appearance and its smartness in movement. Over and above it all, the Yorùbá attach a sort of sacredness to this bird. Hence they sing:

Yíyẹ ní ìyẹ ẹiyẹlé,	The pigoen will always be prosperous,
Dídè ni ídẹ àdàbà lọ́rùn;	The dove will always find peace;
A yẹ mí o,	May I be prosperous,
A sàn mí o	May everything be well with me.

On any occasion when offerings are made to *Orí* (one's counterpart or double), more often than not, a pigeon is offered. Likewise, before an Egúngún goes out from the grove to perform, he immolates a pigeon and allows the blood to drip on his feet as he wishes himself well and prays that he may be endowed with the ability characteristic of the pigeon (*eyelé*) which enables it to fly over dangers.

FISH (ẸJA)

Certain species of fish are also ascribed some symbolic features. Common among these are the mud-fish (*eja àrò*) and another kind of fish *Òkódó*. *Àrò* is a fish believed to symbolise calm and peace. It is treated almost in the same way as the snail (*ìgbín*) already described above, and it is believed that it can soften pain and assuage trouble. Ọ̀rúnmìlà, who is believed to be capable of changing bad fortunes into prosperity, loves the mud-fish.

Òkódó, another kind of fish which is quite resilient, is commonly used, especially by the Ìlàjẹ people (who are mainly fishermen and who know the characteristics and qualities of fishes), as an offering to *Orí* (one's counterpart) as it is portrayed in the following song:

Orí lo ńṣèwà,	It is the head that brings fortune,
Orí ló ńṣèwà fun òkódó,	It is the head that brings fortune to the Òkódó fish,
Orí ló ńṣèwà.	It is the head that brings fortune.

When the fish is used as an offering, the supplicant is requesting for good fortune in all his ways.

SHEEP (ÀGÙTÀN)

This animal is noted for its meek nature; thus when the occasion arises that a substitute sacrifice is prescribed by the oracle, the usual victim is the sheep. It is immolated in the place of man.

COW (ẸRANLÁ)

This is regarded as the highest domestic animal among the Yorùbá. When there is a great national disaster, or when a community is badly oppressed, the usual victim is the cow. From investigation, I discover that wherever cows are offered today, they are generally a substitute for human sacrifice; before the advent of the British and the abolition of human sacrifice, human beings were victims on great occasions.

HUMAN VICTIM (OLÚWỌ̀ OR OLÚỌ̀)

As we pointed out above, a human being was the highest and costliest victim of sacrifice before the nineteenth century. Human beings were offered not because of a sadistic desire for wanton destruction of life or a lack of respect for human life, but mainly because the people's philosophy of life with regard to sacrifice held that it was better to sacrifice one life for the good of the community than for all to perish. A human victim was seen as an ambassador: believed to be 'going to represent the people before, and carry their petitions to, the higher power'.[3]

Human sacrifice was resorted to by the community mostly in time of national crisis and disaster, and such sacrifice was meant to propitiate certain divinities and purify the community. It was considered necessary that the highest and the best must be offered to a divinity that gave protection to a whole community or to assuage the anger of one who has brought calamity upon the community. We shall discuss this further when we consider *treatment of victims* below.

Kola-nut (*Obì*) figures prominently in almost every sacrifice, and it is also a means of divination as we have earlier pointed out. Kola-nuts used for sacrifice are those with four lobes (aláwẹ́ mẹ́rin).

It is a general practice among the Yorùbá to offer kola-nuts to visitors. The offering of kola-nut is a sign of love and understanding. This is aptly put by Parrinder when he said, 'Kola-nuts symbolize friendship, and when split and partaken of by others constitute a pact of loyalty and communion.'[4]

The following sayings among the Yorùbá illustrate further the significance attached to kola-nuts:

(a) *Obì ni won ńpa sí òràn ọlọ́ràn* – It is kola-nut that is killed [split] when someone commits an offence. In a sense, kola-nut signifies a means of bringing about a reconciliation and it also serves as a means of substitution.

(b) *Obì ní íbi ikú, obì ní íbi àrùn* – It is the kola-nut that is used to avert death, it is kola-nut that is used to avert diseases. This statement affirms the people's belief, namely that when a kola-nut is offered to a divinity it (*obì*) is efficacious in warding off death and diseases. Hence it is freely used as a material of sacrifice.

(c) *Ẹbọra kì íkọ ẹ̀bẹ̀ fun obì* – The divinities never turn down an appeal made with the kola-nut. This confirms that the kola-nut is an important element in making an appeal to the divinities.

Palm-oil (*Epo*) is another sacrificial material which symbolises almost the same thing as the snail. It tones down or softens that which would have been otherwise wild and uncontrolable. The Yorùbá have the common saying: *'Epo ní ìròjú ọbẹ̀'* ('Oil is the element that calms the stew'). This statement denotes that the palm-oil acts an agent which calms the wrath of an angry divinity. From observation, we see that oil is used principally at the offerings made to those divinities which are characterised by violence and wild anger, for example, Ògún, Ṣàngó or Ṣọ̀pọ̀nnọ́. Likewise, oil is used in those offerings that are intended for the witches who are also believed to be fiery and bloodthirsty.

When a man uses incantations of some worth, he pours a libation of oil on the ground to calm the spirits of the earth (*imọlẹ̀*). These are believed to be very powerful, and when there is a need to invoke them, oil is generally poured to calm them lest they do harm to man.

NATIVE CHALK (ẸFUN)

Efun is provided and is sometimes used to make some ritual marks on the ground or on the sacred objects or as an important item in the materials offered. It is used especially in the worship of *Ọlọ́sà* or *Olókun* when offerings are made to the spirits of the lagoon and the sea respectively. *Efun* also figures prominently in the worship of *Ọbàtálá* and *Ayélálá*.

ALLIGATOR PEPPER (ATAARE)

Ataare figures prominently in some sacrificial rites. It sometimes accompanies kola-nuts and is eaten with them. In addition, it is believed to facilitate the efficacy of a prayer or a curse. The officiating priest chews the pepper as he prays for a supplicant or curses an offender.

PALM-FRONDS (MÀRÌWÒ)

By convention or tradition the Yorùbá have come to attach sacredness to the young palm-leaves or the frond of the palm-tree. As was noticed in Chapter 5, palm-fronds are used to mark and consecrate the entrances to shrines. Ògún, in particular, is fond of the palm-fronds – *màrìwò* is said to be the 'garment' for Ògún. Wherever Ògún is worshipped, therefore, *màrìwò* must be freely used.

Before the rite of sacrifice can take place, therefore, all the necessary victims and materials for the purpose – be they animals, birds, plants, leaves, articles of dress and many more must be provided by

the supplicant. And on the appointed day and time, these things must
be brought to the officiating priests who now give necessary directives
and lead the worship.

Preparation

Sacrifice requires preparation. Great festival occasions, for example,
the annual festival in respect of a divinity, require a great deal of
preparation by the officiating priests. They have to prepare themselves in order to be worthy and acceptable before the divinities. They
have to observe certain taboos and codes of conduct, avoiding, among
other things, coition, cursing and fighting and they abstain from
taking certain types of food. As an illustration, we cite what the chief
priest of Agẹmọ used to do before the day of sacrifice. In those days
when a human victim was offered, the chief priest and the person
designated to do the immolation (*Ojùwá*) used to go into the special
grove (*àgbàlá*) four days before the actual day of festival. During that
period, they would devote themselves to ritual discipline and prayer.
That practice has not changed much today – the chief priest still goes
into the grove to pray for a whole day before the celebration starts.
Similarly, the Egúngún devotees devote a whole day – the day preceding the Egúngún Festival day – to prayer in the grove. This is the day
known as *Ọjọ Ìkúnlẹ̀*, that is, the day of kneeling down – a day of
intercession.

We were informed by the Ọlọ́ya of Abẹ́òkúta (Madam Mowéádé)
that she usually stays indoors eight days before the Ọya Festival day,
praying that the annual feast and sacrifice may be acceptable and
auspicious.

This practice stems from the belief that anyone who is to officiate on
festival occasions must be ritually clean, faithful and sincere and must
bear no malice against anybody. This calls to mind an experience
which I had in Òwu-Ìjẹbú in 1968, when I visited the Olówu of Òwu.
The people in the town came to their Ọba to discuss the possibility of
reviving the worship of Ọbàlùfọ̀n. I gathered later on that the worship
was suspended because it was difficult to get a man of high probity and
integrity to preside at the shrine of Ọbàlùfọ̀n. The Ọba explained to
the people the high standard required of a presiding priest, and added
'If a man has evil mind and still has the audacity of coming to officiate
at the shrine of Ọbàlùfọ̀n, such a man will not last the year'. This

suggests that a high moral standard is required not only of the officiating priests but also of the devotees.

Having discussed the necessary materials for sacrifice and the position of the priests who should preside and the devotees in general, we may now consider very briefly the normal procedure of the sacrificial rite.

Invocation

Here the priest makes an earnest appeal to the divinity, inviting him to be present and to listen to the call of his children. In doing this, the priest may sound a gong or shake a rattle; he will then pour a libation of water or gin or palm-wine, after which he will pay due regard or homage to his predecessors in office and to those spirits who can bless the worship. This is called '*Ìjubà*' (that is, 'paying homage'). Let us cite an example of a general homage:

The Priest:	*Olójó òní, mo júbà*	The Owner of this day, I pay my homage to you,
People:	*Ìbà á se*	May the homage be accepted
Priest:	*Ìlà oòrùn mo júbà*	The East, I pay my homage
People:	*Ìbà á se*	May the homage be accepted
Priest:	*Ìwò oòrùn, mo júbà*	The West, I pay my homage
People:	*Ìbà á se*	May the homage be accepted
Priest:	*Àríwá, mo júbà,*	The North, I pay my homage
People:	*Ìbà á se*	May the homage be accepted
Priest:	*Gúúsù, mo júbá*	The South, I pay my homage;
People:	*Ìbà á se*	May the homage be accepted
Priest:	*Àkódá, mo júbà,*	The first to be created, I pay my homage to you;
People:	*Ìbà á se*	May the homage be accepted
Priest:	*Asèdá, mo júbà*	The Creator of men, I pay my homage to you;
People:	*Ìbà á se*	May the homage be accepted
Priest:	*Ilè, mo júbà*	The Earth, I pay my homage;
People:	*Ìbà á se*	May the homage be accepted
Priest:	*Èsù Òdàrà, mo júbà*	Esu, the trickster god, I pay my homage;
People:	*Ìbà á se*	May the homage be accepted

Priest:	*X, Y, Z mo júbà*	X, Y, Z (names of ancestors and predecessors), my homage;
People:	*Ìbà á ṣẹ*	May the homage be accepted
Priest:	*Bí ekòló bá júbà ilẹ̀, ilẹ̀ á lanu;*	If the earth-worm pays homage to the earth, the earth will give it access;
	Ọmọdé kì íjúbà kí ìbà pà á	a little child never pays homage and be found destroyed in consequence of it.

In this general homage, the priest pays attention to the Creator, the Controller of the daily happenings, the spirits and divinities in all the four corners of the world and the ancestors; and he hopes or rather believes that once he does this, the sacrifice over which he is presiding will be accepted.

After this general homage, the priest invokes the particular spirit or divinity at whose shrine the offering is made.[5]

It is the people's belief that after the invocation, the divinity is now ready to hear the people's prayers, to receive their gifts and grant their requests.

Presentation

After the invocation, the person who comes to make the offering is asked to stand before the shrine and to state his purpose of bringing the offerings. In other words, the supplicant presents his case before the divinity and prays that his requests may be granted. It is at this stage that he takes in his hands, one after the other, the offerings he has brought – a bottle of gin (if required), kola-nuts and other items. Where an animal is involved, the supplicant holds the rope with which the animal is tethered; he stands before the shrine and enumerates the good things that he desires and prays the divinity to grant his requests. As he prays, all the friends, relatives and the other people invited to the ceremony, say '*Á ṣẹ*' ('May it be so') after each prayer or wish.

The priest now takes over and presents the supplicant and his offerings. He enumerates the items of materials brought by the supplicant. Let us imagine for a moment that the offering is brought by a woman called Málọmọ́ who desires to have a child; the priest will speak in the following manner:

Málọmọ́ ọmọ ré wá síwájúù rẹ;	Málọmọ́ your child comes to you;
Ó ní obìfin,	She has [i.e. offers] white kola-nuts,
Ó nígba omi tútù	She has a calabash of cold water,
Ó ní àgbébọ̀ adìẹ	She has a hen,
Ó ní ìgbín,	She has snails
Ó ní ewúrẹ́	She has a goat,
Ó ní ọ̀pá aṣọ funfun kan	She has one yard of white calico.[6]

After the enumeration of the materials brought by the supplicant, the priest states why she has brought the offerings:

Ẹkún ọmọ ló ńsun,	She is in tears for she has no child,
Àawè àìrí-gbé-jó ló ńgbà	She is fasting for she has no baby to carry on her back;
Òrìṣà, jẹ́kí Málọmọ́ rọ́mọ bí;	Oriṣa, please let Málọmọ́ have a child;
Ọmọ ọkùnrin à-bí-ró	Male children that will stay [live long]
Ọmọ obìnrin à-bí-ró,	Female children that will live long.
Níwòyí àmọ́dún	By this time next year,
Kí Málọmọ́ lè gbọ́mọ pọ̀n	Let Málọmọ́ bear a child on her back
Wá sójúbọ yìí	To come to this shrine rejoicing.

This is followed by the pouring of libation of water on or before the shrine. The priest then breaks one of the kola-nuts and casts it to divine. If the omen is propitious, the result is hailed. One of the four lobes of the kola-nuts will be placed at the shrine while the rest will be shared by those who are present, the priest making sure that he gives one of the lobes to the supplicant who kneels down and with out-stretched hands receives it. As the priest gives this to her he prays saying:

Ọwọ́ò rẹ á gbọ́mọ titun,	You will carry a new baby in your arms,
O kò ní ímú àmúbọ́,	You will not be frustrated or disappointed.

Thus, presentation involves making a statement about the purpose of bringing the offerings, enumerating the materials of sacrifice and praying to the divinity to bless the supplicant.

Immolation

This is the climax of the whole rite of sacrifice. After presentation, the next and most important feature is the handling of the materials and victims of sacrifice by the presiding priest. Immolation is usually done by him or by someone authorised by him. Among the Yorùbá, immolation takes different forms – some more dramatic than others. In some cases, the sacrificial animal is killed by being held on the ground before the shrine while the throat is slashed with a knife. The blood gushing out is either collected in a pot from where it is applied to the symbols of the divinity or it is poured directly on the altar. In some cases, the victim is slain outside the shrine – the earth is dug, and the blood is allowed to flow into it.

Two types of dramatic immolation of a sacrificial animal may be cited here. During the Egúngún Festival in Òkehò near Ọyọ, the Oníjò who is the paramount chief of the community, usually presents a goat to the Alápinni (the chief-priest of Egúngún); the latter, in turn, hands the goat over to the special Egúngún masquerader called Òbẹ́ran (one who slaughters the animal) who carries out the immolation of the animal. In practice the goat is pulled taut by two Egúngún masqueraders with one of them holding down the legs which have been fastened together with a rope, and the other holding a rope which has been tied round the goat's neck. The Obẹ́ran, with a sharpened matchet in hand, stands between these two Egúngún. In one stroke, the goat's head is severed from the body. The blood is allowed to trickle on the images of Alátẹ ọrun and Alápatà (symbols of the most important of the Egúngún). The paramount chief also steps on the blood that has dropped on the ground and dances round to the beating of the bàtá drums.

Another dramatic immolation is that of a dog offered to Ògún (god of iron). For the purpose of easy immolation, the dog is held on a leash or rope tied to a specially prepared cudgel which in turn is tied to the dog's neck. Two people hold the dog, pulling it taut in opposite directions and ensuring that it is laid flat on the ground. The person appointed to carry out the actual immolation holds a very sharp cutlass. He passes over the dog three times, and says, 'Ògún yè'! (Hail Ògún!) and the people respond 'Yè!' each time. After the third time, he raises the cutlass and allows it to descend heavily upon the dog. With this single stroke, the dog is beheaded. If the dog's head is successfully severed from the body in this one stroke, it is a sign that the sacrifice is acceptable to Ògún. And the man who performs the feat then rejoices and sings:

Mo bẹ dé sà sà!   I have cut it through successfully

The people rejoice with him and say:

Wà á tún bẹ́ ẹ nígbà mìíràn   May you be privileged to cut it
                                     next time.

The immolation of birds also takes different forms. Sometimes the bird's throat is slashed through with a knife. Sometimes the bird's head is pressed down between two of the offerer's toes, while he holds its body firmly in his hands; the bird is then jerked up by force and strangled. The hot blood oozing out is poured on the altar or the symbols of the divinity. Another way of immolating a sacrificial bird is by lifting it high and dashing it violently on the ground. Because of these various ways in which fowls are immolated, the Yorùbá have a saying, '*Kò sí ikú tí kò rọ adìẹ lórùn*' ('The fowl has no preference for one form of death or another').

Tradition is clear, however, about the immolation of a pigeon (*eyẹlé*). It is forbidden to kill the pigeon with an ordinary knife. In sacrificing the bird, it is either killed with an improvised knife made from bamboo or the neck of the bird is simply wrung off. At times, a live pigeon is used as a sponge, to which special soap is applied, for washing the head and the whole body. When used in this way, the bird is squeezed and weakened in the process. In some cases, it is expected that the bird must die and be thrown into the river to carry away the supplicant's impurities and misfortunes as the river flows away. And, in some other cases or circumstances, the bird is released alive to fly away, thus carrying with it the supplicant's unhappiness, misfortune, disease or death.

Having discussed the immolation of the lower animals and birds, let us turn our attention to the immolation of human victims that were offered on important sacrificial occasions.

Since human sacrifice has officially become a thing of the past among the Yorùbá, one cannot claim to have first-hand information about how human victims were treated and immolated. The best that one can do in the circumstances is to rely on oral traditions and on what others have written concerning this. According to James Johnson, the human victim is commonly led and paraded through the streets of the town or city of the sovereign who would sacrifice him for the well-being of his government and of every family or individual under it, in order that he may carry off the guilt, misfortune and death of every one without exception. Ashes and chalk would be employed to hide his identity – whilst individuals would often rush out of their houses to lay their hands upon him, that they might thus transfer to him their sin, guilt, trouble and death. . . . The victim was then led into the grove. Here, after he himself has given out or started his last song, which is to be taken up by the large assembly of people, who have been waiting to hear his last words, or his last groan, his head is taken off and his blood offered to the gods. . .[7]

Like James Johnson, P. A. Talbot reports the following:

A person about to act as scape-goat, take upon himself the sins of the people and bring them good fortune, was usually treated with the greatest respect and indulgence by all and given the best of everything. When time came for his death, the Oluwaw, as he was called – who might be either bond or free, rich or poor and was chosen by the priest – was paraded through the streets, when many people took the opportunity of laying their hands on him and transferring their sins to him, he was then led to the grove, and executed – the people waiting outside to hear his last song which was echoed by them. . .[8]

These two accounts deal with human sacrifice among the Yorùbá. Oral traditions among the people also indicate that human victims were sometimes buried alive, or with the head just showing above the ground. Sometimes the victim's limbs were broken and he was left to die from exhaustion before the divinity. The corpse became food for birds and ants. 'The greater the avidity with which carrion birds disposed of the body, the better omen it was believed to be for the cause for which the sacrifice was offered'.[9]

It is noteworthy that when the offerers realised that human victims could and sometimes did curse those who were about to sacrifice them, they used to take precautions to render the victims incapable of reasoning and of cursing. Human victims were gagged before they were killed to prevent them from cursing their murderers. And, if the physical means of preventing this failed, the Yorùbá devised what they called 'Àpagbé' (killing without any repercussion). This is a

Chief Ejigbo of Ilawẹ praying before the symbol of Ọbalufọn. He is touching the symbol of the god with the kolanut offered.

A dog sacrificed to Obinrin Ojowu (a popular divinity at Ijebu-Ode).

Pot of medicine on a tripod. This household medicine is used to ward off, or calm, an attack of Ṣọpọnọ (smallpox).

A household Egúngún called Gbangbalàṣáta at Gbọ̀ngán. Close to the Egúngún is the Ato (the woman who sings the praises of the Egúngún).

means whereby the offerers offered special offerings and prayers at the shrines of the ancestors urging the spirits to undo the curses which possibly might have been pronounced by the victims during the sacrificial rite.

It was also gathered from oral traditions that the priests who presided over the rite involving human sacrifice had a practice of going into penitence after the ceremony. They remained indoors for seven days and refrained from pleasures and social activities, but devoted the quiet time to prayer and meditation urging the divinities and spirits to accept their offerings and overlook their offences.

After immolation, a tense moment has passed. Blood has flowed, and this is a signal that a message has gone from men to the supernatural. The whole atmosphere is then changed. People relax and there is often jubilation.

Treatment of victims or materials of sacrifice

The materials and victims sacrificed are disposed of in different ways. Among the Yorùbá, as among other peoples, blood is regarded as an indispensable constituent of sacrifice. The life of the victim is in the blood; and in consequence of this, the blood that is poured out is always given first to the divinity – that is, poured on or before the symbol of the divinity. In offering the blood, the Yorùbá know and believe that they are offering the life of the animal. And when they give the life of the animal, they want life in exchange. In other words, they want the deity to take the blood or the life of the animal offered in order that they, the supplicants, may live long and enjoy prosperity. This is compatible with the statement of E. O. James that 'the outpouring of the vital fluid in actuality or by substitute, is the sacred act whereby life is given to promote and preserve life, and to establish thereby a bond of union with the supernatural order'.[10]

In some cases, sacrificial blood is used to purify or strengthen a supplicant. For example, when a child is ill, there is a practice of killing a fowl and rubbing some of the blood on the forehead of the sick child. The Ìlàjẹ of Òkìtìpupa Division call this *kíkún ọmọ* (building up the child). This suggests that the child's life is built up by giving blood to the spirits that may have been tormenting the child and causing him to become emaciated. The mark of the blood signifies that the offering is made on behalf of the child who is now to be treated with some deference by the spirits.

Furthermore, when offerings are made to witches, the blood of such sacrificial victims constitutes the essence of what is offered. It is poured into a potsherd (*agbada*) together with palm-oil; the head of the animal, the lower limbs, the entrails and other prescribed materials of sacrifice may also go into the agbada; but the blood is regarded as vital by these human vampires known as witches.

Blood, the most important element in sacrifice, is treated in different ways. It is poured on the symbols of the divinities, or collected in a potsherd and applied to the symbols; sometimes feathers of a sacrificial bird are mixed with the blood and applied to these symbols; at times, the blood so collected is carried to chosen spot to feed the evil spirits. In some cases, however, the earth is dug and the blood is allowed to flow into it and then covered up. When the offering is made to an ancestral spirit, the blood is poured on the grave or before the shrine of the ancestor, and some quantity of blood is smeared on the supplicant's right big toe (if a paternal ancestor) and on the left toe (if a maternal ancestor).

The divinities and the spirits, therefore, drink blood and this is their main share of the sacrificial victims. And when they take blood, they are believed to have taken the whole victim because when blood is drained from a living creature it dies. Blood, it is believed, invokes the pleasure and the blessing of the divinities and the spirits and blots out sins and averts illness and death.

Besides the blood of the sacrificial victim, other parts of the victim are treated in special ways. The internal organs – the liver, the kidney, the lungs, the heart and the intestines – are also regarded as vital portions which, on many occasions, are offered to the divinities. Where sacrifice involves the preparation of the flesh and entrails for food, little bits of the parts enumerated above are usually offered to the divinities while special people, for example, the priests and the elders, have the rest of these internal organs.

The head of the sacrificial animal is also regarded as very important. As we have earlier pointed out, the head goes with the blood in sacrifice of propitiation and of substitution. The blood (which is life) of the animal and its head (which is the symbol of the essence of being) are given in exchange for man's life and head. The offerer is saying in effect, '*Orí ẹran ni ẹ gbà, ẹ máṣe gba orí mi*' ('Take the animal's head and leave mine alone'). Because of this, whenever oracles are consulted and it is revealed that an animal be given to some malignant spirit who intends to take away a person's life, the head of the sacrificial animal must be given to such a spirit. It is a common sight to find at road junctions in villages and towns in Nigeria such heads of sacrificed animals being wrapped in white calico, placed in a potsherd with plenty of oil.

Where human sacrifice was involved, the whole victim was offered to the divinity. There was no cannibalism among the Yorùbá, and thus no indication of the people's sharing of the human victims. Such victims were left to rot away before the symbols of the divinities. In fact, even in those places where cows have been substituted for human beings, sacrificial cows have been left to rot away before the divinities. This is still the practice in Ìlawè-Èkìtì during the Orò-Ọlọ́fin festival when the annual cow is offered. According to the present high priest in Ìlawè, 'if any priest is tempted to cut part of the sacrificial cow for food, such a priest will swell and die within the year'.

At Imọsan near Ìjẹbú-Òde, human victims offered at the shrine of Agẹmọ were allowed to rot away. Later, a change was made whereby a human being and a cow were offered in alternate years. The year in which a human victim was offered was called '*Akọ ọdún*' (male year), and the year in which a cow was offered, *abo ọdun* (female year). When finally human sacrifice was abolished, the people devised the means of offering a bull to mark *akọ ọdún* and a cow to mark *abo ọdún*. What is remarkable here is that, unlike the people of Ìlawè who give all the sacrificed cow to Ọbàlùfọ̀n, the Ìjẹbú devotees of Agẹmọ offer only the blood of the animal to Agẹmọ while the flesh is shared among the priests from the various villages and towns. The Awùjalẹ̀ who is the paramount chief and who supplies the sacrificial cow is given the right leg of the animal.

The Edì Festival in Ilé-Ifẹ̀ furnishes a fascinating example of the treatment of human victims. Before the abolition of human sacrifice, it used to be the practice that a human scapegoat was employed to bear away the sins, impurities, diseases and death from the community. This human scapegoat was known as *Tele*.

The Edì purificatory rite lasts seven days. On the final day, Tele, dressed partly in white gown and partly in grass, would carry away a 'special burden' ritually tied. As soon as Tele appeared in the public, the people who have been waiting outside their houses and lining the route to be taken by Tele, would shout 'Èééòò!' three times. At the third time, they would circle their hands over their heads saying:

Take disease away!
Take misfortune away!
Take pestilence away!
Take death away!

In this act, the people believed that their sins, misfortunes and all calamities had been transferred to and were ceremonially borne away by Tele into the grove. After this dramatic transference of sins, the people hastened back into their houses never to come out till the following day. The human scapegoat was led into the grove where he would be offered up.

This annual rite with its ceremony still continues in Ifẹ. The only modification is that Tele himself does not die but he only bears the 'burden' and leads away a substitute-goat into the grove. But my information has it that there is still a dreadful trick in connection with this ceremony: when Tele has led the goat into the grove and has offered it up, it is his practice to bring back the right leg of the sacrificed goat, and whoever is the first to meet Tele is bound to receive the 'gift' of the leg. The receiver of such a gift, it is alleged, will inescapably die within the year. If Tele fails to meet anybody before daybreak, then he himself will die the death. This means that a human victim is still somehow offered.

Before concluding our discussion of human victims, let us see the voluntary human sacrifice of Elégurù in Ìjèbú-Òde. Tradition has it that in the days gone by, ọsà (the lagoon) was threatening Ìjẹú-Òde. The people in their anxiety consulted the oracle to ascertain what could be done to control the threat. The babaláwo (diviner-priest) on that memorable occasion was Elégurù (alias 'Ẹní ṣe é mọ'). The oracle revealed that a human victim was required as sacrifice. And who was to be the victim? Surprisingly enough, Elégurù said that he was to be both the priest to offer the sacrifice as well as the victim.

At the appointed place and time, Elégurù came. He spread a kind of mat called 'Ẹni àgbá ẹfun' on the 'lagoon'. On the mat he placed all his Ifa paraphernalia; and he himself sat on the mat which started moving away as he was uttering some incantations. As the mat was moving away from the town, so also was the water with it. Finally, Elégurù got to Lúgbókere near the present town of Ejìnrìn where he sank into the lagoon. The Ìjèbú tradition adds that, in consequence of the good deed done by Elégurù, his descendants were, for many years, exempted from paying tax. In this example, we see that a human being played the role of a priest and a sacrificial victim in order to save his people from the menace of the lagoon.

In our discussion of the disposal of materials and victims of sacrifice, it should be pointed out that burning sacrificial victims, if it is ever done, is a rare practice. Hence, it is difficult to agree with scholars who gave prominence to this in their writing. Leo Frobenius, for example, said, 'It is a peculiar and very remarkable thing that the Yorùbás always offer up their beasts as burnt-sacrifices to the Òrìṣà . . .' Later on, he added that it was the hide and a portion of the flesh that were burnt. 'The rest', according to him, 'was prepared as food, a portion of which was given to the Òrìṣà with the sentence "Here is thy Asun" [i.e. votive ashes]. 'The celebrants', he concluded, 'devour the rest among themselves.'[11] Surely there is some confusion here. That which is burnt is supposed to be totally destroyed in flames to the deity. But Frobenius' explanation indicates that that which is burnt is called *Asun* and is presented to the 'Orisha'. What is more, the celebrants share the rest of the meat. This cannot be called a burnt-offering at all – at least not in the sense in which this was practised among the Hebrews.

There is no doubt about it that there is the practice of roasting some choice portions of a sacrificial animal (called *Ẹsun*) which portions are shared between the divinity and the devotees. But this is not reduced to ashes. It is, therefore, an exaggeration on the part of Frobenius when he said, 'The Yorubas always offer up their beasts as burnt-sacrifices.'

Frobenius was not the only one who stressed burnt-offerings among the Yorùbá. Farrow also said, 'In the *Ìràpadà* (that is Redemption offering) the whole victim is burnt with fire, and when consumed, the smouldering ashes are quenched with water and then taken out and deposited on a public road . . .'[12] Lucas, who invariably agrees with Farrow, said, 'The sacrifice (i.e. Redemption) will be burnt with fire and the ashes thrown outside the house'.[13] While Professor Ìdòwú does not dwell much on this aspect of the disposal of sacrificial victim, he mentions it in passing when he says, 'As this sacrifice' (he was discussing Propitiation) 'is never shared with the Òrìṣà, it may be buried, burnt, or treated with oil and exposed.'[14]

It should be emphasised here that in all my investigations among the Yorùbá, nobody confirmed (even when I asked questions specifically about it) that victims of sacrifice are ever burnt to ashes and treated in the way these scholars have claimed. Possibly these writers were influenced by the Hebrew approach to sacrifice.

In concluding this chapter, it should be emphasised that the rite of sacrifice takes specific forms. Offerings are also made in prescribed forms: there is the invocation of the divinity, and the presentation of the materials of sacrifice to the divinity; at the appropriate places and manner, prayers are said. The materials and victims are disposed of in diverse manners depending upon the purposes and circumstances. On happy occasions, people bring thanksgiving or votive offerings, and the atmosphere is always a pleasant one. People eat and drink before their divinities in the midst of music and dancing. But, on unpleasant occasions, for example when there is pestilence or threat of death, the atmosphere is usually tense and solemn, the offerings are made in a haste and in a heavy and pensive mood. The sacrifice offered to the divinity or spirit is total – there is no sharing.

NOTES

1. Mbiti. *African Religions and Philosophy*, p. 59.
2. *Èsúrú-Olókè* – this is the special offering of *ésúrú* (*dioscurea dume torum*) to the Olókè (the spirit believed to dwell in the hill at Ikole-Ekiti).
3. Ìdòwú, *Olódùmarè*, p. 119.
4. Parrinder, *West African Religion*, p. 81.
5. See ch. 5, pp. 100–103, for examples of invocation.
6. Offerings to be offered are dictated by circumstances and the tastes of the divinity concerned. The offering in this case is to Ọbàtálá – the giver of children to the barren.
7. James Johnson, *Yoruba Heathenism*, Exeter, 1899, p. 43.
8. Talbot, *Peoples of Southern Nigeria*, 1969 edition, vol. III, p. 858.
9. Ìdòwú, *Olódùmarè*, p. 119.
10. James, *The Origins of Sacrifice*, p. 33.
11. Leo Frobenius, *The Voice of Africa*, London, 1913, vol. I, p. 191.
12. Farrow, *Faith, Fancies and Fetich*, p. 97.
13. Lucas, *The Religion of the Yorubas*, p. 210.
14. Ìdòwú, *Olódùmarè*, p. 123.

Chapter Ten

FACTORS MILITATING AGAINST TRADITIONAL RITES

Three main factors, it would appear, have influence, in one form or another, on Yorùbá Traditional Religion. These are: (a) the comparatively new religions (Islam and Christianity); (b) Western education and (c) Improved medical facilities.

Islam

It is not easy to date with accuracy when the Islamic religion was introduced into Yorubaland; but according to Gbádébọ̀ Gbàdàmọ́ṣí in one of the recent researches carried out on this subject,[1] 'The entry (of Islam) was unannounced and unplanned', and might have dated back to the seventeenth century because, according to Gbàdàmọ́ṣí, the northern neighbours of the Yorùbá who live, for example, in Kánò and other parts of Hausaland in Northern Nigeria had received Islam as early as the fourteenth century, and the Nupe, the immediate northern neighbours of the Yorùbá were Islamised in the eighteenth century. As many Yorùbá were (and still are) traders, they might have come in contact with these northern Muslim brethren from about the seventeenth century or even earlier. Gbàdàmọ́ṣí claimed that before the eighteenth century, Islam was established in Ketu, a Yorùbá town, and that between 1775 and 1780, during the reign of Ọba Àdèlé I, there were Muslims in Lagos, another Yorùbá town. In fact, the Ọba was expelled from the Lagos throne because of the latitude he gave to the Muslims in his court and for the consequent neglect of traditional worship.[2] 'When he came back to Lagos in 1832, Islam was again firmly planted in his court in Lagos, and Muslims in and outside the court enjoyed his patronage.'[3]

Òwu, before its destruction in 1825, contained some Muslims; and

Badagry evidently had a Muslim community whose colourful celebration of the *Idul Fitr* was watched by Lander on 27 March, 1830. Before 1836, Ìbàdàn was Islamised; and by 1879, Islam had reached Ìjèbú-Òde either by way of Ìlọrin (introduced by Àlí Túbọgun's slave) or through Èpé by the Muslim adherents from Lagos who had already been Islamised as early as 1851.[4]

Our main concern is not with the spread of Islam in Yorubaland; nevertheless, a brief reference will give us an idea of when the influence started being felt. Although we have not discussed the arrival of Islam in all the different parts of the land, yet from our brief survey we know that before 1840 Muslim communities had been established in many places in Yorubaland. The existence in the society of these Muslim communities was bound to create some tension because Islam claimed to be a monotheistic religion and therefore looked down upon Yorùbá Traditional Religion which was described as 'idolatrous'.

The Muslims, in the course of time, made some converts. The adherents of the new faith had to adopt certain ways of life quite different from the previous one and they condemned the traditional religious practices.

The teachers who were really knowledgeable in Arabic and Islam were few, and were held in high regard for their learning, piety and ability to make charms. They went about campaigning against the traditional religion and practices. To start with, they were afraid to pray openly or to say the call to prayer loudly or to think of building a mosque. Despite opposition from the Traditional Religionists, the number of Muslims increased by leaps and bounds. As this happened, opposition to the new religion stiffened, especially when influential Traditional Religionists declared for the new faith. For example, when Balógun Kúkù of Ìjèbú-Òde declared for Islam in 1902, about three hundred other people did likewise. These people were 'converted' to Islam not necessarily out of their own conviction, but from the respect they had for Balógun Kúkù. As time went on, more and more of those converted acquired deeper knowledge and understanding of the new faith and so became Muslim teachers. One of such teachers or mallams who were also powerful preachers was 'Kòkéwúkòbèrè', who not only denounced traditional religion and the Òsùgbó cult in both Abéòkúta and Ìjèbú-Òde, but also appealed to all Traditional Religionists to convert to Islam which he described as the way of salvation. In consequence of his preaching, it is reported that several people came to him for the ritual ablution of conversion.[5]

Kòkéwúkòbèrè's success made the adherents of the traditional religion uncomfortable. It is reported that in Ado-Ekiti, he was assailed by members of the Egúngún cult who 'took delight in harassing the Muslims – flogging them, stripping them of their turbans and sometimes of their dresses'.[6] Opposition arose in consequence of differences in values. The Yorùbá held, and may still hold, strong beliefs in certain divinities and spirits which require certain traditional ritual practices that must not be disregarded. Islam, on the other hand, upholds its teaching of monotheism and detests forms of traditional religious practices, including sacrifice. The main arguments of the Muslims is that the one God, Allah, requires praise to be given to Him; and there is no need for any sacrifice to the various divinities and spirits. Secret societies of all types which were common among the Yorùbá were condemned; traditional festivals in which women were kept indoors were also singled out for condemnation. For these reasons, the Muslim leaders disregarded curfews imposed on women during the Orò festival, and they also deprecated the Ògbóni cult, disregarded the divinities and all their cults, and composed songs to ridicule the 'pagan' practices. All the people who practise these traditional rites were stigmatised as *Kafirs* (unbelievers) by the Muslims.

Thus, in a slow and clever way, a distinction was made between the adherents of the Traditional Religion, referred to as *Kafirs*, and the converts to the new religion. The latter were encouraged to disregard and eschew traditional practices. For example, it is a practice among the Yorùbá that when lightning strikes a house, the inhabitants if they are still alive, or their surviving relatives, should provide sacrifice to propitiate Ṣàngó; but the Muslims discouraged the newly converted from observing such rites.

Traditionally, the *Akòko* tree (*Newboldia laevis*) is regarded as a sacred tree and it marks sacred spots. The Muslims in Badagry decided to desecrate the sacred Akòko tree which marked a very important shrine in the town – they cut off branches and leaves from the tree and used them for common purposes in order to tease the adherents of the Traditional Religion and to discourage them from being loyal to their traditional faith. The latter hit back and tension mounted in the town and the surrounding area.[7]

It would be erroneous to picture the relationship between the expanding community of Muslims and the traditional society as merely one of a series of conflicts. While we cannot deny that there were conflicts, we should not fail to mention that these conflicts were only ripples in the otherwise generally calm and peaceful atmosphere in which both Islam and the traditional religion co-existed. The men who were propagating the religion were Nigerians who, besides preaching, were carrying on their normal trading activities, living with the people and persuading them as much as possible.

Islam in its incursions into the lands of traditional religion in India, South-East Asia and Africa has shown itself, at certain stages of development, to be accommodating towards traditional religion, so that sometimes opponents have accused her of syncretism. But history shows that in the end a time of reformation will come and local Islam will be brought into line with the Islam of the centre.

Christianity

From the available recorded history we know that Christianity came into Yorubaland in 1842 by way of Badagry. The leaders of this missionary effort was the Rev. Thomas Birch Freeman, the energetic Superintendent of Methodist Mission at Cape Coast. And, struck by the initiative of the Methodists, the Local Committee of the C.M.S. in Sierra Leone sent out the Rev. Henry Townsend who got to Abẹ̀òkúta on 4 January, 1843. Both Freeman and Townsend, one after the other, were warmly received both by the liberated slaves (who made request for missionaries) and the paramount chief of the Ègbá, Ṣódẹkẹ́, and his chiefs. The main C.M.S. Mission, led by the Rev. C. A. Gollmer, accompanied by Townsend and Crowther, came out to Yorubaland in 1845. As these missionaries could not proceed to Abẹ̀òkúta immediately in consequence of Ṣódẹkẹ́'s death, they stayed in Badagry and improved the church life there. Of the missionaries' experience it is recorded that:

> There was no open hostility or persecution, but the hold of the traditional religion on the people was very firm. They had welcomed missionaries, not because they wanted Christianity, but because they were weak and poor and they hoped that the missionaries could attract some trade back to the town . . .[8]

From this statement, we know that the traditional religion was very deeply rooted before the advent of the missionaries; it would be no surprise, therefore, if the people found it difficult to accept the new religion. The people in Badagry, according to this record, accepted Christianity for economic reasons, not for spiritual upliftment, nor from the conviction that Christianity was better than the traditional religion.

It is to be borne in mind that the people who advocated the introduction of Christianity were not members of the Yorùbá traditional society but the Westernised liberated slaves who felt that they were missing (in Nigeria) the sort of Western education and Christian fellowship which they used to enjoy in Freetown. They also wanted their people in Nigeria to benefit from the light they had received. When the missionaries came, therefore, they were received mainly by the liberated slaves who were scattered all over important towns and villages, especially Lagos, Badagry and Abẹ̀òkúta. The Ijebu slaves, however, were not favourably received by their people who regarded them as people who had no regard for tradition. The Ijebu felt that once the missionaries and their African supporters established themselves, they would disrupt the traditional beliefs and organisations. This was why the Awùjalẹ̀, the Ọba of Ìjẹ̀bú, 'sent messages from time to time to the Oǹdó, Ijaw, Ẹ́gbá and Ìbàdàn, urging them to drive away the supposed greatest enemies of Yorubaland, the missionaries and their followers, from the country.[9]

Between 1843 and 1846, Christian stations were established in Badagry and Abẹ̀òkúta; and by 1851, after the British had suppressed slave trade in Lagos, the British moved in. There was then free movement of missionaries between Lagos and Abẹ̀òkúta. Even though the early missionaries were well received by Ṣódẹkẹ́ as we have earlier indicated, there was indication that Ṣódẹkẹ́'s chiefs and subjects were not supporting him; it was also reported that 'the fetish priests had taken alarm at Ṣódẹkẹ́'s eager welcome of Christian missionaries and, in their jealous fear of losing their own power had poisoned him'.[10] His death was a setback to missionary activities. But his successor, Ságbúà, also proved friendly to the missionaries; mission houses, churches and schools were built. Sermons were preached and converts were made. Among the first batch of converts were the mother and four nieces of the Rev. Àjàyí Crowther and an Ifá priest. But the report added:

> Though the people vaguely recognised a Supreme God, whom they called Ọlọ́run, and to whom the enlightened Ṣódẹkẹ́ had built a small temple, the worship of the city centred round such

deities as *Ifá* (the god of secrets), Ògún (the god of iron and war), Shango (the god of thunder) and perhaps a powerful spirit believed to dwell in the Olúmọ rock and worshipped in the largest of its caves. Sacrifices were consistently offered, and the people held the gods in awe . . .[11]

Christianity, like Islam, divided the community into two camps – the converts who looked down upon the old traditional religion, and the devotees of the old religion. After a time in Abẹòkúta, young male converts found it difficult to get wives because the old men would not give their daughters in marriage to the young converts on the ground that, having become Christians, the men stood firm and resolved not to marry any girl who would not join them in reading God's Book (the Bible). Attempts were made to poison some of these resolute youths, and Christian girls were also threatened with the mysterious terrors of the *Orò* which for ages had filled Yorùbá women with fear. Christians were beaten and chased with matchets, but they were adamant. The constancy of the Christians as can be seen from the following remarks by Walker, made a deep impression on their persecutors:

> There grew a general feeling of sympathy with the people who could suffer so bravely for their faith. The persecutors were puzzled and asked: 'What is it that the white man gives you to eat that make your hearts so strong'?[12]

We see from this account that there was a big struggle between Christianity and the old faith in Abẹòkúta. It was a pointer to the fact that the Yorùbá had their own religion which they highly cherished before the advent of the missionaries who falsely claimed that they were introducing God to the people for the first time.

This sort of struggle was not limited to Abẹòkúta. The Rev. David Hinderer, who was the first white man to reach Ìbàdàn and was greeted with cheers when he arrived there on 10 May, 1851, experienced a similar thing. Although the head chief, Abèrè, received him warmly, the Ìbàdàn people received him with far less enthusiasm. This was probably because the Ìbàdàn people were naturally warlike and indulged in human sacrifice. The account says:

> Cruelty and human sacrifice were such common features that the surrounding peoples were apt to call them 'the mad dogs of Ìbàdàn' . . . Only two years before Hinderer arrived, a notable

chief had passed away, and seventy human beings were sacrificed over his grave. . . .[13]

It is to be recorded that before the arrival of Hinderer and of Christianity, Islam had been firmly established and the Muslims were many. Some of them who were still trafficking in slaves scented mischief in Hinderer's arrival. So they cleverly urged Abèrè and his council to expel the missionaries because the 'white men had made the people of Abéòkúta like women, so that they no more went out to war.'[14] But this was not a general feeling. The common people who were suffering and who longed for peace and security were glad to listen to Hinderer's message. So he had a handful of followers after three months of work of evangelisation. And, in 1854, on his second visit to Ìbàdàn, he gained more followers, and the Church at Kúdetì was built.

The Ìjèbú, who were very conservative in their traditional practices, detested any interference from any quarters in matters of religion. 'With pride they boasted to the Lagos Government about their religion which was best for them and made them peaceable and prosperous, unlike the white man's religion, which they said, formented war'.[15] Governor Carter developed hatred for Ìjèbú because of the latter's 'imperviousness to British influence, as represented by missionary "propaganda", their "jujuism", slavery and addiction to human sacrifice, every vice a native race could have in which he believed the Ìjèbú to be pre-eminent.'[16] Carter, therefore, used force to introduce 'civilisation' to the Ìjèbú and to oblige missionaries to establish schools as they had done in Lagos, in order to introduce 'a higher standard of morality and a purer form of religion than at present existed amongst those which were ignorant of the Bible.'[17] Eventually, in the famous Ìjèbú Expedition of 1892, the Ìjèbú were defeated. Christianity was, to some degree, imposed upon the people. And Governor Carter justified his action on humanitarian grounds because the Ìjèbú, according to him, 'were heathens of the most uncompromising description, even hostile to missionaries who were of their own race'. The conservative people were defeated despite the sacrifice of two hundred men and woman made by them to a deity believed to be fighting for them. The Ògbóni house was destroyed. Thus a vacuum was created in the spiritual life of a deeply religious people. Many accepted the religion of their conquerors.

On hearing of the Ìjèbú defeat, the Oǹdó people put a stop, in 1893, to the annual human sacrifice to Ọràṁfẹ̀, and accepted British sovereignty voluntarily.[18]

By 1906, more than 7,600 Ìjẹ̀bú had declared for the new faith. And that same year, it was reported that Gbádébọ̀, the Aláké of Abẹ̀òkúta, attended Townsend-Wood Memorial Church and henceforward

> became a regular church goer. In doing this, he cast to the wind the tradition that his face must not be seen by his brother chiefs, and still less by the common people. Instead of consulting the traditional priests at times of drought and illness, the Alàké supplicated to the white man's God at St. Peter's, kneeling before the altar . . .[19]

This testifies to the impingement of the new faith on the traditional religion and on a paramount chief, who was a custodian of the tradition.

Without bothering to go into the whole history of the spread of Christianity in all the different parts of Yorubaland, we can, from what we have gathered so far, give some assessment of the influence of the new religion on the traditional religion. With the arrival of the missionaries in the middle of the nineteenth century, a new set of religious ideas was introduced, and new social grouping established. New converts, in some cases, were largely withdrawn from the community. They set out with the intention of converting the so-called 'heathen' to their own views in all things – religious, moral and social. This might be regarded as reasonable from their point of view, but they obviously assumed that the Yorùbá religion was necessarily inferior to their own, naming it fetichism, idolatry, juju and heathenism. To them, to accept Christianity was the same thing as accepting 'civilisation'. And those who accepted Christianity and civilisation, must, of necessity withdraw from traditional rituals of kinship which were directed to the divinities and the ancestral spirits. The traditional religion expresses the unity of lines and chiefdoms, but the new religion expresses the unity of groups of believers who associate in churches. But the two systems are not mutually exclusive – the Christian still belongs to the family though he does not worship in the traditional way. This means, in effect, that he impairs the solidarity of the community. Thus, with the advent of Christian missionaries, 'a potentially violent intrusion was made into the social and political world of the Nigerian peoples.'[20] This 'violent intrusion' also affected the religious life of the people.

Education and improved medical facilities

The most potent factor that militates against traditional practices is the Western education which is a concomitant of Christianity and which was regarded by missionaries as the gateway to the benefits of the Western world. The missionaries planned 'the trinity of the 3Cs – Christianity, Commerce and Civilisation'.[21] As the missionaries claimed that they were working for spiritual salvation of the people, so also did they claim to be working for their material well-being. When, therefore, the British attacked a place which did not easily yield to Christianity, they claimed that they were fighting for God and for humanity. The white missionaries and the liberated Africans who had accepted Christianity regarded themselves as representatives of British Christian civilisation; for the Yorùbá to be educated and civilised, according to these missionaries, was to adopt the British way of life and to boycott the traditional Yorùbá culture.

All new converts were taught in the mission houses and were encouraged to look down upon their culture. Later, mission schools and colleges soon sprang up in many places in Yorubaland. Such men and women who were taught the Scriptures and the 3Rs (Reading, 'Riting, 'Rithmetic) became transformed and bade *adieu* to the old faith. Some of them who had knowledge of the Scriptures were made to preach against the 'idolatrous' practices of their own people. The converts became 'friends' of the white people, and they belonged to a small social group. In this way, traditional life was deeply undermined and the family structure was disrupted.

The results of such Western education remain with us today. Some educated Yorùbá are detribalised and are Westernised – they become separated from their religious milieu and linked with another social group. Such educated ones would claim that they cannot participate in the traditional festivals which they regard as of 'the devil'. If and when such people come from their place of work or study, they do not move freely with those who observe the traditional rites.

Education encourages movement from the villages and rural areas into cities, and such urbanisation creates some problems and weakens the traditional hold on people. In villages or rural areas, people keep to the traditional pattern of life and the old traditional beliefs and practices are adhered to. But in the towns and cities where people have become sophisticated and badly Westernised, traditional beliefs and practices are ridiculed and regarded as superstitions.

Before the advent of Christianity and Western culture, it was a dreadful, almost tragic, thing for a woman to have twins (*Ìbejì*); such children were regarded as abnormal and one of them used to be killed immediately. But with the advent of Christianity and Western education, this nefarious practice has stopped. Education made people realise that there was nothing abnormal in the birth of twins. Nevertheless, the typical Yorùbá find it difficult not to regard such a birth as abnormal. In consequence of this belief, they adopt the practice of making offerings to propitiate the spirit of *Ìbejì* (tutelary spirit of twins). Such twins are treated differently from other children. At stated times, their mothers prepare certain articles of food like *àkàrà* (bean cake), *àádùn* (cake prepared from corn), *ìrèkè* (sugar-cane), *àgbon* (coconut) and invite other children, particularly twins, in the neighbourhood to come and feast with their twins. Although this is a rather expensive exercise, the mothers who make this provision are assured of the fact that their twins will not be sick and die prematurely nor will the parents face any calamities and sorrow. Hence the women sing gleefully:

Epo ḿbẹ, èwà ḿbẹ o	There is oil [to fry beans] and there are beans
Epo ḿbẹ, èwà ḿbẹ o;	
Àyà mi kò já, e o	There is oil, and there are beans; I am not afraid.
Àyà mi kò já láti bíbejì,	I am not afraid to have twins,
Epo ḿbẹ, èwà ḿbẹ o.	There is oil and there are beans.

An educated Yorùbá Christian woman, will, today, feel reluctant to engage in this type of exercise. From her scientific knowledge of how twins are formed in the womb, she would never subscribe to such a tradition.

Education also brings improved medical facilities. Before the advent of Christianity and Western education, if a man had a headache or a stomach ache or an attack of fever, or if an expectant mother was having a protracted labour – whatever the complaints might be – the traditional procedure was to consult the oracle to ascertain what supernatural powers had been wronged or what taboo had been broken and what sacrifice should be offered. Today, education has changed people's outlook to a great extent. If a person is ill, medical practitioners rather than oracles are usually consulted by educated men who have access to modern medical facilities. In this way, they minimise the offering of sacrifices.

In the past, smallpox was regarded as a grave sign of the visitation of Ṣọ̀pọ̀nnọ́ (a divinity whose scourge is smallpox), and many taboos had to be observed and sacrifice offered if the victim or a community visited was to escape the scourge. With improved medical facilities, people now know the need to be vaccinated against smallpox, and if there is an outbreak of the dreadful disease, medical science has a ready answer. In consequence, immolation of chickens and animals, and the provision of plenty of oil and *èkọ* (cold corn-meal) as propitiatory sacrifice is greatly reduced, though not completely banished.

Concluding remarks

While we have tried to pinpoint what influences Islam, Christianity, Western education and improved medical facilities have on the Yorùbá community, with particular reference to the practice of traditional religion, we also need to ask the pertinent question: how many so-called Muslims or Christians in Yorubaland (or Nigeria or any other part of Africa) could boast of not falling back upon or lapsing into the old traditional religion from time to time as emergencies arise? In trying to give an honest answer to this question, one may tend to contradict oneself. Is it not true that we have a few sincere Muslims and Christians in Yorubaland who, having placed their hands on the plough, have decided never to look back? Is it not also true that many so-called Muslims and Christians find it difficult to bid a final farewell to the traditional religion and its practices?

Ideally, when a man accepts Christ, he accepts Him *altogether*. He becomes a new man (to use the language of Paul) and he makes a *total* surrender to Jesus Christ. He accepts, in faith, the redemption done by Jesus Christ in the sacrifice that He offered once and for all. Similarly, Islam emphasises to its adherents that, 'There is no god but Allah, and Mohammed is his Apostle'. All worship, therefore, is to be accorded to Allah. This, of course, is the ideal; what happens in practical life is another matter. Islam has been with us in Yorubaland for almost two hundred years, and Christianity for about one hundred and forty years. Many of those who openly declare for these two religions, even among the literate, are found to revert, at one time or another, to traditional beliefs and practices. Thus we see that the traditional religion is only scotched, not killed. It is too deeply rooted to be extirpated.

Islam and Christianity, together with Western education, are super-imposed on the traditional religion, and the adherents of the religion find it difficult, if not impossible, to dissociate themselves from the traditional practices into which they were born; hence they revert to it from time to time. They maintain a divided loyalty to both the traditional religion and the new religion to which they have been 'converted'. Thus it is a common thing to find some Christian Yorùbá who have one foot in the Christian religion and another foot in the traditional religion. Such Christians swing to one faith or the other as circumstances dictate. The same thing goes for Muslims. What is uppermost in the mind of a Yorùbá man is to have life – that is, to have peace, happiness, good health, prosperity and longevity[22] and he is ready to utilise whatever means by which such good things are available. It is not unusual to find a Christian Yorùbá seeking spiritual aid from an Imam (a Muslim leader) or to find an Imam seeking aid from the Aládùúra (a Christian prayer group). Moreover, it is common for Christian and Muslim Yorùbá to go back to the traditional religion to seek aid, including offering prescribed sacrifice. If they do not do so openly because of shyness, they do so surreptitiously under cover of night. The important fact that we have to face is that a large percentage of Christians and Muslims among the Yorùbá find traditional sacrifice a necessity because in it they find a salve for their physical and spiritual problems.

Moreover, both Muslim and Christian Yorùbá consult oracles to be sure of the true situation rather than leave matters in the hands of God, as true believers ought to do. And, as pointed out earlier, once oracles are consulted, it is customary that sacrifice will be prescribed; and once people hear of prescribed sacrifice, they normally do not feel comfortable until the sacrifice is offered. Such Christians and Muslims sing with pride:

Àwa ó ṣorò ilé wa o,	We shall fulfil our traditional rites,
Àwa ó ṣorò ilé wa o,	We shall fulfil our traditional rites,
Ìgbàgbó, kò pé é o	Christianity does not prevent us
Ìgbàgbó kò pé	Christianity does not prevent us
Káwa má ṣorò.	From fulfilling our traditional rites.
Àwa ó ṣorò ilé wa o,	We shall fulfil our traditional rites,
Àwa ó ṣorò ilé wa o,	We shall fulfil our traditional rites,

Àwa ó ṣorò ilé wa o;	We shall fulfil our traditional rites;
Ìmàle kò pé, é o	Islam does not prevent us,
Ìmàle kò pé kàwa má ṣorò	Islam does not prevent us from fulfilling our traditional rites.
Àwa ó ṣorò ilé wa o.	We shall fulfil our traditional rites.

It is therefore a common occurrence during traditional festivals like Egúngún, Agẹmọ, Èje, ÒkèBàdàn, Ọbàlùfọ̀n, to mention but a few, to find a large number of Christians and Muslims among the active participants. This means that the traditional festivals and the sacrifices involved are observed not only by the strict adherents of the traditional religion but also by a large number of Christians and Muslims in the community. Unlike the Christian and the Muslim Yorùbá, the true devotees of Yorùbá traditional religion do not usually doubt that their needs would be met by the divinities they worship. It is rare, if it ever happens, to find the adherents of the traditional religion running to the Christian or Muslim leaders seeking spiritual aid. They are constant in their faith, perhaps much more constant than the Christian and Muslim Yorùbá. They do not campaign for membership and they have no written literature to guide their adherents; yet many Christians and Muslims revert to them in moments of need without feeling any sense of inconsistency.

Old customs die hard. The blood of Jesus Christ shed for the sins of the world about two thousand years ago, and declared by the Christian missionaries as adequate for the salvation of all men, seems to have little meaning for the generality of people who were born into and brought up in the traditional Yorùbá way. When confronted with life's problems, a Yorùbá wants to act in a practical way. And one way in which he acts is to find out from the oracle the source of any trouble and how it can be removed. The removal or the prevention usually involves sacrifice. Likewise, when all things are well, for example, when crops do well on the farm, or another year rolls in, or requests are granted, there are thanksgiving offerings to the Supernatural Being who makes the good things possible. People are convinced of the necessity for sacrifice. They do not think that life is possible without due attention being paid to Olódùmarè and to the divinities, the ancestral spirits and other spirits. These spiritual beings who control the world are real to the Yorùbá, and they know that it is the height of wisdom to be on good terms with them, 'to acknowledge their presence; to greet them; to pray to them; to make them little offerings to secure their good-will'.[23]

Thus sacrifice, which is the essence of the religion of the Yorùbá, makes the special relationship of man and the spiritual world visible and concrete. Man regards this act as a privilege given by the Supreme Being to him. He is convinced that while man-to-man relationships may fail, man-to-God relationship never fails. Moreover, offering sacrifice emphasises the fact that man is limited and powerless, incapable of helping himself but that God is omnipotent and is ready to give help to His creatures.

Finally, when a man makes offerings to the Supernatural Being or beings, he does so with the aim of fulfilling certain obligations. His sacrifice is, therefore, an expression of an inner feeling and conviction. He is persuaded that once the sacrifice is made, all will be well with him – he is psychologically and spiritually satisfied that he has fulfilled his obligation and that the spiritual beings who receive the sacrifice will also not fail him. Therefore, as long as man breathes and is conscious of his dependence upon, and responsibility to, the spiritual beings, he will continue to offer sacrifice. The form of this may change, but sacrifice – in essence – will always remain with us.

NOTES

1. T. G. O. Gbadamosi, 'The Growth of Islam among the Yoruba, 1841–1908', Ph.D thesis, University of Ibadan, 1968. To him I am mainly indebted for the dates cited here.
2. Gbadamosi, p. 11. This date is corroborated by M. O. A. Abdul, 'Islam in Ìjèbú-Òde', M.A. thesis, McGill University, 1967, p. 21. The latter, however, referred to the expelled Oba as Kosoko and not Adele I as claimed by Gbadamosi.
3. Gbadamosi, p. 11.
4. Abdul, p. 21.
5. For a description of the conversion ceremony, see Abdul, pp. 43ff, and Gbadamosi, p. 324
6. Gbadamosi, p. 325.
7. *Ibid*, pp. 327 and 328.
8. J. F. A. Ajayi, *Christian Missions in Nigeria, 1841–1891*, Longman, 1965, p. 34.
9. E. A. Ayandele, *The Missionary Impact on Modern Nigeria*, Longman, 1966, pp. 35 and 56.

10. F. D. Walker, *The Romance of the Black River*, London, 1931, p. 46.
11. *Ibid.*, p. 56.
12. *Ibid.*, p. 63.
13. *Ibid.*, p. 78.
14. *Ibid.*, p. 79.
15. Ayandele, p. 56.
16. *Ibid.*, p. 60.
17. *Ibid.*, p. 62.
18. *Ibid.*, p. 69.
19. *Ibid.*, p. 69.
20. *Ibid.*, p. 5.
21. *Ibid.*, p. 8.
22. See J. Ọmọṣade Awolalu, 'The Yoruba Philosophy of Life', *Présence Africaine*, 73, 1970, pp. 20ff.
23. E. Smith, *The Secret of the African*, London, 1929, p. 13.

INDEX